U. S. PUBLIC DIPLOMACY: BACKGROUND AND ISSUES

FOREIGN POLICY
OF THE UNITED STATES

Additional books in this series can be found on Nova's website
under the Series tab.

Additional E-books in this series can be found on Nova's website
under the E-book tab.

FOREIGN POLICY OF THE UNITED STATES

U. S. PUBLIC DIPLOMACY: BACKGROUND AND ISSUES

MATTHEW B. MORRISON
EDITOR

Nova Science Publishers, Inc.

New York

LIBRARY OF CONGRESS CATALOGING-IN-PUBLICATION DATA

U.S. public diplomacy : background and issues / editor, Matthew B. Morrison.
       p. cm.
    Includes index.
    ISBN 978-1-61728-888-3 (hardcover)
    1. United States--Relations--Foreign countries. I. Morrison, Matthew B.
    II. Title: United States public diplomacy.
    JZ1480.U155 2009
    327.73--dc22
                                    2010026185

Published by Nova Science Publishers, Inc. † New York

CONTENTS

PREFACE

Public diplomacy is defined in different ways, but broadly it is a term used to describe a government's efforts to conduct foreign policy and promote national interests through direct outreach and communication with the population of a foreign country. The U.S. has long sought to influence the peoples of foreign countries through public diplomacy. After the 9/11 terror attacks, there was a new interest in promoting effective public diplomacy, as a struggle against extremist ideologies became crucial to the overall fight against terrorism. In recent years, many observers have called for increased resources for and improvement of U.S. public diplomacy efforts. This book examines the background and current issues of U.S. public diplomacy.

Chapter 1 - Public diplomacy is defined in different ways, but broadly it is a term used to describe a government's efforts to conduct foreign policy and promote national interests through direct outreach and communication with the population of a foreign country. Public diplomacy activities include providing information to foreign publics through broadcast and Internet media and at libraries and other outreach facilities in foreign countries; conducting cultural diplomacy, such as art exhibits and music performances; and administering international educational and professional exchange programs. The United States has long sought to influence the peoples of foreign countries through public diplomacy. After World War II, during which the U.S. military conducted most information and communication activities, authority for U.S. public diplomacy was placed in civilian hands. During the Cold War, the United States Information Agency (USIA) led U.S. public diplomacy efforts, with a primary mission of combating Soviet propaganda and the spread of communism. Once the Soviet Union dissolved in 1991, USIA's role was diminished, and its resources were reduced during the 1990s. Finally, USIA was abolished in 1999 as part of a post-Cold War reorganization, with public diplomacy responsibilities folded into the Department of State.

After the 9/11 terror attacks, there was new interest in promoting effective public diplomacy, as a struggle against extremist ideologies became crucial to the overall fight against terrorism. In recent years, many observers have called for increased resources for and improvement of U.S. public diplomacy efforts. A number of challenges and questions, however, currently affect the future of U.S. government communications with foreign publics. Some argue that abolishing USIA was a mistake and that the State Department is ill-suited to conduct long-term public diplomacy. Also, the Department of Defense and the U.S. military have increased significantly their role in communicating with foreign publics. Determining public diplomacy roles, responsibilities, and coordination procedures among civilian and military actors has therefore become a central issue. In addition, with the rise and rapid evolution of Internet communications, the U.S. government must determine how to effectively communicate with foreign publics in an increasingly complex, accessible, and democratized global communications environment.

A number of issues for Congress have arisen concerning U.S. public diplomacy. Determining levels of public diplomacy funding, for programs and personnel, will continue to be of central importance. Establishing capabilities to improve monitoring and assessment of public diplomacy activities, as well as to leverage expertise and best practices outside government, may be important to increasing public diplomacy effectiveness. Questions of possible reorganization of public diplomacy authorities and capabilities, through legislation or otherwise, may be considered. Requirements for effective interagency cooperation and coordination, as well as creation of a national public diplomacy strategy and whole-of-government approaches may be created to improve effective communication with foreign publics. Several pieces of legislation proposed thus far in the 111th Congress concern changes to, improvements in, and funding for public diplomacy. These bills include H.R. 2647 and S. 1707, which have been enacted into law, as well as H.R. 363, H.R. 489, H.R. 490, H.R. 2387, H.R. 2410, S. 230, and S. 894. Congressional consideration of these bills, and continued interest in U.S. public diplomacy, are expected to continue during the 111th Congress's second session.

Chapter 2 - Since the September 11, 2001, terrorist attacks, the U.S. government has spent at least $10 billion on communication efforts designed to advance the strategic interests of the United States. However, foreign public opinion polling data shows that negative views towards the United States persist despite the collective efforts to counteract them by the State Department (State), Broadcasting Board of Governors (BBG), U.S. Agency for International Development (USAID), Department of Defense (DOD), and other U.S. government agencies. Based on the significant role U.S. strategic communication and public diplomacy[1] efforts can play in promoting U.S. national security objectives, such as countering ideological support for violent extremism, we highlighted these efforts as an urgent issue for the new administration and Congress.[2] To assist Congress with its oversight agenda, we have enclosed a series of issue papers that discuss long-standing and emerging public diplomacy challenges identified by GAO and others.[3]

Chapter 3 features a letter to the U. S. Senate.

Chapters 4 through 7 feature testimony before the U. S. Senate.

Chapter 8 features a report to the White House.

In: U.S. Public Diplomacy: Background and Issues
Editor: Matthew B. Morrison

ISBN: 978-1-61728-888-3
© 2010 Nova Science Publishers, Inc.

Chapter 1

U.S. Public Diplomacy: Background and Current Issues*

Kennon H. Nakamura and Matthew C. Weed

Summary

Public diplomacy is defined in different ways, but broadly it is a term used to describe a government's efforts to conduct foreign policy and promote national interests through direct outreach and communication with the population of a foreign country. Public diplomacy activities include providing information to foreign publics through broadcast and Internet media and at libraries and other outreach facilities in foreign countries; conducting cultural diplomacy, such as art exhibits and music performances; and administering international educational and professional exchange programs. The United States has long sought to influence the peoples of foreign countries through public diplomacy. After World War II, during which the U.S. military conducted most information and communication activities, authority for U.S. public diplomacy was placed in civilian hands. During the Cold War, the United States Information Agency (USIA) led U.S. public diplomacy efforts, with a primary mission of combating Soviet propaganda and the spread of communism. Once the Soviet Union dissolved in 1991, USIA's role was diminished, and its resources were reduced during the 1990s. Finally, USIA was abolished in 1999 as part of a post-Cold War reorganization, with public diplomacy responsibilities folded into the Department of State.

After the 9/11 terror attacks, there was new interest in promoting effective public diplomacy, as a struggle against extremist ideologies became crucial to the overall fight against terrorism. In recent years, many observers have called for increased resources for and improvement of U.S. public diplomacy efforts. A number of challenges and questions, however, currently affect the future of U.S. government communications with foreign publics. Some argue that abolishing USIA was a mistake and that the State Department is ill-

---

* This is an edited, reformatted and augmented version of a CRS Report for Congress publication dated December 2009.

suited to conduct long-term public diplomacy. Also, the Department of Defense and the U.S. military have increased significantly their role in communicating with foreign publics. Determining public diplomacy roles, responsibilities, and coordination procedures among civilian and military actors has therefore become a central issue. In addition, with the rise and rapid evolution of Internet communications, the U.S. government must determine how to effectively communicate with foreign publics in an increasingly complex, accessible, and democratized global communications environment.

A number of issues for Congress have arisen concerning U.S. public diplomacy. Determining levels of public diplomacy funding, for programs and personnel, will continue to be of central importance. Establishing capabilities to improve monitoring and assessment of public diplomacy activities, as well as to leverage expertise and best practices outside government, may be important to increasing public diplomacy effectiveness. Questions of possible reorganization of public diplomacy authorities and capabilities, through legislation or otherwise, may be considered. Requirements for effective interagency cooperation and coordination, as well as creation of a national public diplomacy strategy and whole-of-government approaches may be created to improve effective communication with foreign publics. Several pieces of legislation proposed thus far in the 111th Congress concern changes to, improvements in, and funding for public diplomacy. These bills include H.R. 2647 and S. 1707, which have been enacted into law, as well as H.R. 363, H.R. 489, H.R. 490, H.R. 2387, H.R. 2410, S. 230, and S. 894. Congressional consideration of these bills, and continued interest in U.S. public diplomacy, are expected to continue during the 111th Congress's second session.

INTRODUCTION

The United States has long sought to influence the peoples of foreign countries through public diplomacy (PD) efforts. Public diplomacy provides a foreign policy complement to traditional government-to-government diplomacy which is dominated by official interaction carried out between professional diplomats. Unlike public affairs which focus communications activities intended primarily to inform and influence domestic media and the American people, U.S. public diplomacy includes efforts to interact directly with the citizens, community and civil leaders, journalists, and other opinion leaders of another country. PD seeks to influence that society's attitudes and actions in supporting U.S. policies and national interests. Public diplomacy is viewed as often having a long-term perspective that requires working through the exchange of people and ideas to build lasting relationships and understanding the United States and its culture, values, and policies. The tools of public diplomacy include people-to-people contact; expert speaker programs; art and cultural performances; books and literature; radio and television broadcasting and movies; and, more recently, the Internet. In contrast, traditional diplomacy involves the strong representation of U.S. policies to foreign governments, analysis and reporting of a foreign government's activities, attitudes, and trends that affect U.S. interests. There is a growing concern among many in the executive branch, the Congress, the media, and other foreign policy observers, however, that the United States has lost its public diplomacy capacity to successfully respond to today's international challenges in supporting the accomplishment of U.S. national interests.

Public diplomacy capacity and capabilities atrophied in the years following the dissolution of the Soviet Union in 1991. U.S. public diplomacy efforts were carried out primarily by the U.S. Information Agency (USIA), created in 1953, as well as U.S. non-military international broadcasting by entities such as Voice of America, Radio Free Europe, and Radio Liberty. These entities had been well resourced throughout the Cold War; however with the end of the Soviet threat, those resources dwindled as it was believed that there was no ideological fight still to win. Many analysts believe that the United States generally placed public diplomacy on a "back burner" as a relic of the Cold War. In 1999, new legislation abolished USIA and folded its responsibilities into the State Department, again with reduced resources for public diplomacy. After the 9/11 terrorist attacks, and with U.S. combat operations in Iraq and Afghanistan, interest in public diplomacy as a foreign policy and national security tool was renewed. Concerns about the events in the Middle East focused the attention of policy makers on the need for a sound, well-resourced public diplomacy program. This concern was heightened by the realization that the worldwide perception of the United States has declined considerably in recent years with the United States often being considered among the most distrusted and dangerous countries in the world.[1]

As the United States sought to revitalize its PD initiatives, it became clear the changes in the world order and changes caused by the Internet and information technology in general created a new dynamic for U.S. public diplomacy initiatives. The world of international communications and information sharing is undergoing revolutionary changes at remarkable speeds. The rapid increase in available sources of information, through the proliferation of global and regional broadcasters using satellite technologies, as well as the global reach of news and information websites on the Internet, has diversified and complicated the shaping of attitudes of foreign populations. Individual communicators now have the ability to influence large numbers of people on a global scale through social networking, providing a direct challenge to the importance of traditional information media and actors. Traditional media, such as newspapers, have created online interactive exchanges between providers and consumers of information by allowing readers to comment on news reporting. New online social media networks such as weblogs, Twitter, MySpace, and Facebook allow individuals to connect with one-another on a global scale, providing opportunities for "many-to-many" exchanges of information that bypass the "one-tomany" sources that formally dominated the information landscape. In addition, the method of information delivery and receipt has been fundamentally changed, with cell phones and other handheld mobile devices capable of sending and receiving large amounts of written, visual, and audio information. Communication of information through these new media, regardless of how they depict the United States, contribute to the impressions about the United States and its society. It is in this ever expanding and accelerating global communications environment that U.S. public diplomacy and international broadcasting must operate, "competing for attention and for credibility in a time when rumors can spark riots, and information, whether it's true or false, quickly spreads across the world, across the internet, in literally instants."[2]

The attitudes and perceptions of foreign publics created in this new environment are often as important as reality, and sometimes can even trump reality. These attitudes affect the ability of the United States to form and maintain alliances in pursuit of common policy objectives; impact the cost and the effectiveness of military operations; influence local populations to either cooperate, support or be hostile as the United States pursues foreign policy and/or military objectives in that country; affect the ability to secure support on issues of particular concern in multilateral fora; and dampen foreign publics' enthusiasm for U.S. business services and products. Under Secretary of State for Public Diplomacy and Public Affairs, Judith McHale, in discussing the implications of foreign perceptions and attitudes on U.S. foreign policy and national security, said,

> Governments inclined to support U.S. policies will back away if their populations do not trust us. But if we do this right, if we develop relationships with people around the world, if they trust us as a partner, this dynamic will be reversed. Less cooperative regimes will be forced to moderate their positions under popular pressure. To the extent that we succeed, threats we face today will diminish and new partnerships will be possible.[3]

Today, 14 Cabinet-level departments and over 48 independent agencies and commissions participate in at least one form of official public diplomacy, mostly regarding exchanges or training programs.[4] Yet because of the increasing recognition of public diplomacy's key role in the conduct of U.S. foreign affairs, many in the executive branch, Congress, think tanks, nongovernmental organizations, and news media debate different approaches to improving U.S public diplomacy to respond to new challenges, determining public diplomacy authorities and responsibilities, defining and executing public diplomacy strategy, and adequately resourcing public diplomacy.

Organization of This Report

The body of this chapter is divided into five sections.[5] The first section provides background information on U.S. public diplomacy, its legislative foundations, and the history of modern U.S. public diplomacy including the former USIA. The second section discusses the abolishment of USIA and the transfer of its functions to the Department of State. The third section discusses the current structure of public diplomacy within the Department of State as well as its budget and personnel levels. The fourth section gives a detailed overview of some of the major related policy issues and perceived challenges to the effectiveness of U.S. public diplomacy, and proposed reforms and solutions. Finally, the fifth section describes proposed legislation intended to reform and improve U.S. public diplomacy.

U.S. PUBLIC DIPLOMACY BACKGROUND

This section provides an overview of the legislative authorities for the conduct of public diplomacy activities within the U.S. government. It continues with a discussion of the historical context of U.S. civilian-led public diplomacy as it developed since World War I, the creation of USIA in 1953, and its activities and organization. It also provides budget and personnel information for the former USIA.

Legislative Authority

Four acts provide the current foundational authority of the U.S. government to engage in public diplomacy in its many venues, and establishes the parameters and restrictions regarding those authorities: the State Department Basic Authorities Act of 1956; the United States Information and Educational Exchange Act of 1948; the Mutual Educational and Cultural Exchange Act of 1961; and the United States International Broadcasting Act of 1994.

State Department Basic Authorities Act of 1956

The State Department Basic Authorities Act of 1956, as amended (P.L. 84-885; 22 U.S.C. §§ 265 1a, 2669 et seq.), authorizes six Under Secretaries of State for the Department of State, specifically requiring that there be an Under Secretary for Public Diplomacy. Section 1(b)(3) of the Act (22 U.S.C. § 265 1a(b)(3)), in describing the position of the Under Secretary for Public Diplomacy, states that the Under Secretary has "the primary responsibility to assist the Secretary and the Deputy Secretary in the formation and implementation of United States public diplomacy policies, including international educational and cultural exchange programs, information, and international broadcasting." The section enumerates several responsibilities of the Under Secretary, including preparing an annual strategic plan for public diplomacy, ensuring the design and implementation of appropriate program evaluation methodologies, and assisting the United States Agency for International Development (USAID) and the Broadcasting Board of Governors (BBG) in presenting the policies of the United States.

Section 60 of the act (22 U.S.C. § 2732), entitled "Public Diplomacy Responsibilities of the Department of State," requires the Secretary of State to make public diplomacy an integral component in the planning and execution of U.S. foreign policy. The Secretary is to make every effort to coordinate the public diplomacy activities of the federal agencies, work with the Broadcasting Board of Governors to develop a comprehensive strategy for the use of PD resources, and establish long-term measurable objectives. The Secretary is also to work with USAID and other private and public assistance organizations to ensure that information on the assistance the United States is providing is disseminated widely, and particularly to the people in the recipient countries.

United States Information and Education and Exchange Act of 1948

The United States Information and Education and Exchange Act of 1948, as amended (P.L. 80- 402; 22 U.S.C. § 1431 et seq.), also known as the Smith-Mundt Act, served as the post World War II charter for a peacetime overseas information and education exchange activities. Section 501 (22 U.S.C. § 1461) states that the objective of the Act is "to enable the Government of the United States to promote a better understanding of the United States in other countries, and to increase mutual understanding between the people of the United States and the people of other countries." The section authorizes the Secretary of State to prepare and disseminate "information about the United States, its people, and its policies, through press, publications, radio, motion pictures, and other information media, and through information centers and instructors abroad." Section 501, unlike previous government public information efforts, prohibits materials developed under the authorities of this Act from being disseminated within the United States, its territories, or possessions:

OTHER LEGISLATIVE RESTRICTIONS ON DOMESTIC DISSEMINATION OF PUBLIC DIPLOMACY INFORMATION

In addition to restrictions contained in the Smith-Mundt Act, there are a number of other provisions that restrict the use of funds for public diplomacy activities intended for domestic audiences.

1985 Zorinsky Amendment

Section 208 of the Foreign Relations Authorization Act, Fiscal Years 1986 and 1987 (P.L. 99-93; 99 Stat. 431; 22 U.S.C. § 1461-1a), popularly known as the Zorinsky Amendment,[7] limits the use of USIA funds for domestic purposes:

SEC. 208. BAN ON DOMESTIC ACTIVITIES BY THE USIA.

Except as provided in section 501 of the United States Information and Educational Exchange Act of 1948 (22 U.S.C. 1461) and this section, no funds authorized to be appropriated to the United States Information Agency shall be used to influence public opinion in the United States, and no program material prepared by the United States Information Agency shall be distributed within the United States. This section shall not apply to programs carried out pursuant to the Mutual Educational and Cultural Exchange Act of 1961 (22 U.S.C. 2451 et seq.).[8]

Section 1331 of the Foreign Affairs Reform and Restructuring Act of 1998 (Division G of P.L. 105-277; 22 U.S.C. § 655 1) states that after USIA's dissolution, all references to USIA are deemed references to the State Department. Section 1333 (22 U.S.C. § 6552) of the act provides a similar restriction on the use of funds for State Department public diplomacy programs, prohibiting their use for influencing U.S. public opinion and banning domestic distribution or dissemination of program material.

State Department/Foreign Operations Prohibition

Yearly appropriations language for State Department and foreign operations funding includes a related restriction on using funds for "publicity or propaganda." For example, Section 7080 of the Department of State, Foreign Operations, and Related Agencies Appropriations Act, 2009 (Division H of P.L. 111–8, the Omnibus Appropriations Act, 2009; 123 Stat. 831) prohibits using funds for publicity or propaganda purposes "within the United States":

SEC. 7080. No part of any appropriation contained in this Act shall be used for publicity or propaganda purposes within the United States not authorized before the date of the enactment of this Act by the Congress: *Provided,* That not to exceed $25,000 may be made available to carry out the provisions of section 316 of Public Law 96–533.[9]

Section 316 of the International Security and Development Cooperation Act of 1980 (P.L. 96–533; 94 Stat. 3149) authorizes U.S. government assistance for private organizations to promote public discussion of world hunger.

(a).... Subject to subsection (b), any information (other than "Problems of Communism" and the "English Teaching Forum" which may continue to be sold by the Government Printing Office) shall not be disseminated within the United States, its territories, or possessions, but, on request, shall be available in the English language at the Department of State, at all reasonable times following its release as information abroad, for examination only by representatives of United States press associations, newspapers, magazines, radio systems, and stations, and by research students and scholars, and, on request, shall be made available for examination only to Members of Congress.

(b)(1) The Director of the United States Information Agency shall make available to the Archivist of the United States, for domestic distribution, motion pictures, films, videotapes, and other material prepared for dissemination abroad 12 years after the initial dissemination of the material abroad or, in the case of such material not disseminated abroad, 12 years after the preparation of the material.

Section 502 of the act (22 U.S.C. § 1462) also placed limitations on the international information activities of the government so that it would not compete with corresponding private information dissemination if it is found to be adequate, and that the government would not have a monopoly in the production and sponsorship of short wave or any other medium of information.[6] Further, in protecting the private sector and helping it, Section 1005 (22 U.S.C. § 1437) states that a duty of the Secretary of State shall be to utilize, to the maximum extent practicable, "the services and facilities of private agencies, including existing American press, publishing, radio, motion picture, and other agencies through contractual arrangements or otherwise." Further, the government was to utilize the private agencies in each field "consistent with the present and potential market for their services in each country."

Mutual Educational and Cultural Exchange Act of 1961

The Mutual Educational and Cultural Exchange Act of 1961, as amended (P.L. 87-256; 22 U.S.C. § 2451 et seq.), also known as the Fulbright-Hays Act, authorizes U.S. exchange programs as a public diplomacy tool. Section 101 of the Act (22 U.S.C. § 2451) states the Act's four-fold purpose:

- to increase mutual understanding between the people of the United States and the people of other countries by means of educational and cultural exchanges;
- to strengthen the ties which unite us with other nations by demonstrating the educational and cultural interests, developments, and achievements of the people of the United States and other nations, and the contributions being made toward a peaceful and more fruitful life for people throughout the world;
- to promote international cooperation for educational and cultural advancement; and
- to assist in the development of friendly, sympathetic, and peaceful relations between the United States and the other countries of the world.

Under Section 102 (22 U.S.C. § 2452), the President is authorized to take action when he considers that certain steps would strengthen international cooperation. Among the activities authorized by this Act are the following:
- providing grants, contracts, or otherwise for educational and cultural exchanges for U.S. citizens and citizens of other countries;
- providing for participation in international fairs and expositions abroad;

- providing for the interchange of books, periodicals, and government publications, and the reproduction and translations of such material;
- providing for the interchange of technical and scientific material and equipment, and establishing and operating centers for cultural and technical interchanges;
- assisting in the establishment, expansion, maintenance, and operation of schools and institutions of learning abroad, and fostering American studies in foreign countries;
- promoting foreign language and area studies training for Americans;
- providing of U.S. representation at international nongovernmental educational, scientific, and technical meetings; and
- promoting respect for and guarantees of religious freedom abroad and by interchanges and visits between the United States and other nations of religious leaders, scholars, and religious and legal experts in the field of religious freedom.

Section 103 (22 U.S.C. § 2453) authorizes the President to enter into international agreements with foreign governments and international organizations to advance the purposes of this Act, and to provide for equitable participation and support for the implementation of these agreements. Section 104 (22 U.S.C. § 2454) authorizes the President to delegate his authorities to other officers of the government as he determines to be appropriate. The Department of State and USAID are responsible for the vast majority of U.S. sponsored exchanges. However, several other federal agencies, such as the National Institutes of Health, also administer exchange programs under this Presidential delegation.

Section 112 of this act (22 U.S.C. § 2460) establishes a Bureau of Educational and Cultural Affairs in the Department of State to be responsible for managing, coordinating, and overseeing various programs and exchanges, including the J. William Fulbright Exchange Program, the Hubert H. Humphrey Fellowship Program, the International Visitors Program, the American Cultural Centers and Libraries abroad, and several others.

United States International Broadcasting Act of 1994

The United States International Broadcasting Act of 1994, as amended (P.L. 103-236; 22 U.S.C. 6201 et seq.), reorganizes U.S. non-military international broadcasting (hereafter referred to as U.S. international broadcasting). It creates the nine-member Broadcasting Board of Governors (BBG), whose members are appointed by the President with the advice and consent of the Senate, and the International Broadcasting Bureau (IBB), which operates under the BBG to administer Voice of America and Cuba Broadcasting. It also places all U.S. international broadcasting under the authority of the BBG. The mission of the BBG is "to promote freedom and democracy and to enhance understanding by broadcasting accurate, objective and balanced news and information about the United States and the world to audiences abroad."[10] Section 305(d) of the act (22 U.S.C. § 6204) charges the Secretary of State and the BBG with respecting the professional independence and integrity of the international Broadcasting Bureau, its broadcasting services, and the grantees of the Board.

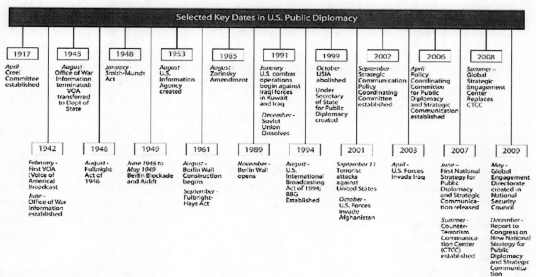

Source: CRS.

Figure 1. Public Diplomacy Timeline (1917 to present)

Section 303 of the act (22 U.S.C. § 6202) establishes standards and principles for U.S. international broadcasting. In the list of principles, the act states that such broadcasting shall include

- news that is consistently reliable and authoritative, accurate, objective, and comprehensive;
- a balanced and comprehensive projection of U.S. thought and institutions, reflecting the diversity of U.S. culture and society;
- clear and effective presentation of the policies, including editorials, broadcast by the Voice of America, which present the views of the U.S. government and responsible discussion and opinion on those policies;
- the capability to provide a surge capacity to support U.S. foreign policy objectives during crisis abroad; and
- programming that meets needs of the people who remain underserved by local media voices.

Moves toward a Permanent U.S. Public Diplomacy Capacity

U.S. government efforts to communicate with foreign publics have historically increased as perceived threats to national security grow, particularly during times of war. During World War I, President Woodrow Wilson established the Committee on Public Information (Creel Committee) which represented the U.S. government's first large scale efforts at information dissemination to both domestic and foreign audiences. President Wilson established the Committee initially to counter German propaganda, but it began disseminating its own distortions of the truth and propaganda to both U.S. and foreign audiences. At the end of the First World War, the Creel Committee was disbanded.

During the Second World War, President Franklin Roosevelt established the Office of War Information (OWI) to provide American and foreign audiences with news of the war, U.S. war policies, and the activities and aims of the U.S. government. Voice of America (VOA), which is the oldest of the U.S. government radio broadcasting services was an integral part of OWI's programs. In 1948, President Harry Truman issued Executive Order 9608, terminating the OWI and transferring its international information functions to the Department of State. VOA, which also was transferred to the State Department, then became the official overseas broadcast arm of the United States.

As the United States became more deeply involved in the Cold War with the Soviet Bloc nations, the United States and the Congress began creating programs to counter Soviet influence and once again compete in a war of hearts and minds. The original Fulbright Act of 1946 was enacted to mandate peacetime international exchange programs. In 1948, Congress passed the Smith-Mundt Act, described previously. While serving as the charter for peacetime overseas information programs, some contend that this act was intended from the outset to provide the authority for the U.S. government to engage vigorously in a non-military battle with the Soviet Union, which then U.S.-diplomat and Soviet specialist George Kennan described as having declared psychological war on the United States, a war of ideology requiring a fight to the death.[11] This was a significant departure in U.S. public information policy in that it provided for a permanent peacetime information effort.

On August 1, 1953, following the recommendations of several commissions, President Dwight Eisenhower created the independent United States Information Agency (USIA) to organize and implement U.S. government international information and exchange programs in support of U.S. foreign policy. [12]

UNITED STATES INFORMATION AGENCY

With its establishment in 1953, USIA became the agency responsible for executing U.S. public diplomacy efforts to understand, inform, and influence foreign publics in promotion of the U.S. interests, and to broaden the dialogue between Americans and foreign publics. USIA's stated goals were

- explaining and advocating U.S. policies in terms that are credible and meaningful in foreign cultures;
- providing information about the official policies of the United States, and about the people, values, and institutions which influence those policies;
- bringing the benefits of international engagement to American citizens and institutions by helping them build strong long-term relationships with their counterparts overseas; and
- advising the President and U.S. government policy-makers on the ways in which foreign attitudes will have a direct bearing on the effectiveness of U.S. policies.[13]

USIA in Washington

During the 46 years of the Cold War, USIA was headed by a Director, a Deputy Director, and three Associate Directors who led its major bureaus: the Bureau of Information, the Bureau of Educational and Cultural Affairs, and the Bureau of Management. USIA's support offices included the Office of Public Liaison, the Office of the General Counsel, and the Office of Research and Media Reaction. The Office of Research and Media Reaction conducted polling activities and also provided daily analysis of overseas press opinion on U.S. foreign policy.[14] USIA regional affairs offices supported and coordinated activities in the field, where USIA was known as the U.S. Information Service (USIS). **Figure 2** below provides an organization chart for USIA.

Bureau of Information

The Bureau of Information produced and distributed to USIS offices in the field a variety of publications in as many as 30 languages supporting U.S. policy objectives, such as an explanation of U.S. drug policy. The Bureau also published books and pamphlets providing information on U.S. history, politics, economy, and culture, and adopted new technologies for information delivery. The Bureau utilized new technologies as they became available, such as teletype, to move informational materials to the field. When the Bureau began utilizing the Internet, availability of printed materials and other types of information grew dramatically. Examples of information sent through electronic media from Washington headquarters included

- the Washington File, which provided official U.S. public statements on U.S. policy;
- a USIA website, and temporary USIA-sponsored, issue-specific websites such as a site covering the Kyoto Climate Change Conference;
- access to the Foreign Affairs Documentation Collection, which contained selected authenticated versions of treaties and other international agreements; and
- an electronic journal with articles that could be downloaded as formatted publications for print distribution on a variety of topics, from providing background on U.S. society and values to NATO-enlargement issues.

In addition, the Bureau's Speakers Program sent several hundred recognized U.S. speakers to foreign countries each year. U.S. embassies could organize speaking engagements on college campuses, with the press, or with the general public. While their trips were sponsored by the U.S. government, these speakers expressed their own views, which proved attractive to audiences, according to many public diplomacy officers:

> When the United States Information Agency existed, there were on-going debates between public diplomacy officers and political officers as to whether official speakers and official events should stick to the party line or incorporate opposing ideas as well.... When USIA- sponsored academics respectfully differed with current policy, the result from the audiences was unalloyed admiration for the courage of the U.S. in showcasing free and open discussion.[15]

The Information Bureau also made speakers available through video and telephone conferences to ensure a more timely discussion of current issues. A link for a video conference using satellites could be established through several embassies at one time.

Bureau of Educational and Cultural Affairs

The Bureau of Education and Cultural Affairs was responsible for the administration of relationships with a variety of educational and cultural exchanges. The Bureau administered both the academic exchanges and the professional and cultural exchanges. Examples of academic exchanges are the Fulbright Program, which provides for the exchange of students, scholars, and teachers between the United States and other countries, and the Hubert H. Humphrey Fellowship Program, which facilitates academic study and internships in the United States for mid-career professionals from developing nations. The professional and cultural exchanges included the International Visitors Program, which brought current and promising leaders of other countries to the United States to travel around the country, meet their counterparts, and learn about and experience U.S. society and culture. The Bureau also ran programs for cultural ambassadors, such as musicians, artists, sports figures, and writers to share American culture with foreign publics.

Bureau of Management

As the name suggests, the Bureau of Management provided agency-wide management support and administrative services. USIA had control of its own human resources program with its own recruiting, employment, assignments and career tracks that were separate from the Department of State. It also controlled its own budget and support of its own operations.

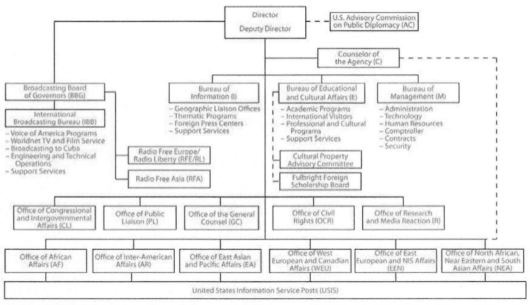

Source: United States Information Agency, *USIA Program and Budget in Brief, Fiscal Year 1999*, p. 3.

Figure 2. Organization Chart for the United States Information Agency in 1999

U.S. International Broadcasting

During the life of USIA, the relationships between USIA and U.S. international broadcasting varied. For many years, all broadcasting services were housed within USIA. Later, surrogate broadcasting was under an independent Board of International Broadcasting (BIB), which had an indirect relationship with USIA leadership. With the enactment of the United States International Broadcasting Act of 1994, as discussed previously, all U.S. international broadcasting services were consolidated under a new Broadcasting Board of Governors (BBG) within USIA.

The BBG had responsibility for supervising, directing, and overseeing the operations of the International Broadcasting Bureau (IBB). The IBB included the worldwide broadcasting services of the Voice of America (VOA) and television's Worldnet, Cuba Broadcasting, an Engineering and Technical Operations Office, and various support services. The BBG also had funding and oversight authority over surrogate radio grantees: Radio Free Europe/Radio Liberty (RFE/RL) and Radio Free Asia (RFA). Among BBG's responsibilities was to review and evaluate the operations of the radios, and assess their quality, effectiveness, and professional integrity. It also was responsible for determining the addition or deletion of the language services under the IBB.[16] In 1999, the U.S. government and surrogate services broadcast hours included

- 660 hours of weekly VOA programming in 53 languages;
- 24 hours-a-day of radio and 4 1/2-hour-per-day television broadcasting in Spanish to Cuba; and
- over 500 hours per week of RFE/RL programming in 23 languages to Central Europe, Russia, Iran, Iraq, and the republics of the former Soviet Union, then referred to as Newly Independent States (NIS).[17]

USIS in the Field

In 1999, USIA operated 190 USIS posts in 142 countries. At that time, 520 USIA Foreign Service Officers staffed these posts with the support of 2,521 locally hired Foreign Service Nationals (FSN).[18] The USIA officers were posted at embassies, consulates, and USIS libraries around the world.

USIS planned and implemented its activities and programs on a country-specific basis, targeting particular audiences identified by the post. Six geographic offices supported and coordinated USIS efforts: the Office of African Affairs, the Office of Inter-American Affairs, the Office of East Asian and Pacific Affairs, the Office of West European and Canadian Affairs, the Office of East European and NIS Affairs, and the Office of North African, Near Eastern and South Asian Affairs (NEA).[19]

There were three principal USIS foreign service positions at an embassy or consulate abroad:

- The Public Affairs Officer (PAO) was responsible for managing the embassy's information and cultural activities. The PAO was the senior advisor to the Ambassador and other embassy officials on public diplomacy strategies for policy implementation, public opinion in the country, and various embassy activities, and oversaw the work of the other public diplomacy officers posted to the embassy.

- The Information Officer (IO) worked with the host country and international media, and was the embassy spokesperson. The IO drafted policy guidance on key issues of public interest, arranged press events, issued press releases, arranged live WORLDNET interactive satellite television/teleconference linking local opinion makers with U.S. government officials or other American specialists on time-sensitive issues. The IO worked with local editors and reporters explaining U.S. policies and issues regarding U.S. society and culture, and provided support for American journalists working in the country.
- The Cultural Affairs Officer (CAO) administered the educational and cultural exchange programs, and arranged programs, lectures, and seminars with U.S. speakers, artists, musicians, and other representatives of U.S. culture. The CAO also worked with local publishers to reprint and translate American books and publications.

Table 1. FY1997-FY1999 Appropriations for USIA and Related Programs ($ in thousands)

Base year for Constant $ Comparison is FY2008	FY1997 Actual	FY1997 Actual in Constant $	FY1 998 Estimate	FY1 998 Estimate in Constant $	FY1 999 Request	FY1 999 Request in Constant $
International Information Programs (includes salaries and expenses for management and support of agency)	442,183	576,253	453,146	584,694	461,728	586,902
Educational and Cultural Exchanges	218,870	285,231	197,731	255,132	199,024	252,979
Technology Center	5,050	6,581	5,050	6,516	5,050	6,419
Broadcasting	355,640	463,470	384,884	496,616	388,690	494,064
Associated NGOs and Funds	42,249	55,057	44,470	57,380	48,500	61,648
Buying Power Maintenance Fund	5,500	7,168	—	—	—	—
TOTAL	**1,099,492**	**1,432,858**	**1,125,281**	**1,451,950**	**1,119,300**	**1,422,742**

Source: United states Information Agency Summary of Positions and Appropriations, 1997-1999, *USIA Program & Budget in Brief, Fiscal Year 1999*, Washington, D.C, p. 13., and CRS calculations.

Table 2. USIA Authorized Personnel Strength 1997-1999

	1997	1998	1999 Request
Domestic	3,350	3,336	3,335
Overseas American	736	739	748
Foreign Nationals	2,849	2,753	2,689
TOTAL USIA POSITIONS	6,935	6,826	6,772

The work of the USIS Officer involved advocating U.S. positions, but also involved working with a much larger segment of the host country's society to discuss both broad U.S. government policy, and more specific issues of mutual interest to that country, such as U.S. import quotas or visa issuance policies. In order to communicate convincingly across a broader segment of contacts, USIS Officers had to "study and absorb the political and cultural climate of the host country, the better to craft messages and offer insights about America which can be coherently read in the local context."[20]

USIA's Budget and Staff Levels

Appropriations

Prior to the dissolution of USIA and the consolidation of its functions into the Department of State, the FY1 999 appropriations request for USIA was approximately $1.12 billion. **Table 1** provides USIA budget and appropriations information sorted by major account.[21]

Personnel

The authorized personnel strength reported by USIA for FY1999 is illustrated in **Table 2**.[22]

ABOLISHING USIA AND TRANSFERRING PUBLIC DIPLOMACY TO THE STATE DEPARTMENT

The Foreign Affairs Agencies Consolidation Act of 1998 (Subdivision A of Division G of P.L. 105-277) (Consolidation Act) abolished USIA.[23] The Act transferred USIA's functions to the Secretary of State. It also created the position of Under Secretary for Public Diplomacy in the Department of State. A number of factors have been identified as important to this transfer of public diplomacy responsibilities, not all of which bore directly on the improvement or importance of having a robust U.S. public diplomacy capability. First, the end of the Cold War meant that the central justification for a strong public diplomacy mechanism, namely, the ideological fight against the Soviet Union, no longer existed. After more than four decades of engaging the Soviet Union and its allies in ideological warfare, the Cold War came to an end with the collapse of the Soviet Union. The United States was the sole superpower, and the spread of democracy seemed to be on the march around the world. Many believed that the United States and the rest of the free world had won the war of ideas, and terms such as the "end of history" became popular. Some considered USIA an expendable "Cold War relic." USIA had a difficult time defining its mission in this new context, attempting to focus on new issues such as trade and economic liberalization.[24]

Second, while some saw a greatly diminished need for public diplomacy resources in general, others perceived a specific weakness in the public diplomacy apparatus represented by an independent USIA that operated separately from the State Department. As one commentator argued, U.S. public diplomacy is characterized by two types of activities: advocating for U.S. foreign policy, and building mutual understanding between Americans and foreign peoples.[25] Arguments for keeping public diplomacy in an organization separate from the State Department often focus on the importance of developing long-term relationships with the people of foreign countries, in order to create a foundation of mutual understanding, values, and interests that prepares the ground for acceptance of specific U.S. policies and actions. Placing those duties too close to the short-term policy activities of traditional diplomats within the State Department might diminish the importance of long-term efforts to achieve mutual understanding. On the other hand, public diplomats also endeavor to explain U.S. actions and policies to foreign publics in a positive light, advocating for the United States on day-to-day, shorter-term issues moving through an foreign news cycles. For these activities, some argue, a closer proximity and relationship to those in the State Department responsible for foreign policy and U.S. actions abroad would improve the synchronization and coordination of public diplomacy with official diplomacy and specific foreign policy. This argument has been bolstered as advances in technology required ever quicker communications in support of policies as news and information is spread instantly to a global audience in a 24-hour-a-day media cycle. The case of abolishing USIA and folding public diplomacy into the State Department has been described as placing quick public diplomacy responses on policy issues ahead of the protection of long-term mutual understanding efforts.[26]

Third, and related to the first two factors, certain Members of Congress and leadership within the executive branch were seeking to reorganize and streamline government in general, as well as to reduce the size and resources of U.S. foreign policy agencies in particular. Concerns about the U.S. national debt, annual federal budget deficits, and the size of government led to initiatives to "reinvent government" and reap a "peace dividend" in the form of agency and bureaucracy consolidation. USIA became part of a group of foreign affairs agencies, along with the Arms Control and Disarmament Agency (ACDA) and the Agency for International Development (USAID), that were targeted as prime candidates for consolidation into the State Department. After an extended period of political wrangling in Congress and the Clinton Administration over issues not related to public diplomacy or arms control,[27] Congress passed the Consolidation Act eliminating USIA and ACDA, with USAID surviving but in a restructured form.

Transfer of USIA Functions to the State Department

Originally, USIA's Bureau of Information Programs and the Bureau of Educational and Cultural Affairs were consolidated into a new State Department Bureau of Information Programs and International Exchanges. The Bureau was responsible for educational and cultural affairs and production of information programs to advocate for U.S. policy positions with foreign audiences. State's Bureau of Public Affairs incorporated the work of running foreign press centers, and the geographic area offices became part of their respective regional bureaus at State. USIA's research office was integrated into the State Department's Bureau of Intelligence and Research.[28]

The Bureau of Information Programs and International Exchanges was subsequently divided, and now consists of the Bureau for International Information Programs, headed by a Coordinator, and the Bureau for Educational and Cultural Exchanges, headed by an Assistant Secretary.

Independence for the Broadcasting Board of Governors (BBG)

Though the Consolidation Act dismantled USIA, it also established the Broadcasting Board of Governors as an independent entity within the executive branch. The Consolidation Act required the Secretary of State and the BBG to respect the professional independence and integrity of the International Broadcasting Bureau (IBB), charged with administering day-to-day broadcast operations, the BBG's broadcasting services, and the grantees of the BBG. This separation, and the requirement to respect the independence and the integrity of the broadcasters, maintained (1) an established deniability for U.S. diplomats when foreign countries objected to a particular broadcast, and (2) a firewall between the Department of State and the broadcasters to prove a degree of independence for the broadcasters. However, the Consolidation Act also recognized the importance of consistency between U.S.-sponsored broadcasting and the broad foreign policy objectives of the United States, as well as the importance of broadcasting as a foreign policy tool. It made the Secretary of State a permanent voting member of the Board and authorized the Secretary to assist the Board in carrying out its function by providing information and guidance on foreign policy issues as the Secretary deems appropriate.[29]

CURRENT STRUCTURE OF PUBLIC DIPLOMACY WITHIN THE DEPARTMENT OF STATE

Many recent recommendations for reform of the public diplomacy structure call for a new agency or other entity to remove public diplomacy from the State Department's responsibilities, or to reorganize or reform State Department organization to better accommodate public diplomacy. This section explains the current structure of public diplomacy organization, as well as the organization of U.S. international broadcasting, and recent budget information.

Public Diplomacy Organization in Washington

Planning, funding, and implementation of public diplomacy programs are led by the Department of State through the Under Secretary of State for Public Diplomacy and Public

Affairs, a position created by Section 1 (b)(3) of the State Department Basic Authorities Act of 1956, as amended (22 U.S.C. § 265 1a(b)(3)).[30] The Under Secretary's organization, carrying the State Department designation of "R," is tasked with leading the U.S. government's overall public diplomacy effort, increasing the impact of educational and cultural exchange, and developing and utilizing new technologies to improve the efficiency of public diplomacy programs.[31] Judith McHale was sworn in as Under Secretary of State for Public Diplomacy and Public Affairs on May 26, 2009.

Three bureaus and two offices report to the Under Secretary:

- the Bureau of Educational and Cultural Affairs (ECA) headed by an Assistant Secretary;
- the Bureau of International Information Programs (IIP) headed by a Coordinator;
- the Bureau of Public Affairs (PA) headed by an Assistant Secretary;
- the Office of Policy, Planning and Resources (R/PPR) headed by a Director, and
- the Office of Private Sector Outreach (R/PSO), also headed by a Director.

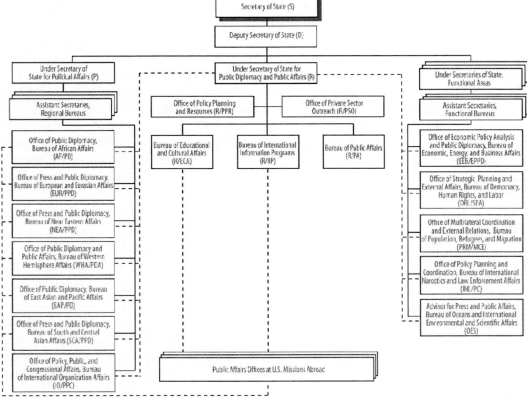

Source: Figure created by CRS, based in part on information from U.S. Department of State, *Foreign Affairs Manual*, and U.S. Department of State website, http://www.state.gov/r/index.htm, and http://www.state.gov/r/partnerships/.

Figure 3. Organization of Public Diplomacy Within the Department of State

Bureau of Educational and Cultural Affairs (ECA)

Like its earlier USIA version, ECA's mission is to foster mutual understanding between the people of the United States and the people of other countries by means of educational and cultural exchanges.[32] To achieve this goal, the Offices of Academic Exchange Programs, Citizen Exchanges, English Language Programs, Exchange Coordination and Designation, Global Educational Programs, and International Visitors implement programs for educational and professional exchange and leadership and professional development.

The Fulbright Program, which is administered by the Office of Academic Exchange Programs, is often considered the flagship of such exchanges. For the 2008-2009 academic year, with total available funding of $262,454,000, approximately 7,000 new Fulbright awards were made. Of these, 1,500 were for U.S. students, 2,700 for visiting students, 1,400 for U.S. scholars, 900 for visiting scholars, and the remainder for awards under the Fulbright teacher program. [33]

The Office of Private Sector Exchanges oversees 15 different categories of citizen exchanges bringing foreign nationals to the United States: Alien Physicians, Au Pairs, Camp Counselors, Government Visitors, International Visitors, Interns, Professors, Research Scholars, Short-Term Scholars, Specialists, Students-Secondary, Students-College/University, Summer Work Travel, Teachers, and Trainees. This office

- designates the sponsoring organizations that implement the international exchange programs;
- oversees organizations' compliance with federal regulations concerning each exchange category; and
- investigates and resolves problems that may arise in the exchange programs and the treatment of the participating international exchange students.

The Office has designated more than 1,400 sponsoring organizations to administer international exchanges.[34] The State Department estimates that more than 300,000 individuals participate in these exchange programs annually; currently there are over 1 million alumni of U.S. exchange programs around the world. These alumni include more than 40 Nobel laureates and more than 300 current and former heads of state or government.[35]

Exchange programs offer highly varied experiences. The Office of Citizen Exchanges implements cultural, professional, sports, and youth programs. For example, the Citizen Exchange Office administers the "Cultural Envoy Program." This program, which seeks to promote cross-cultural understanding and collaboration by sharing American artistic traditions with foreign audiences. It has sponsored dancer/choreographers to teach American dance, Blues musicians, off-Broadway companies, and choirs to show the breadth of American performing arts.[36]

The Obama Administration has expressed its support for exchanges, stating that such programs foster engagement and dialogue among all citizens around the world, particularly with key "influencers" including educators, clerics, journalists, women, and youth. It provides these influencers first-hand experience with Americans and U.S. values and culture.[37]

Bureau of International Information Programs (IIP)

Like its USIA forerunner, the Bureau of Information Programs, IIP administers programs that present information on foreign policy, society, and values to foreign audiences through print and electronic resources in several languages to improve international receptiveness to the United States, its people and national interests. The Bureau also provides policy and technical support for outreach efforts through U.S. embassies and consulates in more than 140 countries.

IIP continues a publication program that produces 40 to 50 publications annually in Arabic, Chinese, English, French, Persian, Russian, Spanish, and other languages, when appropriate, on topics that explore U.S. policy, society, and culture. These IIP produced books range from pocket- sized publications to illustrated "coffee-table" books. Topics include *Free at Last: The U.S. Civil Rights Movement*, *Being Muslim in America*, and *Outline of the U.S. Economy*. IIP also translates literary and non-fiction titles by American authors into several languages and, working through the embassies, establishes joint publishing agreements with local publishers. The translations can be full-length books, condensed editions, anthologies, and special adaptations in book form.

IIP also continues the speakers program and operates American Corners. As most freestanding American Centers were closed in major foreign city centers largely due to security concerns about terrorism, America Corners took their place as embassies partnered with host country institutions such as universities and libraries to house U.S. material and host events for the local population to meet visiting U.S. officials and speakers. Unlike American Centers, which were staffed by U.S. personnel, American Corners are often staffed by the partnered institution's personnel.

IIP has increased its information presence on the Internet in recent years provides videos, blogs, timelines, web chats, articles and news stories on world events, American society, and U.S. policies, in several major languages. Videos on the website generally run for little more than a minute, and discuss a wide variety of subjects from the diversity of religions in America to the experience of a young Chinese American cartoonist growing up in the United States. *Ejournal* is a monthly electronic magazine providing information on a wide variety of subjects such as jury trials, U.S. presidential transitions, and multicultural literature.

IIP also has a ten-person Digital Outreach Team that communicates on popular Arabic, Persian, and Urdu blogs, news sites, and discussion groups to explain U.S. foreign policy and counter misinformation. The Digital Outreach Team members identify themselves as employees of the Department of State as they interact on 25 to 30 Internet sites per week. The team posts short comments as well as longer op-ed pieces and translated videos previously produced by IIP.

The joint ECA-IIP Grants Division provides grants to organizations to carry out educational and cultural programs and free exchange of information.

The Bureau of Public Affairs (PA)

The Bureau of Public Affairs (PA) has a separate mission and audience from IIP's. While IIP's work and products are made for foreign audiences, and by law cannot be developed for domestic consumption, PA's function is to inform the American public about U.S. foreign policy, and to share American concerns and views with U.S. policymakers. The Bureau
- conducts press briefings for domestic and foreign press corps;

- manages the State Department website at State.gov;
- arranges town meetings and schedules speakers to visit communities in the United States to discuss U.S. foreign policy; and
- prepares the historical studies on U.S. diplomacy and foreign affairs matters.

Office of Policy Planning and Resources (R/PPR)

R/PPR provides the Under Secretary with strategic planning and performance measurement capability for public diplomacy and public affairs initiatives so that public diplomacy resources can be allocated to meet national security objectives. The Evaluation and Measurement Unit (EMU) within PPR was created in 2004 to evaluate all public diplomacy programs in Washington and in the field through the development of data collection methods and analytical procedures.

Office of Private Sector Outreach (R/PS O)

R/PSO seeks to develop working relationships with private sector leaders in U.S. companies, universities, and foundations to promote foreign policy objectives such as countering violent extremism, empowering women business and civic leaders, and strengthening international education.

Public Diplomacy in the Field

Each U.S. embassy maintains a public affairs section to manage informational and cultural programs in a host country. The section is tasked with explaining U.S. government policy and actions to that country's officials, media, and people. At large embassies the section's overall responsibilities are shared by a cultural affairs officer (CAO) and an information officer (IO), while at other embassies the duties are handled by the public affairs officer (PAO). The CAO or PAO manages cultural programs designed to educate foreign publics about the United States, and to dispel false conceptions about Americans, American attitudes and beliefs, and life in the United States. These programs include sending foreign individuals to the United States for various periods of time for professional and educational exchange. The Public Affairs section also sponsors trips by American cultural ambassadors as previously mentioned in the ECA discussion, and brings American speakers to the host country to engage the people on important issues. The PAO will also often conduct informal outreach by attending receptions and concerts in the host country, and by hosting receptions for foreign individuals in his or her home.[38]

In addition, the PAO also coordinates the embassy's communications with the media in the host country, and is the only embassy person, besides the U.S. Ambassador, who is authorized to speak directly to the press. The PAO issues press releases on current issues concerning U.S. government policy or action, and responds to inquiries in press conferences and interviews provided to local media. The PAO will inform Washington of this activity as well as provide analysis on the coverage of such activities. The PAO, as well as other Public Diplomacy Officers (PDO), make presentations to various groups and institutions within the host country. The PAO also must perform a number of administrative duties within the embassy, related to supporting the Ambassador, and manage exchange and other public diplomacy programs, budgets, and personnel within the public affairs section.[39]

Differences between USIA and the State Department

There are a number of differences in organization and operations of public diplomacy between the former USIA and the current State Department public diplomacy structure.

Authority

In USIA, the Agency's Director had a direct line of authority to the geographical area offices, and Public Diplomacy Officers (PDOs) were part of a chain of command that descended directly from the Director. At the State Department, in contrast, much of the public diplomacy staff is located in separate public diplomacy offices in the regional and functional bureaus, outside R's organizational structure. These public diplomacy offices within each bureau are designed to place PDOs in close contact with the bureaus' policy-makers, in order to improve integration of traditional and public diplomacy on foreign policy issues. Therefore, while public diplomacy policy and planning fall under the R's authority, public diplomacy staff in the regional and functional bureaus are under the authority of the Under Secretary of State for Political Affairs in the case of regional bureaus, as well as the various under secretaries heading the functional organizations within State.[40]

Funding

Funds for public diplomacy activities are disbursed and expended differently within the State Department in comparison to the former USIA. Funding for public diplomacy has a separate line in the State Department's operating account and is sequestered from other funds within the State Department. Funding for public diplomacy activities and for salaries of Foreign Service Nationals (FSNs) employed in public diplomacy positions is provided through allotments from the budget of the Under Secretary of State for Public Diplomacy and Public Affairs. Under secretaries and assistant secretaries outside R may not transfer public diplomacy funds to other uses within their organizations.[41] Unlike USIA, however, R does not have complete control over public diplomacy funding. Because PDOs located in each of the regional and functional bureaus are in many cases the primary actors undertaking public diplomacy activities in the Department, day-to-day expenditure of public diplomacy funds is dictated by the regional and functional bureaus themselves, not by R.

Assignments and Evaluations

PDO assignments and evaluations are handled differently in the State Department. The USIA Director made all position assignments through USIA's dedicated human resources office, and the Director's direct chain of command implemented all performance evaluations and promotion decisions. Evaluations were based primarily on an Officer's public diplomacy skills and accomplishments. The State Department, on the other hand, uses its Department-wide Human Resources Bureau to make assignments and to evaluate PDOs alongside other FSOs from the other four career cones (Consular, Economic, Management, Political) in the Department. Under the State Department's generalist approach to the careers of its F SOs, the

Department regularly assigns PDOs to non public diplomacy positions, and also fills Public Diplomacy positions with FSOs from other cones. Evaluations of PDOs within State are based on a general set of criteria not specifically related to accomplishment and skill in public diplomacy. The fact that R does not administer employee performance evaluations for the PD officers at posts abroad or in the regional and functional bureaus represents a significant difference from the evaluation structure of the former USIA.[42]

Support in the Field

Critics of the current organizational structure also contend that since the old USIA regional bureaus became part of the Department of State's regional bureaus, PDOs assigned to U.S. posts and missions abroad no longer get the same support from the State Department regional and functional bureaus.

> The "area directors" for each region of the world supervised a staff of FSOs in a single Washington office who were all experienced public diplomacy professionals and who had served abroad, usually in that region. These area offices were efficient in evaluating field requests because they understood in detail what the circumstances were that the PAO was operating in, and they were prompt in responding to the PAO.[43]

BROADCASTING BOARD OF GOVERNORS

With the enactment of the United States International Broadcasting Act of 1994 (P.L. 103-236), all U.S. international broadcasting services were consolidated under a new Broadcasting Board of Governors (BBG) within USIA. In 1998, Congress passed legislation establishing the BBG as an independent entity within the executive branch at the same time it abolished USIA. The BBG, which acts independently of the Department of State, is composed of nine members, with the Secretary of State serving as a voting member *ex officio* and providing foreign policy information and guidance to the Board. By ensuring broadcasting independence while at the same time institutionalizing guidance from the Secretary of State, the legislation struck a balance between U.S. international broadcasting that is credible in the view of foreign audiences and support for the foreign policy objectives of the United States. The President appoints the remaining eight members to three-year terms, and the members are confirmed by the Senate.

The BBG has responsibility for supervising, directing, and overseeing the operations of the International Broadcasting Bureau (IBB). The IBB, whose director is appointed by the BBG, supervises the worldwide broadcasting services of the Voice of America (VOA) and Worldnet television broadcasts, Cuba Broadcasting (Radio and TV Marti), an Engineering and Technical Operations Office, and various support and transmission services to the broadcasters. The BBG also has funding and oversight authority over surrogate radio[44] grantees: Radio Free Europe/Radio Liberty (RFE/RL) which also operates Radio Farda (Iran) and Radio Free Iraq; Radio Free Asia (RFA); and the Middle East Broadcasting Network which operates Radio Sawa and Alhurra television. Among BBG's responsibilities is reviewing and evaluating the operations of the radios, and assessing their quality, effectiveness, and professional integrity. It is also responsible for determining the addition or deletion of the language services under the IBB.[45] See **Figure 4**.

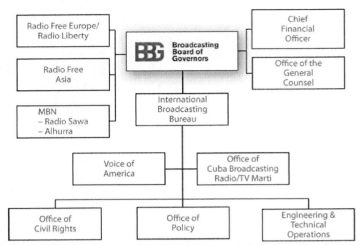

Source: Broadcasting Board of Governors, http://www.bbg.gov/about/index.html.

Figure 4. Organization of U.S. International Broadcasting

Table 3. FY2008-FY2010 Public Diplomacy Appropriations in U.S. Department of State ($ in thousands)

	FY2008 Actual	FY2009 Estimate	FY20 10 Request
Diplomatic and Consular Programs (D&CP):			
Regional Bureaus	280,613	293,928	302,998
Bureau of International Information Programs	51,547	58,829	66,425
Functional Bureaus	26,197	20,691	62,987
Payment—Foreign Service National Separation Liability Trust Fund	2,238	2,238	5,472
FY2008 Supplemental	20,000	—	—
FY2009 Supplemental	4,000	3,320	
Central Program Increases	—	19,688	62,396
PUBLIC DIPLOMACY FROM D&CP TOTAL	**364,595**	**398,694**	**500,278**
Educational and Cultural Exchanges	501,347	538,000	633,243
National Endowment for Democracy	—[a]	115,000	100,000
East-West Center	19,342	21,000	11,730
Eisenhower Exchange Fellowship Program	—	500	500
Israeli Arab Scholarship Program	232	375	375
Sec. 810 United States Information and Educational Exchange Act Fees	7,568	6,000	6,000
Representation Allowances	1,805	1,859	1,859
PUBLIC DIPLOMACY OVERALL TOTAL (includes D&CP)	**890,889**	**1,081,428**	**1,253,985**

Source: U.S. Department of State, *Congressional Budget Justification, Fiscal Year 2010*, p. 13.

a. Funded by the Democracy Fund in FY2008 in the estimated amount of $99,190,000. U.S. Department of State, Summary and Highlights, International Affairs Function 150, Fiscal Year 2009 Budget Request, p. 3.

PUBLIC DIPLOMACY BUDGET

Funding for public diplomacy is located in annual State Department/Foreign Operations appropriations legislation, which includes funds appropriated for public diplomacy within the State Department and separate funding for international broadcasting.

State Department

The State Department includes its requests for funding of public diplomacy under the Diplomatic and Consular Programs heading in appropriations legislation, as well as under a number of other headings, such as Educational and Cultural Programs. **Table 3** denotes public diplomacy appropriations for FY2008-2009 and the FY2010 request.

International Broadcasting

Table 4 below shows appropriations for the BBG for FY2008-2009, and the FY2010 request.

Public Diplomacy Personnel

Table 5 provides staff numbers in the major areas of public diplomacy function within the State Department. The FY2009 request included appropriations to fund an additional 20 public diplomacy positions for both domestic and overseas positions in IIP, as well as new locally engaged staff overseas.

Table 4. FY2008-FY2010 Appropriations for International Broadcasting
($ in thousands)

	FY2008 Actual	FY2009 Enacted	FY2009 PendingSupp.	FY2009 Total	FY20 10 Request
International Broadcasting Operations	673,343	704,187	—	704,187	732,187
Broadcasting Capital Improvements	10,661	11,296	—	11,296	13,263
INTERNATIONAL BROADCASTING TOTAL	**684,004**	**715,483**	—	**715,483**	**745,450**

Source: U.S. Department of State, *Summary and Highlights, International Affairs Function 150, Fiscal Year 2010 Budget Request,* p. 63.

Table 5. 2008-2010 Public Diplomacy Positions, U.S. Department of State

	FY2008	FY2009	FY2010 Request
Regional Bureaus	2,370	2,370	2,370
Educational and Cultural Exchanges	362	381	410
Bureau of International Information Programs	263	263	263
Central Program Increases	—	20	20
Functional Bureaus/Other Support	39	39	59
TOTAL PUBLIC DIPLOMACY POSITIONS	**3,034**	**3,083**	**3,122**

Source: U.S. Department of State, *Congressional Budget Justification, Fiscal Year 2009*, p. 13.

Note: The term "Public Diplomacy Positions" includes all direct-hire full-time employees in Foreign Service and Civil Service positions, but does not include Locally Engaged Staff (LES).

OTHER GOVERNMENT AGENCIES COMMUNICATING WITH FOREIGN PUBLICS

While the State Department is the recognized lead for U.S. public diplomacy efforts, a number of government agencies engage in communications with foreign publics by virtue of their missions. The Department of Defense (DOD) and the Agency for International Development (USAID) are two organizations with clear foreign policy aspects to their activities. A number of other agencies conduct exchanges under the Mutual Educational and Cultural Exchange Act of 1956 (MECEA), and, with the advent of instant global communication through satellite and Internet media, more agencies must consider the effect of their messaging on foreign publics than before. An overview of DOD and other agencies' efforts follows.

Department of Defense Communications

The Department of Defense (DOD) has focused increasingly on improving its communications with foreign publics, as well as measuring and assessing the effect its words and actions have on populations living in the areas where U.S. military operations are taking place. It has attempted to shift its focus in many cases from traditional military operations and missions to the non-kinetic, information- and influence-based activities contemplated within concepts of "strategic communication," integrating communication and influence guidance throughout operational planning and execution. DOD has defined the term "strategic communication" as

> [f]ocused United States Government efforts to understand and engage key audiences to create, strengthen, or preserve conditions favorable for the advancement of United States Government interests, policies, and objectives through the use of coordinated programs, plans, themes, messages, and products synchronized with the actions of all instruments of national power.[46]

Two observations may be made about this definition. First, although the term "strategic communication" (SC) is attributed to DOD activities to a much greater extent than other government agencies, its definition of the term includes the efforts of the entire U.S. government. Second, the definition describes a process of activity, not an organizational structure within DOD or any other government agency. In DOD, activities related to strategic communication are primarily supported by three capabilities: (1) Information Operations (IO), and primarily within IO, Psychological Operations (PSYOP); (2) Public Affairs (PA); and (3) Defense Support to Public Diplomacy (DSPD). Military Diplomacy (MD) and Visual Information (VI) also support SC-related activities. In addition, while the term "public diplomacy" as used by the State Department describes communications with foreign populations, strategic communication involves DOD interacting with and influencing foreign publics, military adversaries, partner and non-partner governments, other U.S. government agencies, and the American people.

Department of Defense Strategic Communication Activities

DOD undertakes a number of specified activities through SC-support organizations such as PSYOP, PA, and VI, and has in recent years increased its communication efforts on the Internet as well as in areas where kinetic military operations are ongoing, including Iraq and Afghanistan. It has also attempted to improve the understanding of foreign societies in order to better communicate with these publics. Beginning in 2007, for instance, DOD created small teams of social scientists and anthropologists, known as Human Terrain Teams, and embedded them in brigades in Iraq and Afghanistan. These Teams are responsible for providing insights into the customs and values of local populations.[47]

In addition, responding to the release of the 2007 National Strategy for Public Diplomacy and Strategic Communication, which called for relevant agencies to provide information on activities related to the goals and concepts in the Strategy (see National Strategy and Interagency Coordination Efforts, below), DOD identified a number of specific SC-related programs and activities. These included a number of government-to-government and military-to-military activities, but DOD also described programs for interaction with foreign publics, and related activities. As DOD considers messages conveyed through actions a major part of strategic communication in addition to those delivered through words, it included the Department's humanitarian assistance activities as important to interaction with foreign populations, and also described the activities of its PA organization that publicize such assistance to explain the source of that assistance. Deeds-based SC activities also included the Global Maritime Partnership, which involves deployment of Navy warships and hospital ships to conduct civil-military operations in foreign countries as well as deliver humanitarian assistance.

A number of programs designed to support the effort to counter terrorist and extremist groups also were listed. The Trans-regional Web Initiative (TRWI) directed Combatant Commands (COCOMs) to create regionally focused websites with tailored communications to foreign audiences and measure and assess their effectiveness. The Department created the Expanded Trans-Regional PSYOP Program (ETRP) to unify and synchronize communications themes and objectives across all theatres, guiding individual COCOM-created communications to selected foreign audiences in each region. ETRP authorized communications through audio-visual, telephonic, and web-based applications. DOD has also created Regional Centers for Security Studies,[48] which provide educational opportunities in the United States and Germany for key foreign audiences on regional security issues. These centers create networks of influential alumni who "serve as a vanguard of indirect strategic communications efforts."[49]

DOD is also seeking to measure and assess more effectively the effects of its actions and messages on foreign populations, and to develop improved communications. DOD has identified a number of activities and capabilities required to achieve these goals, including the following:

- utilizing network science in addition to opinion polling to identify key audiences, key issues, and effective communications activities;
- using new software to track and analyze Internet activity to identify trends, developing issues, and local, regional, and global sentiment;
- identifying and tracking the statements, actions, and attitudes of key foreign opinion leaders;
- utilizing independent inspector teams to interact directly with foreign populations to determine communication and influence problems and to alter actions and words to improve explanation and acceptance of DOD actions; and
- mapping social communications systems for reference in building communications strategies.[50]

Department of Defense Strategic Communication Doctrine and Coordination Efforts[51]

DOD created the office of the Deputy Secretary of Defense for Support to Public Diplomacy in 2007 to coordinate DOD communications with other government entities. With reports surfacing that the office was providing guidance to military commanders that did not meet DOD's standards of accuracy and transparency, Michele A. Flournoy, appointed in early 2009 as Undersecretary of Defense for Policy, abolished the office and the Deputy Assistant Secretary position. In its place as a coordinating entity for strategic communication strategy and activities within DOD, Undersecretary Flournoy created the Global Strategic Engagement Team (GSET) headed by Rosa Brooks, Senior Advisor to the Undersecretary.

The GSET is currently in the midst of reviewing the overall DOD approach to enterprise-wide strategic coordination; existing SC-related capabilities and activities; recent DOD documents regarding SC concepts, principles, goals, and best practices;[52] and avenues for creating formal SC doctrine. Ms. Brooks has also instituted a Global Strategic Engagement Coordinating Committee, represented by the various organizations that provide crucial support to DOD's strategic communication efforts, including PA, Legislative Affairs, IO, Joint Staff, and the Office of the Undersecretary of Defense for Policy itself. This Committee provides the opportunity for policy discussion and oversight, creation of a common orientation toward SC issues and coordination, as well as senior-level SC review and direction. Ms. Brooks's team is directing reviews of existing SC capabilities such as IO to analyze their activities and doctrine in support of wider SC coordination and integration efforts. As this process has begun recently, DOD officials anticipate a timeline of several months before the initial review process is finished.

USAID

It is acknowledged that USAID, because of its administration of foreign assistance, has an important role in public diplomacy. The Agency creates long-standing relationships between the United States and the people of other countries, relationships that are capable of influencing foreign publics to view U.S. policies and actions as beneficial and to cooperate with U.S. government initiatives. Since the 9/11 terrorist attacks, USAID claims it has increased its outreach to foreign publics to better explain the humanitarian and assistance programs intended to improve the living conditions and development of vulnerable populations. USAID employs its own public diplomacy officers, called Development Outreach and Communication Officers, to carry out USAID's mission to inform host country publics about U.S. assistance efforts.[53] These Officers develop mission-specific communication strategies based on audience research and including goals, objectives, action plans, and budgets required to carry them out.[54] USAID provides its Communications Officers with specialized training and has developed a field manual for communicating with foreign publics.

USAID works with the State Department through the State-USAID Joint Policy Council and Management Council to coordinate the two agencies' public diplomacy efforts. In addition, the Secretary of State is encouraged to work with USAID and other private organizations in ensuring when practicable that assistance provided through USAID, whether it is in the provision of commodities and services or funding large civil works projects, is clearly marked "from the American people," with the logo of USAID.[55]

Additional Actors

While State and USAID sponsor nearly four-fifths of U.S. and foreign participants in educational and cultural exchange programs,[56] other government agencies are responsible for the remaining participants in exchange programs authorized under the Mutual Educational and Cultural Exchange Act of 1961. Examples include the short-term exchange of scientists program at the National Cancer Institute, and the Architectural and Transportation Barriers Compliance Board with its 74 foreign participants in 2007. These exchanges, while not having been designed strictly as public diplomacy initiatives, nevertheless have the same effect with foreign participants meeting, working with, and living in the United States.

A number of congressionally mandated NGOs, many founded during the Cold War, continue to receive appropriated funds to perform work in support of U.S. foreign policy objectives. These NGOs seek to develop long-term relationships and to improve foreign populations' understanding of and attitudes toward the United States. Among these organizations are the National Endowment for Democracy (NED), the Asia Foundation, the East West Center at the University of Hawaii, and the Eisenhower Exchange Fellowship Program.

Although most U.S. government agencies do not have a mandate to communicate with foreign publics, Internet and satellite broadcasting technologies make any public messages and statements instantly available to a global audience. Thus, when the Secretary of the Treasury discusses the state of the U.S. economy and steps that the Department is proposing, or the Administrator of the Environmental Protection Agency discusses pollution standards or the Agency's position on climate change, all are communicating to foreign publics even if that is not the intent.

NATIONAL STRATEGY AND INTERAGENCY COORDINATION EFFORTS

There have been numerous attempts to create government-wide strategies and to foster interagency coordination for public diplomacy and strategic communication in recent years, but none has been regarded as successful. The National Security Council established a Strategic Communication Policy Coordinating Committee in 2002, and tasked it with creating a national strategy for strategic communication. Although a draft strategy was produced, it was not released, and this Policy Coordinating Committee was disbanded with the advent of the war in Iraq.[57] President George W. Bush created the Office of Global Communications in July 2002, with a similar assignment to provide strategic direction to U.S.-government communications, but instead it performed only day-to-day public affairs functions, providing guidance on policy messaging. It was disbanded in 2005.

In April 2006, National Security Advisor Stephen Hadley authorized creation of a new Policy Coordinating Committee for Public Diplomacy and Strategic Communication (PCC), to be led by the Under Secretary of State for Public Diplomacy and Public Affairs, with support from the Deputy National Security Advisor for Strategic Communication and Global Outreach. The PCC was intended to act as the principal interagency coordination body for U.S. government communications with foreign publics, and is comprised of representatives from the State Department, DOD, the Department of the Treasury, the National Security Council, the intelligence community, and other agencies. The Global Strategic Engagement Center, established by former Under Secretary of State for Public Diplomacy and Public Affairs James K. Glassman, acts as a subject-matter advisory group for the PCC, and also serves as a response unit for counterterrorism communications. It is staffed by civilian personnel from the State Department, the Central Intelligence Agency, and other agencies, as well as by active-duty military personnel.

In 2007, the PCC released the National Strategy for Public Diplomacy and Strategic Communication. It articulates three strategic objectives for U.S. government communications with foreign publics:

1. America must offer a positive vision of hope and opportunity that is rooted in our most basic values.
2. With our partners, we seek to isolate and marginalize violent extremists who threaten the freedom and peace sought by civilized people of every nation, culture and faith.
3. America must work to nurture common interests and values between Americans and peoples of different countries, cultures and faiths across the world.

It identifies three main target audiences: (1) key influencers, those who can effectively guide foreign societies in line with U.S. interests; (2) vulnerable populations, including the youth, women and girls, and minority groups; and (3) mass audiences, who are more connected to information about the United States and the world than ever before through new and expanding global communications media. The Strategy identifies three public diplomacy priorities:

- expand education and exchange programs, "perhaps the single most effective public diplomacy tool of the last fifty years";
- modernize communications, including a heightened profile for U.S. officials in foreign media, increased foreign language training for U.S. diplomats, and utilization of Internet media such as web chats, blogs, and interactive websites; and
- promote the "diplomacy of deeds," publicizing U.S. activities to benefit foreign populations through humanitarian assistance, health and education programs, and economic development, as well as U.S. government activities that show respect for foreign culture and history.[58]

As the first steps toward better interagency coordination and unity of effort with regard to public diplomacy and strategic communication, the Strategy asked each relevant agency to develop an agency-specific plan to implement the objectives of the Strategy, as well as to increase information sharing with other agencies to encourage clear and consistent messaging across all U.S. government communications to foreign publics.

Although the Strategy was considered a step forward in government-wide coordination of communications efforts, it was criticized for failing to clearly define agency roles and responsibilities, and implementation of the Strategy has been lacking, especially with regard to the creation and coordination of agency-specific plans.[59] In addition, the PCC does not convene regularly, although Rosa Brooks, Senior Advisor to Undersecretary of Defense for Policy Michele Flournoy, currently meets regularly with Under Secretary of State for Public Diplomacy and Public Affairs Judith McHale to discuss interagency issues and plans concerning public diplomacy and strategic communication. In light of these deficiencies, Congress has mandated creation of a new strategy for public diplomacy and strategic communication. Section 1055 of the National Defense Authorization Act for Fiscal Year 2009 (P.L. 110-417) requires the President to submit by the end of 2009 a report on a federal government strategy for public diplomacy and strategic communication to specified congressional committees. For more information see the section entitled "Recent Legislative Action."

The National Security Council (NSC) also provides fora for interagency public diplomacy and strategic communication coordination. When events occur that may impact counterterrorism efforts or that generally require coordinated response, the NSC convenes the International Crisis Communication Team, which includes NSC, White House, DOD, and State Department representatives, as well as other agency representatives as needed, to coordinate a government- wide communication response. In addition, in May 2009, President Obama announced the creation of a Global Engagement Directorate (GED) within the NSC, "to drive comprehensive engagement policies that leverage diplomacy, communications, international development and assistance, and domestic engagement and outreach in pursuit of a host of national security objectives... ."[60] As part of the activities of the GED, NSC holds weekly interagency policy committee meetings that can directly concern public diplomacy and strategic communication issues.

CURRENT ISSUES CONCERNING U.S. PUBLIC DIPLOMACY

A number of issues currently present challenges to the future implementation of U.S. public diplomacy efforts. These issues relate to the following:

- leadership;
- strategy at the national level;
- roles, responsibilities, and interagency coordination;
- organizational issues within the State Department;
- personnel matters;
- exchanges and other outreach activities;
- U.S. international broadcasting;
- leveraging outside expertise and best practices;
- monitoring and evaluation of public diplomacy; and
- restrictions on domestic dissemination of public diplomacy information.

Congress might wish to take these issues into account when considering new legislation or conducting oversight over U.S. public diplomacy and strategic communication. A number of Members of Congress have already proposed legislation in the 111th Congress that touches upon a number of the issues discussed in this section.

Leadership

As with many other efforts at reform and improvement of government effectiveness, leadership, both at the presidential and agency level, is crucial. This seems to hold especially true with regard to the U.S. government's communications with foreign publics, as the President is the government's most high-profile communicator. President Obama has made communicating to the world a priority thus far in his Administration. He has made major speeches in Europe, Russia, Egypt, and Ghana, and has given an exclusive interview to the television broadcaster Al Arabiya, a leading source of information programming in the Middle East. He has addressed directly his vision that the United States will engage with the world in an atmosphere of mutual respect and shared values and goals. In the White House, he has created a Global Engagement Directorate within the National Security Council that, the President has asserted, will rely on government communications as well as other non-military elements of national power to meet national security objectives.

According to some, however, the President's leadership has not manifested itself sufficiently in reform-minded proposals necessary to improve the public diplomacy apparatus within the State Department, the interagency coordination process for communications with foreign publics, and the effectiveness of U.S. public diplomacy on the whole. Foremost in the comments of some was the lack of agency-level leadership for public diplomacy, as the position of Under Secretary of State for Public Diplomacy and Public Affairs was left vacant for the first four months of the Obama Administration (as it was at many times during past Administrations).[61] Some feared this delay could signify that changes to public diplomacy, at least within the State Department, would not receive top priority from the new

Administration. In May 2009, President Obama filled the Under Secretary position, appointing Judith McHale. Although Under Secretary McHale has extensive experience in broadcasting both domestically and abroad, some observers noted her lack of experience with the State Department's bureaucracy, taking it as a possible sign that the Obama administration does not expect to raise the profile of public diplomacy within the State Department and across other pertinent agencies. Furthermore, some criticized Under Secretary McHale's lack of experience with traditional public diplomacy activities, the expansion and improvement of which many see as crucial to reestablishing the effectiveness of U.S. public diplomacy overall.[62] Although it certainly remains to be seen what impact Under Secretary McHale will have on public diplomacy within her organization at the State Department, it may be that the Obama Administration, as some have suggested, is content with concentrating major communications efforts intended for foreign audiences in the White House, and in the President himself. (See "Agency Roles and Interagency Coordination", and "State Department Organizational Issues," below, for more discussion on the State Department's role.)

National Strategy

The National Defense Authorization Act for Fiscal Year 2009 (P.L. 110-417) requires the President to report to Congress, no later than December 31, 2009, on the creation of a new national strategy for public diplomacy and strategic communication. This strategy will replace the June 2007 National Strategy for Public Diplomacy and Strategic Communication, which has been criticized by some as deficient in both construction and implementation. Several studies have considered creation of a new national strategy for communicating with foreign publics and have provided recommendations. Analyzing these recommendations, there seems to be an emerging consensus on the need for a new U.S. national strategy to address certain core public diplomacy issues in order to ensure effective communications with foreign publics. These issues include (1) effectively placing U.S. public diplomacy within the global communications environment; (2) providing a reconsidered, more sophisticated approach to public diplomacy and strategic communication; (3) and ensuring the integrated, flexible, whole-of-government implementation of public diplomacy strategy to meet the objectives of U.S. foreign policy.

Global Communications Environment

Much discussion about U.S. public diplomacy concerns the nature of the global communications environment, and the position both of the U.S. government and the United States as a whole in that environment. Personal communications technology is relatively inexpensive and increasingly available to higher numbers of people, and communications technology and new media are expanding rapidly. Non-state actors, including NGOs, corporations, and individuals, can now exert exponentially higher communications capabilities through the improvement in speed and capacity of the Internet. The Internet has given rise to new phenomena in communications technology. According to one report, for example, an individual blogger can today reach more people globally than could the British Broadcasting Service (BBC) or the Voice of America (VOA) thirty years ago.[63] The Internet has also raised the importance of so-called "many-tomany" communications media, where networks of actors can both receive messages from and send messages to each other in a continuous two-way conversation. This differs from traditional "one-to-many" communications, through which one information source provides one message to large numbers of people. Also, the "many-to-many" communications model has made message influence a matter of convincing potential consumers to choose to receive information from a plethora of communications sources. Rather than consuming programming and information from a limited number of sources that "push" information to large numbers of people, now foreign publics can "pull" information from the sources they deem to be most representative of their interests or most trustworthy. In addition, while the influence of traditional media has fallen as the Internet has grown in importance, many new actors have moved into traditional broadcasting, with a proliferation of new satellite broadcast networks having gained a large share of listeners and viewership in recent years.

These developments in new communications media have complicated the work of U.S. public diplomacy, reducing the guaranteed audience the United States used to enjoy, and increasing the number of information sources where the U.S. government seeks an influential message presence. These challenges exist alongside the perceived need for improving traditional public diplomacy activities. From the several calls to expand and improve traditional U.S. international broadcasting, as well as to expand the United States' ability to conduct in-country, person-toperson public diplomacy, it is apparent that a new national strategy would require an approach that meets the challenges of traditional outreach and contemporary communications media and technology simultaneously. Internet communications, including social media networks such as Twitter and Facebook, have characteristics of both broadcast communications, such as the ability to communicate written and spoken words, still images, and motion pictures to a wide audience, and in-country, person-to-person outreach, which engenders personal relationships connected in networks of individuals connected by common interests, not just common geography. Thus, the new U.S. national strategy could attempt to integrate outreach approaches from these two traditionally separate communications areas to create effective outreach solutions for the challenges created by the global communications environment.

New Approach to Communicating with Foreign Publics

Pointing to various perceived deficiencies in recent U.S. public diplomacy efforts, some observers have suggested implementing a newly considered, sophisticated approach to public diplomacy that provides frameworks, tools, and techniques to meet clear strategic objectives in order to improve the government's ability to communicate with foreign populations.

Adherence to Traditional Public Diplomacy Principles

Certain recommendations have stressed the importance of the central principles underpinning theories of effective public diplomacy activities. These include the principle that communications with foreign publics should be open and truthful, and any covert communications activities that must be undertaken by the U.S. government should be effectively separated from the communications undertaken by public diplomacy actors.[64] Also, the United States should "listen" to foreign publics, that is to say, U.S. public diplomacy activities should encourage and sustain two-way communications between U.S.

public diplomacy actors and members of foreign populations, especially those "key influencers" within such populations.[65] U.S. public diplomacy efforts would adhere to these principles as they meet identified objectives, including cultivating common understanding between citizens of the United States and foreign populations, and promoting shared values and interests. According to some, increasing common understanding could include teaching Americans more about the cultures, languages, and interests of foreign countries and peoples.[66] In the opinion of some analysts, integrating such principles into a national strategy to be implemented by all relevant government agencies could represent a step forward for U.S. government communications with foreign publics.

Adaptive and Culturally Sensitive Communications

Many recommendations call for a more nuanced approach to U.S. public diplomacy efforts, placing emphasis on understanding how different foreign publics perceive U.S. government messages and whether they trust U.S. government messengers. For example, there are calls for U.S. public diplomacy to be more delicate in the way it promotes and defends America to foreign publics. Some argue that U.S. government communicators must determine whether touting and promoting American values, such as human rights, rule of law, democracy, or free trade, might backfire due to the perception of foreign publics that U.S. policies do not follow those values, either at home or abroad. Some have also suggested that any defense of certain unpopular U.S. policies and actions in foreign countries, especially in a manner that some characterize as arrogant or dismissive, should in some cases be eschewed altogether as it damages the long-term trust of U.S. government messages by foreign populations. When U.S. policies are unpopular within a given foreign population, public diplomacy messages could instead focus on the drawbacks and deficiencies of U.S. adversaries and opponents in the corresponding country or region. Other recommendations suggest better utilization of non-U.S. government messengers, especially individuals identified as "key influencers," to deliver messages that will aid U.S. interests and allow U.S. government actors to stay out of the spotlight.[67]

Under this approach, determining which type of messenger to utilize in any given situation would be made continuously based on knowledge of the cultural and political climate within a given target population developed over the long term.[68] In addition, the strict controls over U.S. government messages and information have clashed with the need for Public Diplomacy Officers to have access and permission to employ every tool of communication with foreign publics. Flexible, adaptive communications might provide the most potential for success in achieving U.S. public diplomacy and related foreign policy objectives. Increased public diplomacy resources and training, both to enhance traditional public diplomacy capabilities as well as to take advantage of new communications techniques and technologies, could provide a more complete public diplomacy toolkit, thus improving the flexibility of communications response proposed. [69]

Comprehensive Approach and Long-Term Focus

Some have called for U.S. public diplomacy strategy and approaches to concentrate on comprehensive and long-term objectives in support of U.S. foreign policy. Some observers of U.S. communications with foreign publics describe the focus in recent years on communications in support of counterterrorism as necessary, but in some ways too narrow and shortsighted in terms of the proper exercise of overall U.S. public diplomacy.[70] Although the terrorism threat and engagement with the Muslim world must take some precedence in the current national security environment, there are warnings that overemphasis of communications efforts on isolated issues and regions might cause the weakening of relationships with the publics of other important countries and regions. Some argue that because the greatest impact of public diplomacy efforts is the creation of deep, long-term relationships with foreign publics that build a lasting trust of the U.S. government as an honest messenger, resources and personnel for public diplomacy must be deployed in sufficient amount and numbers in all regions of importance. Such comprehensive, global coverage could improve the likelihood that when the next crisis arises, the U.S. government will have a ready-made network of relationships with the relevant foreign publics on which it can rely for, if not outright support, at least an honest discussion of the issues and an accepting outlet for U.S. messaging.[71] Even in an age of instant global communications from nearly unlimited sources, therefore, the existence of long-term networks of communication between trusted U.S. public diplomacy actors and members of foreign publics, based both on geographical and virtual connections, could improve the effectiveness of U.S. communications.[72]

Integrated, Whole-of-Government Implementation

Some experts have claimed that U.S. public diplomacy and strategic communication is not guided by a national strategy that integrates communications efforts across government or within other foreign policy and national security objectives. Without a national strategy, agencies pursue their own communications interests, leading to disunity of voice, redundant messaging, and the possibility of communications working at cross-purposes.[73] Each relevant government agency could be required to provide a plan for communicating with foreign publics, and these plans could serve as the basis for government-wide coordination of public diplomacy efforts. (See Agency Roles and Interagency Coordination, below.)

Certain recommendations for improving public diplomacy and strategic communications call for integration of communications issues within already existing strategies for other uses of U.S. national power, including traditional diplomacy, foreign assistance, and national defense. Such integration might increase the incidence of policy makers considering public diplomacy issues at the creation of policies, instead of bringing U.S. public diplomacy actors into situations after the fact to quell opposition to U.S. actions from foreign publics.[74] In May 2009, the Obama Administration announced the creation of the Global Engagement Directorate (GED) within the National Security Council. The GED is intended to coordinate several different elements of national power, including communications, to achieve national security goals. Although the GED is still in its nascent stages, it may serve as a locus for the implementation of a new national strategy for public diplomacy and strategic communication, integrated into other strategic platforms, as has been recommended.

Agency Roles and Interagency Coordination

The Department of State is the lead agency and the primary practitioner of public diplomacy within the U.S. government. Yet, as previously explained, several U.S.

government agencies participate in at least one form of official public diplomacy or strategic communication activity. Most of these agencies primarily participate in engagement with foreign publics through foreign exchange programs, and DOD and USAID communicate in various ways with foreign publics based on their respective international missions. U.S. international broadcasting, overseen by the Broadcasting Board of Governors (BBG), is another major independent public diplomacy actor.[75] Many observers suggest that while multiple government actors have a proper role to play in public diplomacy, those roles need definition, and the corresponding activities require coordination.[76] Such efforts might encourage conflict between agencies currently engaging with foreign publics, as questions of authority and turf come to the fore.

Complicating the determination of proper public diplomacy roles and coordination of effort across government is the fact that many agencies do not expressly focus on communicating with foreign publics. Certain agencies may not have specific authority or programs for communicating with foreign publics. Given the global and instant nature of communications, however, their public statements can reach the foreign populations, and their actions in some cases could affect those populations' attitudes toward the United States. Identifying the effect each agency has on foreign publics might be required before any roles can be defined and coordinated. Another difficulty arises from the use of different terminology regarding communications with foreign publics. While the State Department has long relied on the term "public diplomacy" to describe its communications with foreign publics, DOD has adopted the term "strategic communication" to describe its activities. Also, the term "engagement" has entered the lexicon of terms describing U.S. government interface with foreign populations. Placing activities that are similar in nature under categories with different terms and definitions could continue to obstruct attempts to delineate the foreign-public communications roles of the numerous agencies involved in such activities.

Although some recommend strengthening State Department authorities and leadership for public diplomacy and strategic communication, the importance of ensuring that other agencies have the capability to communicate effectively with foreign publics has also been recognized. This seems to apply especially to agencies and departments that possess as part of their reasons for existence some sort of engagement with the people of foreign countries. Thus, DOD and USAID, as examples, have strong needs for maintaining a communications capacity, because they operate in foreign countries, their work affects foreign publics, and they must be able to explain the intentions and policies behind their activities.[77] A coordinated communications effort could maintain the State Department as lead public diplomacy actor, communicating with foreign publics on the overall range of foreign policy issues affecting those populations, as well as informing foreign publics on the culture and other aspects of the United States and the American people that would aid deeper mutual understanding and cooperation. Other government agencies operating abroad would then supplement such communications with specialized information pertaining to the work they are performing in each foreign country, to enhance the effectiveness of their particular projects and missions.[78]

DOD: Filling the Communications Gap

Many observers, including some Members of congressional committees, have criticized DOD's expansion into non-military communications and public diplomacy that they believe the State Department should undertake. One of the oft-stated reasons for this expansion is the degradation of the State Department's capacity to conduct public diplomacy and other traditionally civilian- led international activities due to the lack of resources and funding. DOD strategic communication spending, on the other hand, has increased, totaling at least $10 billion since the 9/11 terror attacks.[79] Spending on information operations (IO) has increased from $9 million for FY2005 to a nearly $1-billion request for FY2010.[80] For its part, DOD officials, including Secretary of Defense Robert Gates, have expressed their desire for State and other pertinent civilian agencies to receive the resources they need to effectively carry out their responsibilities. DOD in general explains that public diplomacy activities are the responsibility of the State Department, and that DOD has merely a support role in that area. Yet DOD continues to "fill the gap" when it comes to the perceived deficiencies of State Department public diplomacy capacity and efforts.[81]

Some of this gap-filling may occur because of the importance of communications with foreign publics in areas where U.S. armed forces are carrying out military operations and security is a factor, primarily in Iraq and Afghanistan, and the difficulty U.S. civilian agencies have operating in such environments. There are signs, however, that DOD communications with foreign publics might continue to increase. As counterterrorism and counterinsurgency have gained importance in overall U.S. military planning and strategy, communicating with and "winning the hearts and minds" of foreign populations that may produce terrorists and insurgents have become increasingly important to the success of the mission. Regional combatant commands such as the United States Africa Command (AFRICOM) have placed significant importance on strategic communication and public diplomacy activities. DOD program spending on non-military communications to foreign publics under IO has increased from $9 million to nearly $1 billion in annual funding since FY2005, according to the House Appropriations Committee.[82] Because DOD does not break out strategic communication or public diplomacy figures in its annual budget requests, overall DOD spending on communicating with foreign populations is not known.

Whatever the reasons for the expansion of DOD engagement with foreign publics, many analysts see problems with it. The House Appropriations Committee recently commented on its concerns:

> The Committee has serious concerns about ... the Department's assumption of this mission area [certain new information operations programs] within its roles and responsibilities. Much of the content of what is being produced ... is focused so far beyond a traditional military information operation that the term non-traditional military information operation does not justly apply. At face value, much of what is being produced appears to be United States Military, and more alarmingly non-military propaganda, public relations, and behavioral modification messaging.[83]

This statement seems to parallel the historical aversion to military communications with foreign publics that resulted in the State Department's primacy in public diplomacy. This was a primary reason for creating the civilian USIA after World War II to lead U.S. public diplomacy efforts.

Other criticisms focus on DOD's dual role in communicating with foreign publics. While both civilian agencies and the U.S. military public diplomacy seek to inform foreign publics about America and U.S. policies in a truthful manner, the military also engages in communications designed specifically to achieve military objectives, including military deception. DOD has also been involved in "supposed efforts to minimize target audience knowledge of United States' government sponsorship of certain production materials,"[84] including the planting of news stories in foreign media, as well as operation of news and entertainment websites such as Magharebia.com that do not carry a ".mil" or ".gov" designation and whose government sources are not obviously labeled. DOD has not always made clear delineations between public diplomacy and military operation communications within its organization, and some claim that the military's dual messaging role may lead to confusion, broken trust, and rejection of U.S. government communications in foreign publics.

Coordination Difficulties

Even if agency roles for public diplomacy across the U.S. government were to become more clearly defined, there will likely still be a substantial amount of work required to effectively coordinate public diplomacy and related communications efforts among all agencies. As explained previously, the Office of Global Communications in the White House did not provide strategic direction for communications with foreign publics as originally intended. Most observers have not characterized the Strategic Communication and Public Diplomacy Policy Coordinating Committee (PCC), headed by the Secretary of State, as successful in fostering interagency coordination of communications with foreign publics, or in implementing the June 2007 National Strategy for Public Diplomacy and Strategic Communication. The Global Strategic Engagement Center (GSEC) has not been resourced to effectively carry out directives emanating from the PCC. One recommendation for improving interagency coordination would create a robust coordination organization within the National Security Council (NSC), with a Deputy National Security Advisor for Strategic Communication (DNSA) heading a new Strategic Communication Policy Committee. This DNSA would possess legal authority to assign agency roles and to direct funding for public diplomacy and strategic communication, with a direct relationship to an Associate Director for Strategic Communication in the Office of Management and Budget (OMB). As discussed above, the President has created the GED within NSC to facilitate coordination of global engagement, but it is not clear if this interagency process will lead to a shift of authorities for public diplomacy or other activities to the NSC. Some have concerns over a new NSC structure, as it might simply add another stakeholder in an already complicated web of public diplomacy and strategic communication actors and activities.[85] Other recommendations call instead for the reinforcement of State's lead authority over public diplomacy and strategic communication, by requiring the PCC to meet at regular, frequent intervals, and ensuring that complete information on all U.S. government open and covert communications activities, including those undertaken by DOD and the intelligence agencies, is reported to R for interagency coordination purposes. GSEC would be staffed and resourced at higher levels to act as a fully operational secretariat supporting the PCC by building networks of public diplomacy actors across all pertinent government agencies to enable coordinated efforts.[86]

State Department Organizational Issues

There are several criticisms currently leveled at the public diplomacy organization and authorities within the Department of State. Critics contend that these organizational problems present major stumbling blocks to improving the effectiveness of U.S. public diplomacy as well as public diplomacy's stature within overall U.S. foreign policy.

The Culture of Official Diplomacy in the State Department

The most fundamental criticism is that the State Department's culture of official diplomacy, centering on the protocols of diplomat-to-diplomat interaction and short-term policy considerations, is not entirely compatible with the practice of public diplomacy. Unlike official diplomacy, public diplomacy discussions often take place in informal environments amongst a multitude of participants, only one of which is the U.S. government. The intended audiences of U.S. public diplomacy efforts are highly diverse, containing a spectrum of viewpoints present in any society, unlike the controlled and exclusive foreign government audience a traditional diplomat encounters. While the conduct of traditional diplomacy can focus on specific issues of bilateral relations with another country's government, public diplomacy is intended to focus foremost on long-term relationships with several different sectors of a foreign population that may or may not produce any specific advancement of current U.S. policy objectives or result with regard to U.S. interests.

Also, some have identified a clash between the State Department's bureaucratic process of communication and the practice of public diplomacy outreach. Owing to the sensitivity of official diplomatic communication, some analysts argue, the State Department has developed a multilevel clearance process that can be time-consuming and restrictive. In contrast, they explain, effective public diplomacy officers are reliant on the ability to communicate freely and flexibly with foreign publics, often in informal settings and in an informal manner. Because public diplomacy officers within the State Department are burdened with a cumbersome clearance process, some say the effectiveness of their outreach is hampered. There have been suggestions that public diplomacy communication be given a pared-down clearance process to enable responsive engagement with foreign populations on important issues.[87]

These basic differences in concept, conduct, and results can lead to a lack of importance placed on public diplomacy, some argue, within those parts of the State Department and U.S. embassies that do not have direct experience with outreach to foreign publics.[88] It can also lead to the misunderstanding that public diplomacy is primarily a tool used to placate foreign publics when they react negatively to U.S. government activities and official bilateral relations in promotion of its foreign policy. Many commentators state that public diplomacy leaders often do not play an equal role with other decision makers when foreign policy is made, leading to public diplomacy that is largely reactive in nature, diminishing its effectiveness.[89]

Other observers assert, however, that while there have been some problems with the integration of public diplomacy into the State Department since the abolition of USIA in 1999, placing public diplomacy within the State Department structure is the best way to ensure that U.S. foreign policy is being promoted in a coordinated fashion through both official diplomatic efforts and communications with foreign publics. They also state that the integration of public diplomacy officers with officers from the other foreign service cones within the State Department has increased the familiarity of the State Department with public diplomacy in a way that could not have occurred otherwise. As foreign service officers from other career tracks get public diplomacy experience from their rotations outside their cones, they will be able to gain an appreciation for public diplomacy that they can apply once they return to positions in their chosen career tracks.[90]

Public Diplomacy in the State Department Hierarchy

Some have suggested that placing the head of public diplomacy in an Under Secretary position, and thus subject to the direction of Secretary of State, is equal to subordinating public diplomacy to traditional, official diplomacy, with concomitant detrimental effects on the importance of public diplomacy as a tool of foreign policy. Converting the Under Secretary position to a Deputy Secretary position has been suggested as one possible way of raising the profile of public diplomacy to the highest levels of policy making within the State Department. Other recommendations focus on improving the authorities of the Under Secretary and her organization ("R," in State Department parlance) within the current structure.[91] As explained in the Background section of this chapter, the Under Secretary does not enjoy overriding operational control over public diplomacy activities, personnel, and resources in Washington or at U.S. missions overseas. Unlike the geographic area offices that were at the USIA Director's disposal, public diplomacy staffs within State's regional bureaus answer to the regional Assistant Secretaries and the Under Secretary for Political Affairs. At embassies, public diplomacy officers are subject to the primary direction of the Chief of Mission, and they report back to Washington through the regional bureaus, not through R. To remedy some of these perceived problems, some analysts have recommended that the President provide new authorities to the Under Secretary for Public Diplomacy and Public Affairs in the areas of public diplomacy policy, budgets, and utilization of public diplomacy personnel. Creation of dedicated Deputy Assistant Secretaries (DAS) for Public Diplomacy within each of the regional bureaus could also create a more robust capability for strategic approaches to outreach tailored to each geographic region and country. A DAS in each bureau would provide the Under Secretary a higher-level group of officers who could potentially better carry out strategic initiatives conceived within R. Junior public diplomacy officers in each regional DAS 's organization could handle more routine public diplomacy duties to free the DAS to play a more important role in the overall work and direction of each regional bureau.[92]

At U.S. foreign missions, it has been suggested, the Public Affairs Officer (PAO) heading public diplomacy efforts could administer a discretionary fund solely for public diplomacy activities, monitored by R, creating a dedicated resource and focus on public diplomacy within each embassy.[93] At least one report has made a far-reaching recommendation to create regional public diplomacy hubs, based on the current handful of media hubs, that would establish separate facilities for public diplomacy organized along a regional structure similar to that of DOD's combatant commands. These regional hubs would coordinate U.S. public diplomacy efforts in a particular region, and would act as the primary Washington-field coordination and feedback nexus for public diplomacy.[94] This concept of public diplomacy hubs would seem to place importance on the separation of public diplomacy from other U.S. mission activities, although the public diplomacy function would remain within the State Department's purview through its foreign missions.

A New Agency for Public Diplomacy?

Although numerous perceived problems with the State Department's public diplomacy organization have been identified, it appears that most experts are not willing to promote re-creating USIA or setting up a new government agency in order to restore the separation of public diplomacy from the State Department. Senator Sam Brownback introduced legislation in the 110th Congress that would have created a National Center for Strategic Communications, which would have served as the new focal point for public diplomacy and strategic communication for the U.S. government.[95] Under this proposal, the public diplomacy apparatus within State would have been transferred to the Center, and the Center would also have had a defined leadership role in interagency coordination for communications with foreign publics. Broadcasting would have been placed under the leadership of the Center as well.

For a number of reasons, however, most expert opinion appears focused on making improvements to the State Department's organizational structure removing the public diplomacy function to a new agency. First, standing up a new government agency would take a significant amount of time.[96] Second, creating new bureaucracies is not seen as an optimal solution—creating a new bureaucracy that does not consolidate older organizations, but actually separates organizational structures into separate bureaucratic entities. A new agency for public diplomacy would require a new management bureau to replace the State Department's management organization that the Under Secretary for Public Diplomacy and Public Affairs currently relies upon. A new inspector general for the public diplomacy agency would also need to be created, among other things.

Third, many observers have noted the current debate over the public diplomacy roles and responsibilities of several government agencies, especially between the State Department and DOD, as an impediment to successfully creating a new agency. It could be expected that any problems with the determination of roles and the improvement of interagency coordination would be intensified with any effort to create a new agency, as different government actors would likely seek to further protect their perceived authorities in the area of communications with foreign publics. Interagency coordination would likely not improve through legislation designating a new agency as the lead on public diplomacy and strategic communication, given that current legislative language clearly designating the State Department as lead on such communications has not resolved questions about roles and authorities thus far.

Personnel: Recruitment, Training, and Utilization

The size, utilization, and fitness of the Department of State's public diplomacy workforce is a central issue for the discussions on improving U.S. public diplomacy. A primary area of concern is the number of personnel carrying out public diplomacy duties within the Department of State. Although the number of foreign service officers overall have increased recently, the number of officers specializing in public diplomacy is at a significantly low level, in comparison to the apex of USIA's activities during the Cold War. Public Diplomacy Officer (PDO) numbers have dropped consistently during the decade after USIA's abolition. Overall numbers of civil servants and locally engaged staff (LES) assigned to public diplomacy duties have also declined substantially. Several analysts have called for increases in the number of personnel for public diplomacy assignments, as high as 100% over current numbers, to augment the human capital required to cultivate a culture of mutual understanding and shared values with foreign publics. These increases would include more LES, who can provide a ready-made, deep-seated connection to their own people. Increases in public diplomacy personnel could also create a human resources "float" that would allow all public diplomacy slots to be filled while also providing a certain percentage of public diplomacy officers with opportunities for public diplomacy training.

Recruiting and Training

Some analysts argue for improving public diplomacy recruiting and training. They note that the State Department does not actively recruit individuals who already have public diplomacy experience or skills. The U.S. Advisory Commission on Public Diplomacy recently found that the Foreign Service Officer Test and Oral Assessment do not specifically test for communication skills and public diplomacy instincts. According to the Commission, hiring experienced officers could rapidly improve outreach efforts.[97] Improving public diplomacy capabilities at the entry- level positions, however, will not immediately address another deficiency in public diplomacy personnel: the current shortage of mid-level officers, which arose due to accelerated promotion and retirements among PDOs. Some experts have called for the short-term appointment of former public diplomacy officers to fill this mid-level gap.[98]

Many have called for improving public diplomacy training. While public diplomacy courses available to foreign service officers have increased in recent years, many argue that too many courses focus on administration, such as managing exchange programs, and too few on public diplomacy theory, techniques, and execution. There are several calls for an increase in foreign language training for to address deficiencies in language skills among Officers in public diplomacy posts.[99] Private-sector partnership training has been encouraged to support the leveraging of private sector communications capacity and expertise. Some commentators suggest increased alternative training, including distance learning at post and on-the-job programs. Increased LES training, both abroad and in Washington, has also been recommended.[100]

Effective Use of Public Diplomacy Officers

There are numerous concerns over the utilization of PDOs. First, many observers believe that PDOs do not spend enough time in public diplomacy positions. They note that the rate of public diplomacy position vacancies within the Department and at foreign posts has ranged near 20% during recent years,[101] while at the same time a large percentage of PDOs are placed in nonpublic diplomacy positions. Some PDOs must wait until their third or fourth rotations before being assigned a public diplomacy position, yet many public diplomacy positions are filled by FSOs from the other cones (consular, management, economic, and political). Because of these conditions, some argue that public diplomacy expertise and experience have been critically reduced. Suggestions for remedying this situation include requiring early-career public diplomacy postings for PDOs; increasing the number of public diplomacy rotations for each PDO; lengthening public diplomacy rotations for PDOs; and allowing PDOs with specific cultural and language skills to rotate exclusively within the geographic area appropriate to their expertise.[102] Other analysts counter, however, that outside-cone rotations are necessary to maintain the generalist approach to a career in the Foreign Service, which the State Department values highly.

Second, some have criticized the State Department for allowing public diplomacy positions to be heavily burdened with administrative responsibilities. They assert that the Public Affairs Officer (PAO), the senior public diplomacy officer at a U.S. embassy, has been transformed into a manager generally supporting the ambassador, unable to focus on outreach or strategic public diplomacy planning. Similarly, some reports claim that junior- and mid-level public diplomacy officers also are expected to focus primarily on administrative tasks.[103] This perceived lack of importance placed on active outreach is reinforced by the lack of career incentives to demonstrate commitment to public diplomacy activities. The U.S. Advisory Committee on Public Diplomacy reported in 2008 that the Department of State's employee evaluation report (EER), used to determine promotions, does not contain a section devoted to public diplomacy. Also, in the work requirements statements (WRS) of some public diplomacy officers, only one of 11 job requirements described substantive public diplomacy outreach, while nine were squarely administrative in nature. Some of these seeming anomalies in assessment might factor into problems for career advancement, as PDOs are "promoted at the lowest rate of any track."[104]

Outreach Activities

Some observers have suggested that outreach to foreign publics must increase in general, both in the overall number and frequency of public diplomacy activities and in the techniques and tools of communications for public diplomacy. These increases are recommended for both educational and cultural exchange and international information programs; they include both traditional, in- person activities in foreign countries, and the "virtual" presence of U.S. public diplomacy on the Internet and other related forms of communications media.

Exchange Programs

There is widespread consensus that educational and cultural exchange programs supported by the U.S. government are highly effective public diplomacy tools. Exchanges target influential audiences within foreign publics, and provide them with experiences of American society. They build an environment of mutual understanding by creating a cadre of both American and foreign citizens who develop a first-hand knowledge of another culture, and they create long-term relationships that can be drawn upon to enhance cooperation and understanding between the United States and foreign countries. Many analysts have recommended increases in exchanges in order for the United States to further benefit from the long-term connections they create. Although exchanges funding and participation have increased in recent years, and the number of visas for foreign exchange participants coming to the United States have also begun to rise after a period of decline, some have called for significant increases in exchanges funding, up to 100% over current levels.[105] Certain increases have occurred in exchanges involving individuals from Muslim-majority countries as well as American Muslims, but some analysts have cautioned against concentrating exchanges increases in just one or a few regions. Exchange participation between Americans and foreign nationals from developing countries have also increased.[106]

English Language Education

Some observers have focused on the importance of increasing English language education for foreign populations provided by U.S. missions abroad, contending that the reduction in such language instruction represents a significant lost opportunity to engage foreign publics and to encourage long-lasting connections with and goodwill toward the United States. They claim that other countries are much more successful teaching foreign publics their respective native languages, including the United Kingdom, which devotes a greater amount of resources to English language instruction than the United States.[107] U.S. missions abroad have engaged in more English language instruction in recent years,[108] but there are calls for greater increases, as well as better efforts to leverage the connections made to foreign publics in the language classes to create robust, active language-graduate alumni groups in a similar fashion to alumni of foreign exchanges. Because fees may be charged to provide English language classes to foreign publics, it is suggested that U.S. missions could expand language instruction without requiring as much new funding as other projects, making the types of long-term connections possible through language education that is much more cost-effective. Although keeping costs low for English language classes is considered important, one recommendation for increased language education suggests that the United States needs also to increase the number of official U.S.-mission staff instructors instead of hiring subcontractors, to ensure instructor quality.[109] Permanent staff instructors could be expected to increase country, cultural, and native language expertise within U.S. mission staff through direct contact with the population.

America Centers/America Houses

During the Cold War and the existence of USIA, the United States operated a large number of "America Centers," facilities that were open to foreign publics and provided a substantial physical U.S. presence in the centers of large foreign cities. At these Centers foreign citizens could avail themselves of libraries and reading rooms, English language instruction, U.S. speaker programs on a wide range of topics, and exhibitions of American films, among other outreach programs. Although some of these types of facilities still exist, most have been closed. With the end of the Cold War, many observe, America Centers were considered expendable. Added to the decreased emphasis on public diplomacy's overall importance, security concerns for all U.S. government facilities abroad came to the fore after the bombings of the U.S. embassies in Kenya and Tanzania in 1998. Legislation passed soon after these bombings required U.S. missions abroad to be "co-located" on one secure campus, unless a specific waiver is granted.[110] Several America Centers, most often located in city centers and separate from the main U.S. embassy complex, were not housed in facilities that met the requirements of these new security rules. To make up for the loss of the America Centers, U.S. embassy complexes now house Information Resource Centers (IRCs), but the IRCs have much less to offer foreign publics than did the America Centers. Also, because U.S. embassies have been hardened against terrorist attacks and have developed more stringent security measures, members of foreign publics have more difficulty accessing IRCs as compared to the open access to former America Centers. Many IRCs require foreign citizens to make appointments with IRC staff before they may visit. In addition, many U.S. embassies have moved well outside city centers, limiting further the number of individuals visiting the IRCs.[111]

Some analysts see the closure of America Centers as a key deficiency in U.S. outreach to foreign publics, because such Centers served high numbers of foreign citizens and were critical points of contact for the United States to build long-term relationships with foreign publics.[112] Some have pointed out that as the United States has retreated from outreach in important countries and regions, other countries, including Iran, have increased their presence and influence in the same places. It has been recommended, therefore, that the U.S. government seek to reestablish America Centers in the downtown areas of large cities in countries where important U.S. foreign policy interests can be served.[113] These recommendations state that while security at America Centers is a key consideration, security interests should not trump engagement with foreign publics. Some have called for waivers of the co-location requirement in order to allow America Centers to exist as freestanding facilities, with the understanding that such Centers may be closed if the security situation involves too much risk. A Senate report on U.S. public diplomacy called for temporary closure of Centers experiencing security issues, not an outright abandonment of the facilities as has occurred in the past.[114]

Information Resources and Internet Presence

Some observers recommend resurrecting certain international information programs that have atrophied in recent years, such as programs to translate books from English into Arabic. Calls have also been made for publishing more and more effective U.S. informational materials and interactive applications on the Internet, given its potential to reach mass audiences. Such materials could include new online libraries, online English language instruction, and robust websites containing more publications.[115] These recommendations parallel suggestions for increasing outreach activities online, including augmenting the capabilities of the State Department's Digital Outreach Team, which responds to misinformation about the United States on prominent online discussion sites, as well as investing more heavily in the most up-to-date communications technologies, both in hardware and software.[116] Determining how to best reach targeted audiences with such information, understanding what information and formats will best serve U.S. foreign policy interests, and building trust in U.S. government messages will be challenges to effective online information outreach just as they are to traditional outreach accomplished through a physical presence. If anything, these challenges might be more difficult to address given the lack of control over the receipt and effect of messages on the Internet, preventing their misuse or distortion, and determining what effect such messages had through valid feedback.[117]

International Broadcasting

The current state of U.S. international broadcasting is also the subject of debate. First, some argue that U.S. international broadcasting needs to be better integrated with U.S. foreign policy activities, strategies, and goals, in order to more effectively advance U.S. national interests. Since the United States International Broadcasting Act of 1994 created an independent Broadcasting Board of Governors (BBG), there has been a perception among some that U.S. international broadcasters might make programming decisions that distract or detract from U.S. public diplomacy efforts at both the government-wide and individual U.S.

mission levels.[118] This perception has persisted despite the inclusion of the Secretary of State as a voting member of the BBG. Affording the State Department, or perhaps a new government agency for international broadcasting, the authority to more directly supervise broadcasting programming might develop international broadcasting into a more effective tool for advancing U.S. interests. The primary counterargument to such integration of international broadcasting is based on journalistic integrity. Some argue that unless international broadcasting is independent of the political, policy- driven influences of government agencies, international broadcasting will lose its credibility and thereby become less useful in gaining the trust of foreign publics. They assert that independent international broadcasting is imperative to provide an example of a free press in a democracy to foreign publics where little or no free press exists.[119]

Criticism of the Organization of International Broadcasting

Some observers criticize the organization of U.S. international broadcasting as well. They assert that the current structure of numerous independent U.S. broadcasters, some directly supervised by the International Broadcasting Bureau (IBB), and some operating as surrogate grantees, has produced inefficiencies and redundancies across a spectrum of organizational factors. These include duplication of services and programming, a lack of coordination among the broadcasters on program content, and a non-integrated technology infrastructure that results in inefficient use of resources. Because each broadcaster retains a substantial amount of independent discretion over what it will broadcast, some criticize the lack of an overall strategy for U.S. international broadcasting itself.[120] Perceived problems exist concerning over- or under-programming in certain foreign languages, lack of efficient utilization of new communications media, and deficient programming models and audience research. Some commentators have recommended a complete review of U.S. international broadcasting to determine whether a streamlining of the organizational structure is needed to consolidate broadcasters in order to encourage creating and implementing clear strategy and reducing redundancies.[121] Others, however, counter that promotion of U.S. government-run broadcasting services in general undermine U.S. policies concerning the problems of state-run media, government enterprises that in many countries still represent biased, non-reliable sources of information, and suggest privatizing surrogate U.S. broadcasters to ensure credibility.[122]

There are also concerns regarding individual U.S. international broadcast entities. Some have questioned the resourcing of VOA in recent years, claiming that the new Middle East broadcast entities have swallowed up a considerable portion of funding that could otherwise have been used to bolster VOA programming, especially programming in Arabic.[123] At the same time, two of the new Middle East broadcasters, television broadcaster Alhurra and its counterpart Radio Sawa, have had numerous problems and have garnered considerable criticism. Observers have characterized the management and oversight of the broadcasters as poor. Critics have characterized the overall performance of Alhurra as deficient, as it attempts to gain market share of audiences in competition from Arab broadcast powerhouses such as Al Jazeera and Al Arabiya. Alhurra has been forced to restrict the open discourse on its channel due to criticism from Congress and elsewhere after it allowed terrorist organizations and Holocaust deniers to freely promote their views on air; the result of the restricted discourse, it is argued, has damaged Alhurra's credibility with the Arab public. The BBG for its part has claimed that Alhurra enjoys the highest audience of any non-Arab broadcaster in the Middle East.[124] Radio Sawa's effectiveness has been questioned given that its ratio of broadcast content is heavily skewed toward popular music instead of substantive news and informational programming.

Leveraging Non-public Sectors: Expertise, Best Practices, and Innovation

Some studies and reports have recommended increasing the utilization of private and non-profit sector (together, "non-public sector") expertise, resources, best practices, and innovation as an important strategy for improving the capacity, effectiveness, and timeliness of U.S. public diplomacy.[125] These recommendations highlight the fact that the communications and information technology expertise of the U.S. private sector is highly sophisticated and advanced. Private sector individuals and organizations can provide existing, tested information products and tools to the government, thereby allowing the U.S. government to quickly leverage outside expertise to improve public diplomacy efforts. They also point to the current global communications environment, in which individual actors and NGOs in the United States can act as important communicators, suggesting that the U.S. government should coordinate with such communicators in order to ensure maximum effectiveness and clarity of messages from U.S. sources. At least one study states that partnership between U.S. public diplomacy and the non-public sector should be a core principle guiding government communications with foreign publics.[126]

Creating an Independent Support Organization

Although the Under Secretary for Public Diplomacy and Public Affairs currently has an Office of Private Sector Outreach (R/PSO) within her organization, there are recommendations for an independent support organization to increase public diplomacy expertise, best practices, and innovation for use by the U.S. government through partnership with the private sector.[127] Such an organization would allow the U.S. government to build close working relationships with nonpublic sector communications experts from academia, NGOs, and business.[128] The support organization could directly employ such experts, with varying lengths of appointments, instead of merely contracting or providing grants to non-public sector organizations or individuals, ensuring greater impetus toward integrated, coordinated communications research, planning, and other activities. In this way, advocates argue, such an organization would expand the scope of public/non-public partnerships currently undertaken by R/PSO, which does not focus on cooperation with individual communications and public diplomacy experts as such.

Such an independent public diplomacy support organization, as envisioned by some observers, would take on a number of duties, including the following, among others:

- conducting research on innovative techniques and new technologies for U.S. public diplomacy efforts, and leveraging and experimenting with the latest forms of new media for use by U.S. public diplomacy practitioners;
- strengthening U.S. government capability to formulate, coordinate, and execute strategic public diplomacy planning within individual government agencies to

implement requirement of the upcoming national strategy for public diplomacy and strategic communication;

- utilizing research data on results of public diplomacy and other communications efforts to synthesize best practices, and serve as a comprehensive clearinghouse for government public diplomacy actors to access such practices;

- in addition to its independent functions, contracting with government agencies to provide program-specific public diplomacy services;

- partnering with and making grants to private organizations to engage in new public diplomacy efforts, as well as to evaluate effectiveness of such efforts; and

- raising funds from outside sources to fund innovative communications initiatives that could serve dual government/business purposes.[129]

Supporters of such an organization anticipate that it will encourage early government adoption of new communications techniques and proven best practices, and encourage interagency cooperation in a "turf-free" environment.[130]

Research, Monitoring, and Evaluation of Public Diplomacy Activities

It has been repeated often in recent years that global opinion of the United States has declined drastically, and that there have been huge shifts in that opinion, from overwhelming support after the 9/11 terrorist attacks to general dissatisfaction with U.S. actions regarding the war in Iraq and counterterrorism efforts, among other issues. The worsening polling data have been linked to the challenges currently facing U.S. public diplomacy and of the failure of that public diplomacy to improve the U.S. standing in the conception of foreign publics.[131] Recently, however, some worldwide polls have show favorable increases in the image of the United States among foreign publics, with connections being made between that rise and the high initial favorability of President Obama around the world.[132] Yet some have warned that polling data, which can provide fleeting information on opinion based on a snapshot in time, is not sufficient to explain the success or failure of U.S. outreach to foreign publics. Polling numbers, they argue, cannot substitute for sophisticated evaluation of the U.S. relationship with respective foreign publics and the effectiveness of U.S. public diplomacy efforts.

In addition to polling, it is asserted that the United States must build a comprehensive system of evaluating the performance of public diplomacy efforts, determining effectiveness by matching results to stated strategic objectives and goals enumerated in a national strategy. Only once such goals are set out, some argue, will useful performance measurements be produced.[133] Even with a national strategy in place, however, challenges remain for gathering data regarding U.S. public diplomacy activities and analyzing such data to determine their successful performance. Some observers have commented that U.S. missions abroad do a poor job of recording data for use in evaluating outreach efforts, lacking the resources, guidance, and processes necessary to compile useful feedback information. One report states that the reliability of data gathering and evaluation at foreign posts is harmed by public diplomacy officers' fear that reporting any outreach efforts to be ineffective may have detrimental effects on their careers and opportunities for promotion.[134]

In recent years the Office of Management and Budget (OMB) has rated public diplomacy efforts as "not performing," based on the fact that the results of those efforts were not demonstrated. OMB has, however, rated the evaluation efforts of the Bureau of Educational and Cultural Exchange (ECA) as "fully performing," finding a clear system of indicators for measuring success. ECA's system for evaluation includes reliance on data gathered from exchange participants and a well developed and sustained network of exchange alumni, measuring both the outcome and impact of different exchanges on participants and their respective home communities and countries. ECA's methods of evaluation might not be expected to translate to other public diplomacy activities for which audiences are large and disparate, messages are often much more diffuse, and impact on target audiences is more difficult to assess. Nevertheless, it seems that ECA's evaluation system has been drawn on as an example for creating the Evaluation and Measurement Unit (EMU) in R's Office of Policy, Planning, and Resources. EMU's approach to research and evaluation seems to be promising. Both the Public Diplomacy Impact (PDI) project, evaluating performance, and the Mission Activity Tracker (MAT), gathering data on all public diplomacy activities, are intended to comprehensively document public diplomacy activities and measure their impact on a global scale. Many observers want the State Department to ensure that such research and analysis is translated into user-friendly guidance, tools, and techniques for improving public diplomacy at the country level. Some also suggest creating techniques to test the effect of public diplomacy programs prior to full implementation with foreign publics, to avoid unforeseen problems and pitfalls.[135]

Research and evaluation of both U.S. public diplomacy activities conducted on the Internet, and the vast number of communications undertaken by other actors on the Internet, from governments to individuals, is seen as a critical issue for U.S. public diplomacy. This is due to the daunting nature of assessing the impact of individual messages within an ever expanding universe of communication, and the perception that effective Internet messaging is becoming increasingly central to any effective communications strategy. It has been recommended that the U.S. government should invest in developing and improving the science and application of social network analysis and automated sentiment analysis in order to provide U.S. public diplomacy new tools for understanding and harnessing the instant, global, networked communications environment of the Internet. Although such analytical tools may not ensure the dominance of U.S. government messaging, they may provide public diplomacy practitioners with the advantage of superior information as they attempt to gain influence online.[136]

Prohibiting Domestic Dissemination of Public Diplomacy Information: Smith-Mundt Act

As explained earlier in this chapter, current law restricts the State Department's domestic dissemination of public diplomacy information and its authority to communicate with the American public in general. These legislative provisions are intended to protect the American people from the State Department's attempts to influence foreign populations, ostensibly preventing to some extent the U.S. government's propagandizing of its own people. Some have argued that the domestic dissemination provision in Section 501 of the Smith-Mundt Act was also intended to protect the business interests of the U.S. media by ensuring the State Department would not fill its news-reporting role, and to guard against the growth of influence of the employees of the State Department, believed in the post-World War II years to be filled with communist sympathizers.[137]

The Smith-Mundt provisions have come under increasing criticism in recent years, and are seen as anachronisms in the current global communications environment. There have been calls to remove the Smith-Mundt Act's prohibition of domestic dissemination and related restrictions in order to bring U.S. government communications legislation in line with the realities of the current global communications environment. A number of perceived problems with these restrictions have been identified. The State Department provides information to and conducts outreach with foreign publics using the Internet, which, given the Internet's global availability, can be accessed domestically by U.S. citizens. U.S. international broadcasting, also covered by the restrictions, uses satellite and Internet broadcast technologies that can be accessed in the United States. Even when interpreting the domestic dissemination restrictions to prohibit only *intended* dissemination of public diplomacy information domestically in order to find no violation of the law by the State Department, the effectiveness of the restrictions, it is argued, has been fundamentally undermined by these pervasive global communications technologies. At the same time, however, the State Department is required to take measures to comport with these legislative restrictions, which may also reduce the overall effectiveness of its public diplomacy activities. Use of certain new communications technologies and techniques may be curtailed to avoid the risk of inadvertently propagandizing the American public. The State Department must also keep its public diplomacy and public affairs operations separate, even though both functions are headed by the Under Secretary of State for Public Diplomacy and Public Affairs, and communicate on the same issues for "separate" audiences.[138] In addition to the possible detrimental effects of the State Department's public diplomacy efforts, the Department of Defense has interpreted the Smith-Mundt Act's restrictions on domestic dissemination of information to apply to its communications efforts as well. Congress has recently asked DOD to review this interpretation to determine whether it is justified, given the possibility that such interpretation has limited DOD's capability to communicate with foreign publics.[139]

There are some possible advantages to maintaining the Smith-Mundt restrictions, however. They might, for instance, promote a differentiation of foreign versus domestic messages that serves to maintain a tailored approach to public diplomacy. By banning the production of public diplomacy information for domestic use, these provisions encourage information products and outreach programs that focus exclusively on foreign publics. Without such domestic prohibitions, U.S. public diplomacy efforts may become dominated by a preoccupation with communicating to the American people for political effect, to the detriment of creating effective, targeted communications to specific foreign populations.[140] This may exacerbate a perceived weakness in U.S. outreach to foreign publics overall, namely, the lack of country-level and regional public diplomacy strategies based on deep understanding of cultures and effective local communication approaches. On the other hand, those calling for amending the Smith-Mundt Act's domestic dissemination restriction argue that the American people would benefit from a more transparent understanding of their government's communications efforts in foreign countries. Some have suggested that direct dissemination of public diplomacy information to Americans may help build a domestic constituency for foreign affairs, international development, and diplomatic efforts in general, the lack of which has long been lamented as a primary reason for the relative inattention to providing resources for more robust conduct of U.S. foreign policy.[141]

RECENT LEGISLATIVE ACTION

Congress has recently proposed and enacted legislation that would make changes to U.S. public diplomacy. Enacted during the 110th Congress, Section 1055 of the National Defense Authorization Act for Fiscal Year 2009 (P.L. 110-417) is a key provision that requires the President to submit by the end of 2009 a report on a federal government strategy for public diplomacy and strategic communication to specified congressional committees.[142] The report must include the following elements:

- A comprehensive interagency strategy that
  - integrates specific foreign policy objectives with overall communications with foreign publics;
  - considers consolidating and elevating government leadership for public diplomacy and strategic communication, and the possibility of creating a single office to direct government-wide efforts; and
  - improves interagency coordination on public diplomacy and strategic communications.
- A study of whether an independent support organization for public diplomacy and strategic communication should be created to provide guidance and assessment to the federal government.
- A description of the roles and responsibilities of the National Security Council, Department of Defense, and Department of State regarding public diplomacy and strategic communication, as well as how these organizations currently coordinate efforts.

Section 1055 requires an another report from the President to be submitted two years after the first report providing the status of implementation of the strategy, progress toward achieving strategic benchmarks, and any changes made to the strategy. In addition, the section directs the Secretary of Defense to submit by the end of 2009 to the Armed Services Committees a report on the current organizational structure within DOD for advising the Secretary of strategic communication, and the possibility of creating an advisory board within DOD (with representation from other relevant agencies) responsible for strategic communication and public diplomacy strategic direction and communication priorities.

Several pieces of legislation proposed thus far in the 111th Congress concern changes to, improvements in, and funding for public diplomacy. The Foreign Relations Authorization Act, Fiscal Years 2010 and 2011, H.R. 2410 (111th Congress), which contains a subtitle on "Public Diplomacy at the Department of State," as well as other several other pertinent provisions, is a central bill related to public diplomacy. [143] Several other bills are devoted to or include provisions directly related to U.S. public diplomacy efforts, covering a broad array of concerns, many of which are directly parallel to the important issues discussed in the previous section of this chapter.[144] These bills include provisions regarding strategy for communications with foreign publics; agency roles and interagency coordination; personnel and human resources issues; increased outreach activities and exchanges; reforming the organization of U.S. international broadcasting; research, monitoring, and evaluation; leveraging the best practices knowledge and public diplomacy expertise both within government, and from private sector/nongovernmental actors, possibly through an independent support organization; and creating exception to the restrictions on domestic dissemination of information prepared for public diplomacy purposes by the Department of State. In addition, certain committee reports on Defense authorizations and appropriations for FY2010 include reporting requirements concerning DOD's communications with foreign publics. Provided below are descriptions of legislative provisions related to public diplomacy and strategic communication, organized by issue.

Strategy for Public Diplomacy and Strategic Communication

S. 1707 (P.L. 111-73): Section 101 (c)(6)(C) of the Enhanced Partnership with Pakistan Act of 2009 provides the sense of Congress that the United States should have a coordinated strategic communication strategy for engagement with the people of Pakistan to meet the bilateral cooperation goals of the act.

H.R. 2647 (P.L. 111-84): Section 1242(b) of the Senate version of the National Defense Authorization Act for Fiscal Year 2010 requires the President to submit an annual counterterrorism strategy report. Paragraph (1)(G) requires the report to include a description of strategic communication and public diplomacy activities undertaken to counter terrorist recruitment and radicalization.

H.R. 490: Section 2(b) requires the Secretary of State to submit a "quadrennial review" to the Senate Foreign Relations and House Foreign Affairs Committees by October 1, 2012, and every four years thereafter. Such review would consist of a comprehensive examination of U.S. government foreign affairs activities, including public diplomacy efforts. Section 2(d)(4) provides that the quadrennial review's contents would include recommendations for improvements in public diplomacy initiatives.

H.R. 2387: Section 4(a)(2) of the Strategy and Effectiveness of Foreign Policy and Assistance Act of 2009 requires the President to report to Congress on long-term strategies for U.S. national security and foreign affairs, including a description of how public diplomacy efforts are "related to a long-term strategy that advances national security objectives and needs of the United States."

H.R. 2410: Division B of this bill is entitled the Pakistan Enduring Assistance and Cooperation Enhancement (PEACE) Act of 2009. It authorizes implementation of a public diplomacy strategy for Pakistan that would highlight the weaknesses of extremists operating in Pakistan, degrade the ability of extremist groups to get their messages to the Pakistani people, and increase person-to-person and technical and cultural exchange between U.S. citizens and business and their Pakistani counterparts.

S. 894: Section 4(a)(6) of the Success in Countering Al Qaeda Reporting Requirements Act of 2009 requires the President to report on all U.S. government strategic communication and public diplomacy efforts to counter terrorist recruitment and radicalization as part of reporting on overall counterterrorism strategy.

Interagency Coordination

H.R. 489: Section 3 of the Strategic Communication Act of 2009 requires a report from the Secretary of State that would include information on current efforts to coordinate U.S. government strategic communication and public diplomacy, international broadcasting, and military information operations. The Section also requires reporting that would discuss the possibility of creating an strategic communication organization within the National Security Council to lead interagency coordination.

H.R. 2410: Section 211 would amend Section 60 of the State Department Basic Authorities Act of 1956 (22 U.S.C. § 2732) to give the primary responsibility for coordinating unified public diplomacy activities to the Secretary of State.[145] The Section provides for creation of an interagency coordination working group, to meet at least once every three months, to be chaired by the Secretary of State and to include representatives of other relevant agencies. These relevant federal agencies would be required to designate a representative to conduct ongoing consultations and coordination concerning public diplomacy. The Section does not provide a seniority requirement for such representatives.

Agency Roles and Responsibilities

H.R. 2410: Section 211 would amend Section 60 of the State Department Basic Authorities Act of 1956 (22 U.S.C. § 2732) to require federal agencies involved in public diplomacy to report to the President annually on the public activities undertaken by each respective agency, and directs the President to provide such reports to the Secretary of State. Such reports would be expected to provide a clearer explanation of the current public diplomacy roles of different agencies, and provide opportunities to better define or to alter such roles.

State Department Public Diplomacy Organization

H.R. 489: Section 3 of the Strategic Communication Act of 2009 directs the Secretary of State to submit a report assessing the possibility of elevating public diplomacy personnel within the hierarchy of the State Department, including designating certain public diplomacy officials (presumably within the regional and functional bureaus) as Deputy Assistant Secretaries or Senior Advisors to the Assistant Secretary, and elevating the Coordinator of International Information Programs to the Assistant Secretary level.

DOD Communications Activities

H.Rept. 111-166 on H.R. 2647 (P.L. 111-84): The report of the House Armed Services Committee on the National Defense Authorization Act for Fiscal Year 2010 requires detailed information on the strategic communication workforce within DOD, including analysis of the skills and competencies of strategic communication personnel, strategic communications gaps being filled by contractors, and assessment of top-level guidance on strategic communication recruiting, policy, organization, and management. The Committee's report also directs DOD to provide information on its military public diplomacy, including a list of all activities that may be considered to fall within the category of public diplomacy. It further requires description of the performance metrics for such activities; current management of military public diplomacy (given the recent disestablishment of the Deputy Assistance Secretary of Defense—Support to Public Diplomacy); coordination of military public diplomacy with regional theater plans; and assessment of the feasibility of a DOD-State Department exchange for informational and public diplomacy programs.

H.Rept. 111-230 on H.R. 3326: The House Appropriations Committee included a section on DOD's Information Operations in its report on the FY2010 DOD appropriations bill. The Committee states that DOD's budget justification for its Information Operations request of $1 billion is "woefully inadequate," especially given the massive increase in requested funding that totaled only $9 million for FY2005. The Committee also explains its concerns over DOD's moves into non-military communications with foreign publics, and the questionable effectiveness of the programs. In a classified annex, the Committee lists a number of Information Operations programs that DOD should terminate immediately, and reduces funding accordingly, by $500 million. The Committee also states that the remaining funding will not be available until DOD reports on all Information Operations programs, including information on strategies, goals, target audiences, and measuring effectiveness, as well as detailed budget and spend information.

S.Rept. 111-35 on S. 1390: The Senate Armed Services Committee, in its report on the Senate version of the National Defense Authorization Act for Fiscal Year 2010, focused on the wide array of strategic communication activities that DOD undertakes, and the estimated $10 billion DOD has spent on strategic communication since 9/11. It states that DOD does not break out budget figures for strategic communication, and that the Committee cannot determine what parts of DOD are carrying out the programs, and cannot conduct proper oversight for the programs. It requires the Undersecretary of Defense—Policy and the Undersecretary of Defense—Comptroller to develop detailed strategic communication budgets for 2011, clearly explaining the objectives and funding levels for its strategic communication and public diplomacy activities.

Personnel/Human Resources

H.R. 2311: Section 2 of the United States-China Diplomatic Expansion Act of 2009 provides funding for hiring new local public diplomacy staff for the U.S. foreign mission in China.

H.R. 2410: Section 212 provides for the establishment of a Public Diplomacy Reserve Corps, made up of mid- and senior-level former Foreign Service officers to fill the current shortage of mid-level public diplomacy officers within the Foreign Service. Reserve officers would serve for six-month to two-year appointments. Section 301 requires the Secretary of State to expand the Foreign Service in general by 1,500 officers over the next two fiscal years. This number would likely include new public diplomacy officers.

America Centers, Libraries, and Increased Outreach

S. 1707 (P.L. 111-73): Section 101 (a)(5) of the Enhanced Partnership with Pakistan Act of 2009 authorizes the President to provide assistance to Pakistan to strengthen U.S. public diplomacy. Section 101(b) lists activities that would be supported by such assistance, including, in paragraph (5)(A), strengthening public diplomacy to combat militant extremism and increase understanding of the United States through encouraging civil society leaders to speak out against extremist violence.

H.R. 2311: Section 2 of the United States-China Diplomatic Expansion Act of 2009 provides new funding for public diplomacy programs and related information technology infrastructure in China.

H.R. 2410: Section 213 provides for the reestablishment of America Centers, recognizing the current shortfalls of the International Resource Centers (IRCs) and the decreased U.S. presence in important foreign city centers.[146] Such Centers would be run as free-standing facilities through partnerships with qualified local or regional organizations. The Secretary of State is required under the section to consider waiving the security co-location requirements of Section 606(a)(2)(B) of the Secure Embassy Construction and Counterterrorism Act of 1999 (22 U.S.C. § 4865(a)(2)(B)). Section 214 would amend Section 1 (b)(3) of the State Department Basic Authorities Act of 1956 (22 U.S.C. § 265 1a(b)(3)) to require the Under Secretary for Public Diplomacy and Public Affairs to establish libraries and resource centers in connection with U.S. foreign missions. Section 214 states that such libraries and centers should be open to the public, and should include among their cultural outreach screenings of appropriate U.S. films. The information in such facilities and such U.S. films should be available online to the extent practicable. Section 215 provides for grants to encourage distribution of American independent documentary films in foreign countries, and distribution of foreign documentaries in the United States.

H.R. 3701: Section 2 of the More Books for Africa Act of 2009 finds the need for books to be more readily available in Africa, and Section 3 states the sense of Congress that providing books to Africa is a powerful tool of public diplomacy. Section 4 provides for establishment of the More Books for Africa Program in USAID to provide not fewer than 3,000,000 books from the United States per year.

H.R. 3714: Section 2(b) of the Daniel Pearl Freedom of the Press Act of 2009 requires the Secretary of State to create the Freedom of the Press Grant Program, which would provide grant funding to nonprofit and international organizations to promote press freedom worldwide through training and professionalization of skills for foreign journalists. The Under Secretary of State for Democracy, Human Rights, and Labor would administer the Program in conjunction with the Under Secretary of State for Public Diplomacy and Public Affairs.[147]

S. 587: Section 12 of the Western Hemisphere Energy Compact provides $5 million in funding for public diplomacy activities concerning renewable energy in the Western Hemisphere, with at least 50% of funding to be provided for educational programs through local civil society organizations.

Increased Exchanges

S. 1707 (P.L. 111-73): Section 101 (b)(5)(B) of the Enhanced Partnership with Pakistan Act of 2009 authorizes the President to provide assistance to Pakistan for increasing exchange activities under the Fulbright Program, the International Visitor Leadership Program, and the Youth Exchange and Study Program.

H.R. 2647 (P.L. 111-84): Section 1263 of the of the Victims of Iranian Censorship (VOICE) Act (Subtitle D of Title XII of Division A) provides for the creation of the Iranian Electronic Education, Exchange, and Media Fund. This Fund, to be administered by the Secretary of State, would support the development of technologies and programs to increase the Iranian people's access to media, especially through the Internet. Paragraphs (3) and (4) of subsection (d) include in the authorized uses of funding the creation of Internet-based distance-learning programs and U.S.-Iranian exchange programs.

H.R. 1969: Section 402 of the Vietnam Human Rights Act of 2009 states that it is the policy of the United States that U.S. exchange programs with Vietnam should promote the advancement of freedom and democracy in that country.

H.R. 2311: Section 5 of the United States-China Diplomatic Expansion Act of 2009 authorizes funding for Chinese language exchanges.

H.R. 2410: The bill contains provisions for new exchange programs in Title II, Subtitle B. These include exchanges and related educational programs for students from Central Asia, Mexico and South and Central America, and Sri Lanka; professional development exchanges for Liberian women legislators and Liberian women congressional staff, as well as Afghan women legislators; and establishment of a U.S.-Caribbean educational exchange program. Title VII of H.R. 2410 provides for the establishment of the Senator Paul Simon Study Abroad Foundation, a government corporation that would provide grants to increase the number of American students studying abroad, especially in nontraditional countries, to increase U.S. citizens' knowledge of other countries and foreign language skills.[148] Division B of H.R. 2410, the Pakistan Enduring Assistance and Cooperation Enhancement (PEACE) Act of 2009, authorizes increased educational exchanges between the United States and Pakistan.

H.R. 2985: This legislation requires the Secretary of State to establish the Ambassador's Fund for Strategic Exchanges to bring foreign "political, economic, civil society, and other leaders to the United States for short-term exchange visits to advance key United States strategic goals." Exchanges would take place in groups of 8-10 visitors, over five to eight days, and focus on certain broad strategic goals. Funding would come from ECA and U.S. embassies in a cost- sharing arrangement.

H.R. 3328: The Gandhi-King Scholarly Exchange Initiative Act of 2009 provides for the establishment of an exchange program between India and the United States. The Gandhi-King Scholarly Exchange Initiative would provide multiple opportunities for exchange according to Section 3(a) of the act, including a public diplomacy forum focusing on the work of Mohandas Gandhi and Martin Luther King, Jr., a professional training initiative for conflict resolution, and student exchanges.

S. 230: Section 503 of the International Women's Freedom Act of 2009 would amend Section 102(b) of the Mutual Educational and Cultural Exchange Act of 1961 (22 U.S.C. 2452(b)) to include a provision to support international exchanges that promote the respect for and protection of women's rights abroad.

S. 384: Section 301 of the Global Food Security Act of 2009 would amend Part I, Title XII of the Foreign Assistance Act of 1961 (FAA; P.L. 87-195) to include provisions for assistance to university partners for improvement of agriculture abroad. It would add a new Section 298 to the FAA, which would give authority to the President to provide assistance for agriculture programs through universities. Section 298(b) lists types of support, including paragraph (5) of the subsection, which includes agricultural education opportunities through international exchanges.

S. 589: This bill provides for the establishment of an Office of Volunteers for Prosperity in the U.S. Agency for International Development (USAID), which would administer a newly created Global Service Fellowship Program. The Program would be designed to "promote international volunteering opportunities as a means of building bridges across cultures, addressing critical human needs, and promoting mutual understanding."

International Broadcasting

H.R. 2647 (P.L. 111-84): Section 1262 of the Victims of Iranian Censorship (VOICE) Act (Subtitle D of Title XII of Division A) authorizes $15 million for the BBG's International Broadcasting Operations Fund, and $15 million to its Capital Improvements Fund, for expenditures to increase U.S. international programming in Farsi to Iran. Uses authorized include efforts to stop the Iranian government's blocking of U.S. international broadcasting to Iran, and creation and expansion of Farsi programming.

H.R. 363: This bill, the United States Broadcasting Reorganization Act of 2009, would abolish the Broadcasting Board of Governors and the International Broadcasting Bureau, and transfer international broadcasting authorities to a new United States International Broadcasting Agency. A bipartisan Board of Governors, appointed by the President, would oversee U.S. international broadcasting within the Agency. Among its functions would be to review broadcasting activities and their effectiveness within the context of U.S. foreign policy objectives and American guiding principles, such as freedom and democracy. The act requires the new Agency to submit annual reports to the President and Congress on broadcasting activities with emphasis on this review function for meeting foreign policy objectives.

H.R. 1969: Section 401 of the Vietnam Human Rights Act of 2009 provides funding to stop the government of Vietnam from jamming the signal of Radio Free Asia.

S. 230: Section 502 of the International Women's Freedom Act of 2009 would amend Section 303(a)(8) of the United States International Broadcasting Act of 1994 (P.L. 103-236) to add respect for women's rights to the broadcasting standards of the Broadcasting Board of Governors.

Research, Monitoring, and Evaluation

H.R. 489: Section 3 of the Strategic Communication Act of 2009 provides for establishment of a Center of Strategic Communication that would be tasked with, among other things, developing monitoring and evaluation tools and techniques, and performing analysis on foreign public opinion, cultural influence, and media influence.

H.R. 2410: Section 214(c) requires the Advisory Commission on Public Diplomacy to report to the House Foreign Affairs and Senate Foreign Relations Committees, one year after enactment of H.R. 2410, on the effectiveness of libraries, resource centers, and online outreach authorized by the section. Section 216 requires the Commission to review and assess the effectiveness of U.S. public diplomacy policies, activities, and programs every two years, and report to the Secretary of State and the House Foreign Affairs and Senate Foreign Relations Committees on its findings. As part of its the review, the Commission would be entitled to receive any information it requests from federal agencies involved in public diplomacy or strategic communication activities and from the Broadcasting Board of Governors.

Increasing Public Diplomacy Best Practices and Expertise

H.R. 489: Entitled the Strategic Communication Act of 2009, this bill authorizes the Secretary of State to solicit offers from organizations specializing in research and analysis to create a Center for Strategic Communication. The Secretary would choose one organization to establish the Center as a tax-exempt corporation. The Center would be tasked with providing information and analysis to government decision makers on communications with foreign publics; developing communications plans and programs, leveraging private sector and academic institution expertise and resources; and providing public diplomacy services to the government utilizing nongovernmental organizations and private sector knowledge. The Secretary of State would designate a liaison to coordinate between the Center and the State Department, as well as DOD, the Department of Justice, the Department of Homeland Security, and the Director of National Intelligence. The act provides the Center $250 million from the State Department budget each fiscal year.

H.R. 2410: Although it does not call for a new independent support organization for public diplomacy, Section 216 would amend Section 604(a)(2) of the United States Information and Educational Exchange Act of 1948 (22 U.S.C. § 1469(a)(2)) to improve the public diplomacy expertise of Commission members by requiring that at least four members possess "substantial experience in the conduct of public diplomacy.... " Section 303 authorizes the Secretary of State to establish a Lessons Learned Center within the State Department to serve as a "central organization for collection, analysis, archiving, and dissemination of observations, best practices, and lessons learned by, from, and to Foreign Service officers.... " The Center would be tasked with creating a system for evaluating performance of State Department and Foreign Service activities, which would likely include public diplomacy activities.

Provisions Related to Restrictions on Domestic Dissemination of Public Diplomacy Information

H.Rept. 111-166 on H.R. 2647 (P.L. 111-84): The report of the House Armed Services Committee on the National Defense Authorization Act for Fiscal Year 2010 encourages DOD to conduct a legal review of the Smith-Mundt Act's restriction on domestic dissemination of public diplomacy information as it applies to DOD. The Committee states its opinion that the restriction does not apply to DOD, and should not be allowed to hamper DOD's Internet-based strategic communication, which the Committee currently finds to be inadequate and unable to properly respond to enemies' online communications in real time.

H.R. 363: Section 4 of the United States International Broadcasting Act of 2009 would restate Section 305 of the United States International Broadcasting Act of 1994 to set out authorities and functions of a new United States International Broadcasting Agency. Subsection (b) provides for an exception to the general prohibition on domestic dissemination of information materials intended for distribution abroad, making broadcasting to the Middle East available to U.S. satellite and cable operators. It also makes an U.S. international broadcasting in any language available to U.S. satellite and cable operators if a foreign broadcaster in a corresponding country has access to U.S. operator transmissions. Also, Section 8 of the act would amend Section 501 of the Smith-Mundt Act, the provision that contains the restriction on domestic dissemination, to allow the Secretary of State to make information available to foreign publics on the Internet "without regard to whether such material can be accessed domestically."

End Notes

[1] Congressman William Delahunt, "Opening Statement for Subcommittee Hearings on Global Polling Data on Opinion of American Policies, Values and People," House Committee on Foreign Affairs Subcommittee on International Organizations, Human Rights, and Oversight, Washington, March 6, 2007. From March 6, 2007 to May 17, 2007, the Subcommittee on International Organizations, Human Rights, and Oversight held five hearings examining polling data about attitudes toward the United States in various parts of the world and the reasons for these attitudes.

[2] Under Secretary of State for Public Diplomacy and Public Affairs Karen Hughes, Remarks at the Council on Foreign Relations, New York City, May 10, 2006.

[3] Under Secretary of State for Public Diplomacy and Public Affairs, Judith A. McHale, "Public Diplomacy: A National Security Imperative," Address at the Center for a New American Security, Washington, June 11, 2009.

[4] Interagency Working Group on U.S. Government-Sponsored International Exchanges and Training, *FY2008 Annual Report*, Washington, D.C., 2008, p. 14, http://www.iawg.gov/reports/inventory/.

[5] This chapter focuses primarily on the public diplomacy authorities, organization, resources, and activities of the Department of State and the issues concerning reforming and improving the public diplomacy capabilities of the Department. Although the Department of Defense (DOD), the United States Agency for International Development (USAID), and several other U.S. government agencies communicate with populations abroad, the primary legal authorities and governmental organization for such engagement rest within the State Department, and the State Department remains the central focus and starting point of most calls for reform of the United States' approach to communicating with foreign publics. Individual public diplomacy and strategic communication issues, such as countering violent extremism and radical ideologies in the Islamic world, are referenced when integral to overarching public diplomacy issues but would require dedicated reports to be treated comprehensively.

[6] Ibid., Sec. 502.

[7] Senator Edward Zorinsky proposed S.Amdt. 296 to S. 1003 (99th Cong.), the Senate version of the Foreign Relations Authorization Act, Fiscal Years 1986 and 1987. The amendment, with the addition of the introductory clause of the first sentence, was included in the House version of the bill that became P.L. 99-93.

[8] Sec. 232 of Foreign Relations Authorization Act, Fiscal Years 1994 and 1995 (P.L. 103-236; 108 Stat. 424) added a new sentence to the end of this section, which states, "The provisions of this section shall not prohibit the United States Information Agency from responding to inquiries from members of the public about its operations, policies, or programs."

[9] 123 Stat. 910.

[10] Broadcasting Board of Governors website, http://www.bbg.gov/about/documents/BBGFactSheet2-09.pdf.

[11] Under Secretary of State for Public Diplomacy and Public Affairs James K. Glassman, Keynote Address at the 2009 Smith-Mundt Symposium, Washington, January 13, 2009.

[12] On May 1, 1953, President Eisenhower issued Executive Order 10476, Administration of Foreign Aid and Foreign Information Functions, and Executive Order 10477, Authorizing the Director of the United States Information Agency.

[13] United States Information Agency, *United States Information Agency*, Washington, D.C., October 1998, p. 5.

[14] The Office of Research and Media Reaction published the *Early Report* each morning, the mid-day *Daily Digest*, and periodic *Special Reports* prepared for particular U.S. government agencies upon request in disseminating its analysis.

[15] Patricia H. Kushlis and Patricia Lee Sharpe, "Public Diplomacy Matters More than Ever," *Foreign Service Journal*, vol. 83, no. 10 (Oct. 2006), p. 32.

[16] United States Information Agency, *USIA Congressional Budget Justification, Fiscal Year 1999*, "Broadcasting," p. 1.

[17] United States Information Agency, *Fact Sheet*, Washington, D.C., February 1999, http://dosfan.lib.uic.edu/usia/usiahome/factshe.htm.

[18] Ibid.

[19] USIA Budget in Brief for 1999, op cit. pp. 1, 14.

[20] Mike Canning, *The Overseas Post: The Forgotten Element of Our Public Diplomacy*, The Public Diplomacy Council, Washington, D.C., December 1, 2008, p.4, http://www.publicdiplomacycouncil.org/uploads/canningoverseasposts.pdf.

[21] USIA Budget in Brief for 1999, op cit. pp. 13-14.

[22] Ibid., p. 14.

[23] The Consolidation Act also abolished the Arms Control and Disarmament Agency, and folded its functions into a new Bureau of Arms Control and Disarmament within the State Department.

[24] Nancy E. Snow, *United States Information Agency*, Foreign Policy in Focus, a Project of the Institute for Policy Studies, Volume 2, Number 40, Washington, D.C., August 1997, p. 2, http://www.fpif.org/briefs/vol2/v2n40usia_body. html.

[25] Neil R. Klopfenstein, *USIA's Integration into the State Department: Advocating Policy Trumps Promoting Mutual Understanding*, National Defense University, National War College, Washington, D.C., 2003, pp. 4-8.

[26] Ibid, pp. 12-13.

[27] The Clinton Administration which sought to lower the debt and "reinvent government", also wanted Congress to approve the Chemical Weapons Convention and pay U.S. arrearages to the United Nations to forestall losing its vote in the General Assembly. In agreeing to move ahead with consolidation proposals, the Clinton Administration got the vote on the Chemical Weapons Convention and an agreement with Senator Helms on paying U.N. arrearages.

[28] United States Department of State, *The Budget in Brief, Fiscal Year 2000*, p. 8.

[29] The Statement of Managers in Conference Report 105-825, which accompanied H.R. 4328 (105th Cong.), the Omnibus Consolidated and Emergency Supplemental Appropriations for Fiscal Year 1999, contained two paragraphs discussing the congressional intent regarding all of Division G, the Foreign Affairs Reform and Restructuring Act of 1998. Earlier, on April 28, 1998, Congress passed H.R. 1757 (105th Cong.), the Foreign Affairs Reform and Restructuring Act of 1998. On October 21, 1998, the President signed H.R. 4328 and vetoed H.R. 1757, because of anti-abortion provisions in H.R. 1757. Both bills contained provisions for the abolition of the same foreign affairs agencies, and the transfer of the agency's functions, personnel and appropriations to the Department of State. Conference Report 105-432, which accompanied H.R. 1757, contains a more detailed discussion of the intentions of Congress regarding the relationship between U.S.-sponsored international broadcasting activities and the Department of State than does Conference Report 105-432. U.S. Congress, Conference Committees, H.Rept. 105-432 (Washington: GPO, 1998), pp. 125-130.

[30] Sec. 1313 of the Foreign Affairs Agencies Consolidation Act of 1998 (Subdivision A of Division G of P.L. 105-277) added the provision creating this under secretary position.

[31] Website for the Under Secretary of State for Public Diplomacy and Public Affairs, http://www.state.gov/r/.

[32] Bureau of Educational and Cultural Affairs Website, Department of State, Washington, http://exchanges.state.gov/.

[33] E-mail received from the Bureau of Educational and Cultural Affairs, Department of State, January 1, 2009.

[34] E-mail response from the Bureau of Educational and Cultural Affairs, June 4, 2009.

[35] Bureau of Educational and Cultural Affairs website, http://exchanges.state.gov/about.html.

[36] For descriptions of various Cultural Envoy Programs administered by the Office of Citizen Exchanges, see the Bureau of Educational and Cultural Affairs website, http://exchanges.state.gov/cultural/index.html.

[37] Department of State, Congressional Budget Justification United States Department of State. Fiscal Year 2010, Washington, D.C., May 2009, p. 526.

[38] Department of State, *Inside a U.S. Embassy* (Washington: American Foreign Service Association, 2005), pp.28-29.

[39] Ibid.

[40] CRS interview with Jim Bigert, Office of Policy, Planning and Resources, Under Secretary for Public Diplomacy and Public Affairs, October 2, 2008.

[41] Ibid.

[42] Bill Rugh, *Enabling Public Diplomacy Field Officers to Do Their Jobs*, The Public Diplomacy Council, Washington, D.C., December 20, 2008, pp. 5-6.

[43] Ibid, p. 5.

[44] Surrogate services broadcast into areas that do not have a free press and media, and broadcast as if they are a domestic, uncensored radio or television station broadcasting in that country. The broadcasts are in the language of the area and present local and national news not covered in a state-controlled domestic media. Besides news stories, surrogate services often cover religion, science, sports, Western music, and banned literature and music. These broadcasts also give voice to dissidents and opposition movements through interviews and background stories.

[45] United States Information Agency, USIA Congressional Budget Justification, Fiscal Year 1999, p. 1 in the Broadcasting section.

[46] DOD Dictionary of Military Terms, "strategic communication," http://www.dtic.mil/doctrine/jel/doddict/data/s/18179.html.

[47] See U.S. Army's Human Terrain System website, http://humanterrainsystem.army.mil/.

[48] Section 184(b)(2) of Title 10 of the U.S. Code lists the five established Centers: The George C. Marshall European Center for Security Studies, Garmisch-Partenkirchen, Germany; The Asia-Pacific Center for Security Studies, Honolulu, Hawaii; The Center for Hemispheric Defense Studies, Washington, D.C.; The Africa Center for Strategic Studies, Washington, D.C.; and The Near East South Asia Center for Strategic Studies, Washington, D.C.

[49] Deputy Assistant Secretary of Defense Michael S. Doran, Support to Public Diplomacy & Deputy Assistant Secretary of State H.E. Pittman, Joint Communication, *Memorandum for Under Secretary of State for Public*

Diplomacy and Public Affairs: DOD Response to U.S. National Strategy for Public Diplomacy and Strategic Communication, undated memorandum, p. 11.

[50] See Department of Defense, *Strategic Communication Joint Integrating Concept*, Version 0.9, August 26, 2008.

[51] Certain information in this section is derived from discussions with DOD officials in the Offices of the Undersecretaries of Defense for Policy (OUSD(P)) and Intelligence (OUSD(I)), as well as the Office of the Assistant Secretary of Defense for Public Affairs (OASD(PA)).

[52] DOD has produced a number of documents discussing SC concepts, principles, goals, and best practices in recent years. These include the 2006 Quadrennial Defense Review Strategic Communication Execution Roadmap, which includes 55 tasks to be completed by the Department to address issues in SC identified in the 2006 QDR. The Roadmap contains a plan of action and milestones for completion of such tasks by "Offices of Primary Responsibility." In August 2008, DOD published a six-page document entitled Principles of Strategic Communication. It was written by representatives of DOD, the Department of State, and outside educators and practitioners. The principles included in this publication were intended to standardize SC education and promote understanding and dialogue concerning SC while DOD develops formal doctrine and policy. Also completed in August 2008, DOD produced the latest version of the Strategic Communication Joint Integrating Concept (JIC), which lays out in detail the challenges, solutions, capabilities, and resources required for a joint force commander to implement a comprehensive approach to strategic communication alongside other government actors. In September 2008, U.S. Joint Forces Command released the Commander's Handbook for Strategic Communication, which provides principles, current organization, processes, and best practices for SC. The Handbook is divided into five main chapters, dealing with SC challenges, established policy and guidance, current practices and initiatives, planning and assessment, and operational implications. According to DOD representatives, these documents are currently informing the process of reviewing strategic communication within the Department.

[53] Government Accountability Office, *U.S. Public Diplomacy: Key Issues for Congressional Oversight*, GAO-09-679SP, May 2009, p. 6.

[54] Ibid., p. 16.

[55] Intelligence Reform and Terrorism Prevention Act of 2004 (P.L. 108-458; 22 U.S.C. § 2732(d). It seems from the language of this subsection that there is technically no requirement that U.S. assistance be marked in this way, and some have highlighted practical, security, and effectiveness concerns for the marking of assistance. See written testimony of Kristen M. Lord, submitted for the record in U.S. Congress, House Committee on Foreign Affairs, Subcommittee on Terrorism, Nonproliferation and Trade, *Flag on the Bag?: Foreign Assistance and the Struggle Against Terrorism*, 111th Cong., 1st sess., November 18, 2009.

[56] Interagency Working Group on U.S. Government-Sponsored International Exchanges and Training, *Inventories of Programs*, Department of State, Washington, D.C., 2008, p. 17, http://www.iawg.gov/rawmedia_repository/ 63ded484_d6ef_4862_af8e_41a344873a91.

[57] Government Accountability Office, *U.S. Public Diplomacy: Interagency Coordination Efforts Hampered by the Lack of a National Communication Strategy*, GAO-05-323, p. 10.

[58] Strategic Communication and Public Diplomacy Policy Coordinating Committee, *U.S. National Strategy for Public Diplomacy and Strategic Communication*, June 2007.

[59] See, e.g., Government Accountability Office, *U.S. Public Diplomacy: Key Issues for Congressional Oversight*, GAO-09-679SP, May 2009, pp. 12-14.

[60] The White House, *Statement by the President on the White House Organization for Homeland Security and Counterterrorism*, May 26, 2009, http://www.whitehouse.gov/the_press_office/Statement-by-the-President-on-theWhite-House-Organization-for-Homeland-Security-and-Counterterrorism/.

[61] See Matt Armstrong, "Updating the Under Secretary Incumbency Chart," http://mountainrunner.us/2009/05/ tracking_the_office.html.

[62] See, e.g., Marc Lynch, "Why Judith McHale Would Be a Bad Public Diplomacy Choice," Foreign Policy, January 23, 2009,
http://lynch.foreignpolicy.com/posts/2009/01/23/rumors_of_a_bad_public_diplomacy John Brown, "Can America Change Hearts and Minds?", the Guardian, April 22, 2009, http://www.guardian cifamerica/2009/apr/21/obama-public-diplomacy-judith-mchale; Spencer Ackerman, "Judith McHale on Public Diplomacy's Role in National Security," Washington Independent, June 11, 2009, http://washingtonindependent.com/ 46590/judith-mchale-on-public-diplomacys-role-in-national-security; Patricia Kushlis, "Judith McHale and the White House Press Corps," WhirledView, July 29, 2009, http://whirledview.typepad.com/ whirledview/2009/07/judithmchale-and-the-white-house-press-corps-1 .html.

[63] Kushlis and Sharpe, p. 27.

[64] Canning, p. 3.

[65] Hady Amr and P.W. Singer, "To Win the 'War on Terror,' We Must First Win the 'War of Ideas': Here's How," ANNALS of the American Academy of Political and Social Science, vol. 618, no. 1 (July 2008), p. 215; Kristen M. Lord, *Voices of America: U.S. Public Diplomacy for the 21st Century*, Brookings Institution, Nov. 2008, p. 39.

[66] Defense Science Board, *Final Report of the DSB Task Force on Strategic Communication*, Jan. 2008, p. 21; Lord, *Voices of America*, pp. 38-39.

[67] Humphrey Taylor, "The Not-So-Black Art of Public Diplomacy," *World Policy Journal*, vol. XXIV, no. 4 (Winter 2007/2008), pp. 52, 54-56; Kristen M. Lord, John A. Nagl, and Seth D. Rosen, *Beyond Bullets: A Pragmatic Strategy to Combat Violent Extremism*, Center for a New American Century, June 2009, pp. 12, 15.

[68] See generally Defense Science Board, p. 20; Lord, *Voices of America*, pp. 14, 39.

[69] Lord, *Voices of America*, p. 14.

[70] Canning, p. 7.

[71] Kushlis and Sharpe, p. 29.

[72] Defense Science Board, pp. 18, 20.

[73] Tony Blankley and Oliver Horn, *Strategizing Strategic Communication*, Heritage Foundation, WebMemo no. 1939, May 29, 2008, p. 2.

[74] Tony Blankley, Helle C. Dale, and Oliver Horn, *Reforming U.S. Public Diplomacy for the 21st Century*, Heritage Foundation, Backgrounder no. 2211, Nov. 20, 2008, p. 4.

[75] For a discussion of current issues concerning U.S. international broadcasting, please see "International Broadcasting," below.

[76] See, e.g., Lord, *Voices of America*, p. 32.

[77] Philip Seib and Carola Weil, *AFRICOM, the American Military and Public Diplomacy in Africa*, USC Annenberg School for Communication, Policy Briefing, Mar. 2008, p. 2.

[78] See generally Lord, *Voices of America*, p. 33.

[79] U.S. Congress, Senate Committee on Armed Services, *National Defense Authorization Act for Fiscal Year 2010*, report to accompany S. 1390, 111th Cong., 1st sess., S.Rept. 111-35 (Washington: GPO, 2009), p. 182.

[80] U.S. Congress, House Committee on Appropriations, *Department of Defense Appropriations Bill, 2010*, report to accompany H.R. 3326, 111th Cong., 1st sess., H.Rept. 111-230 (Washington: GPO, 2009), p. 67.

[81] Kushlis and Sharpe, p. 30.

[82] H.Rept. 111-230, p. 67.

[83] Ibid.

[84] Ibid.

[85] Defense Science Board, p. xvi; but see Lord, *Voices of America*, p. 33.

[86] Lord, *Voices of America*, p. 33.

[87] Shawn Zeller, "Damage Control: Karen Hughes Does PD," *Foreign Service Journal*, vol. 83, no. 10 (Oct. 2006), p. 20; Lord, *Voices of America*, p. 35.

[88] Blankley, Dale, and Horn, p. 5, Executive Summary p. 1.

[89] Some have attributed this to a lack of Public Diplomacy Officers in positions of policy-making importance, as well as placement of non-Public Diplomacy Officers in significant public diplomacy positions. United States Advisory Commission on Public Diplomacy, *Getting the People Part Right: A Report on the Human Resources Dimension of U.S. Public Diplomacy*, June 2008, Executive Summary; Zeller, p. 22.

[90] Cf. William A. Rugh, "PD Practitioners: Still Second-Class Citizens," *Foreign Service Journal*, Vol. 86, no. 10, (Oct. 2009), p. 30 (explaining and subsequently dismissing the argument).

[91] Blankley, Dale, and Horn, p. 10; Lord, *Voices of America*, p. 33.

[92] Lord, *Voices of America*, p. 35.

[93] Canning, p. 11.

[94] Lord, *Voices of America*, p. 34.

[95] *Strategic Communications Act of 2008*, S. 3546 (110th Cong.).

[96] Christopher Paul, *Whiter Strategic Communication?*, Rand Corporation Occasional Paper, 2009, p. 10.

[97] *Getting the People Part Right*, pp. 8, 10.

[98] Joe Johnson, "How Does Public Diplomacy Measure Up?", *Foreign Service Journal*, vol. 83, no. 10 (Oct. 2006), p. 50; Lord, *Voices of America*, p. 35.

[99] Robert J. Callahan, "Neither Madison Avenue Nor Hollywood," *Foreign Service Journal*, vol. 83, no. 10 (Oct. 2006), p. 35; Canning, p. 10; *Getting the People Part Right*, Executive Summary.

[100] Lord, *Voices of America*, p. 41; Johnson, "How Does Public Diplomacy Measure Up?", p. 51.

[101] Blankley, Dale, and Horn, p. 6.

[102] Canning, pp. 8-9; Lord, *Voices of America*, p. 35; Callahan, p. 36.

[103] Canning, p. 10; *Getting the People Part Right*, Executive Summary, p. 29.

[104] *Getting the People Part Right*, p. 19.

[105] American Academy of Diplomacy & the Henry L. Stimson Center, *A Foreign Affairs Budget for the Future: Fixing the Crisis in Diplomatic Readiness*, Oct. 2008, p. 24.

[106] Kushlis and Sharpe, p. 30; Department of State information received in response to a request for information on international exchanges, June 12, 2009.

[107] U.S. Congress, Senate Committee on Foreign Relations, *U.S. Public Diplomacy—Time to Get Back in the Game*, 111th Cong. 1st sess., S.Rept. 111-6 (Washington: GPO, 2009), pp. 14-15.

[108] Defense Science Board, p. 6.

[109] *Time to Get Back in the Game*, pp. 7-8.

[110] Secure Embassy Construction and Counterterrorism Act of 1999 (Title VI of H.R. 3427 (106th Cong.) enacted by reference in Section 1000(a)(7) of P.L. 106-113; 22 U.S.C. § 4865 note).

[111] *Time to Get Back in the Game*, pp. 4, 7, 10-11.

[112] Ibid., pp. 5-7; *Foreign Affairs Budget for the Future*, p. 16.

[113] Although it can be expected that the focus on establishing Centers would be on Muslim-majority countries given the current national security environment, some commentators have also suggested reinvestment in Binational Centers in Latin America. The Binational Centers were begun as partnerships between private organizations in Latin American countries and the United States, which operated with resources and programs similar to those of the America Centers. Canning, p. 13. This recommendation to reengage in Latin America even while other geographic regions are demanding more attention underscores an approach to public diplomacy that stresses long-term relationships and the belief that U.S. engagement must have global coverage in order to play a vital role in meeting the foreign policy and national security challenges that will present themselves in the future.

[114] *Time to Get Back in the Game*, pp. 7-8.

[115] Lord, *Voices of America*, p. 32; Defense Science Board, p. xvii; Amr and Singer, p. 208.

[116] Defense Science Board, p. xvii.

[117] Some of these issues are further discussed under the "Leveraging Non-Public Sectors" and "Research, Monitoring, and Evaluation" sections of this chapter.

[118] Zeller, p. 24; Lord, *Voices of America*, p. 40.

[119] Zeller, p. 26.

[120] Johnson, "How Does Public Diplomacy Measure Up?", pp. 48-49.

[121] Ibid.; Defense Science Board, p. xviii.

[122] Stephen Johnson, Helle C. Dale, and Patrick Cronin, Strengthening U.S. Public Diplomacy Requires Organization, Coordination, and Strategy, Heritage Foundation Backgrounder no. 1875, August 5, 2005, Executive Summary p. 2; Amr and Singer, p. 218.

[123] Peter Krause and Stephen Van Evera, "Public Diplomacy: Ideas for the War of Ideas," *Middle East Policy*, vol. XVI, no. 3 (Fall 2009), p. 110.

[124] Broadcasting Board of Governors, "Broadcasting Board of Governors Corrects ProPublica's Report on Alhurra Television," press release, June 30, 2008, http://www.bbg.gov/pressroom/pressreleases-article.cfm?articleID=244.

[125] See, e.g., Defense Science Board; Lord, *Voices of America*.

[126] Lord, *Voices of America*, p. 40.

[127] Blankley and Horn, "Strategizing Strategic Communication," p. 3; Lord, *Voices of America*, pp. 1-2; Defense Science Board, p. xiii.

[128] Lord, *Voices of America*, p. 17. Senator Sam Brownback introduced legislation in the 110th Congress that would have established a similar organization. *Strategic Communications Act of 2008*, S. 3546 (110th Cong.).

[129] See Lord, *Voices of America*; Defense Science Board.

[130] Ibid., see also Blankley and Horn, p. 3.

[131] *Time to Get Back in the Game*, p. 6.

[132] See, e.g., The Pew Global Attitudes Project, *Confidence in Obama Lifts U.S. Image Around the World*, July 23, 2009, http://pewglobal.org/reports/pdf/264.pdf; GfK Custom Research North America, "America Is Now the Most Admired Country Globally," October 5, 2009, http://www.gfkamerica.com/newsroom/press_releases/single_sites/ 004729/index.en.html.

[133] Amr and Singer, p. 216. See generally Government Accountability Office, *U.S. Public Diplomacy: Key Issues for Congressional Oversight*, GAO-09-679SP, May 2009, p. 13 (arguing for "campaign-style approach to PD that includes robust assessment capabilities).

[134] Lord, *Voices of America*, p. 41.

[135] Johnson, "How Does Public Diplomacy Measure Up?", pp. 45-46; Lord, *Voices of America*, p. 40.

[136] Defense Science Board, pp. 55, 59.

[137] Matt Armstrong, "Rethinking Smith-Mundt," *Small Wars Journal*, July 28, 2008, http://smallwarsjournal.com/blog 2008/07/ rethinking-smithmundt/.

[138] *Report on the Smith-Mundt Symposium of January 13, 2009*, Armstrong Strategic Insights Group, LLC and the Center on Communication Leadership, Mar. 12, 2009, p. 11.

[139] U. S. Congress, House Committee on Armed Services, *National Defense Authorization Act for Fiscal Year 2010*, report to accompany H.R. 2647, 11 1th Cong., 1st sess., H.Rept. 111-166, part 1 (Washington: GPO, 2009), p. 377.

[140] *Smith-Mundt Symposium Report*, p. 7.

[141] Ibid., pp. 8-10.

[142] House Foreign Affairs Committee; Senate Foreign Relations Committee; House and Senate Armed Services Committees; and House and Senate Appropriations Committees.

[143] H.R. 2410 includes the provisions of several other bills related to public diplomacy. Bills incorporated as part of H.R. 2410 include H.R. 473, H.R. 909, H.R. 1886, H.R. 1976, H.R. 2131, and H.R. 2475.

[144] Enacted bills are co-designated by their Public Law numbers.

[145] Section 60 of the 1956 act already requires the Secretary of State to make "every effort" to coordinate the public diplomacy activities of other federal agencies.

[146] S.Res. 49 (111th Cong.), agreed to in the Senate by unanimous consent on May 19, 2009, expresses the sense of Congress expressing the importance of public diplomacy to U.S. foreign policy, especially the reestablishment of America Centers outside U.S. embassy compounds.

[147] See also S. 1739; H.R. 2410, Section 1109(c).

[148] The companion bill in the Senate establishing this Foundation is S. 473 (111th Cong.).

In: U.S. Public Diplomacy: Background and Issues
Editor: Matthew B. Morrison

ISBN: 978-1-61728-888-3
© 2010 Nova Science Publishers, Inc.

Chapter 2

U.S. Public Diplomacy: Key Issues for Congressional Oversight[*]

United States Government Accountability Office

Abbreviations

BBG	Broadcasting Board of Governors
CSIS	Center for Strategic and International Studies
DOD	Department of Defense
ECA	Bureau of Educational and Cultural Affairs
PCC	Policy Coordinating Committee
State	Department of State
USAID	U.S. Agency for International Development
VOA	Voice of America

May 27, 2009

Congressional Committees

Since the September 11, 2001, terrorist attacks, the U.S. government has spent at least $10 billion on communication efforts designed to advance the strategic interests of the United States. However, foreign public opinion polling data shows that negative views towards the United States persist despite the collective efforts to counteract them by the State Department (State), Broadcasting Board of Governors (BBG), U.S. Agency for International Development (USAID), Department of Defense (DOD), and other U.S. government agencies. Based on the significant role U.S. strategic communication and public diplomacy[1] efforts can play in promoting U.S. national security objectives, such as countering ideological support for

---

[*] This is an edited, reformatted and augmented version of a U. S. Government Accountability Office publication dated May 2009.

violent extremism, we highlighted these efforts as an urgent issue for the new administration and Congress.[2] To assist Congress with its oversight agenda, we have enclosed a series of issue papers that discuss long-standing and emerging public diplomacy challenges identified by GAO and others.[3]

While the prior administration issued a national communication strategy in June 2007, the National Defense Authorization Act for Fiscal Year 2009 requires that the President issue a new comprehensive strategy by December 2009 to guide interagency efforts. The issues discussed in the enclosures to this chapter should be considered in the development of the new strategic plan, related agency and country-level plans, and other areas such as State's human capital and security policies. Key issues include the following:

- **Strategic and operational planning**—The United States' current national communication strategy lacks a number of desirable characteristics identified by GAO, such as a clear definition of the problem, desired results, and a delineation of agency roles and responsibilities. We believe the inclusion of these and other key elements could have helped address several of the challenges and issues discussed below. Prior GAO reports have discussed the need for agency-specific and country-level plans that support national-level planning efforts. We found that such supporting plans have generally not been developed. In the absence of an improved strategy and supporting plans, it remains doubtful that agency programs are strategically designed and executed in support of common goals.

- **Performance measurement**—While agencies have made some progress in developing performance measurement systems, limited data exist on the ultimate effect of U.S. outreach efforts relative to the top-level goals outlined in the national communication strategy.

- **Coordination of U.S. communications efforts**—Although several mechanisms have been established to coordinate U.S. strategic communication policy and programs, concerns remain regarding the roles and responsibilities of State and DOD; the extent of outreach to the private sector; and whether new leadership mechanisms or organizational structures are needed.

- **State's public diplomacy workforce**—State faces a number of human capital challenges that influence the effectiveness of its public diplomacy operations. Specific challenges include staffing shortages, a shortage of experienced public diplomacy officers to fill mid-career positions, administrative burdens and staffing policies that limit the time public diplomacy officers can devote to outreach efforts, and ongoing foreign language proficiency shortfalls. Collectively, these challenges and concerns raise the risk that U.S. interests are not being adequately addressed.

- **Outreach efforts in high-threat posts**—Security concerns around the world have led to building practices and personnel policies that have limited the ability of local populations to interact with Americans inside and outside the embassy. For the past several years, State has experimented with alternative outreach mechanisms such as American Corners to alleviate this forced isolation. These efforts raise significant policy, funding, and operational questions, which remain to be fully addressed.

- **Interagency efforts to adopt a new approach to public diplomacy**— Dynamic shifts in how target audiences obtain and use information have led many public diplomacy practitioners to conclude that the United States must more fully engage emerging social networks and technologies (such as Facebook and Twitter) in order to remain relevant. Referred to as "Public Diplomacy 2.0," this new approach to strategic communications is exploring ways to operate in this evolving information environment. However, substantial questions exist regarding the challenges associated with this new approach.

We reviewed current agency documents related to the issues discussed in the attached enclosures. We discussed these issues with State, BBG, USAID, and DOD officials in Washington, D.C. We reviewed reports related to public diplomacy by various research institutions. We also applied national planning criteria developed by GAO to the United States' current national communication strategy to highlight deficiencies that we believe should be addressed in the President's new interagency strategy. Further information on the scope and methodology for this particular analysis can be found in appendix I.

We conducted this performance audit from October 2008 through May 2009 in accordance with generally accepted government auditing standards. Those standards require that we plan and perform the audit to obtain sufficient, appropriate evidence to provide a reasonable basis for our findings and conclusions based on our audit objectives. We believe that the evidence obtained provides a reasonable basis for our findings and conclusions.

We provided a draft of this chapter for review and comment to State, BBG, USAID, and DOD. Each agency declined to provide formal comments. State, BBG, and USAID provided technical comments, which we incorporated in the report, as appropriate.

signature

Gene L. Dodaro
Acting Comptroller General of the United States
Enclosures

List of Congressional Committees
The Honorable Carl Levin
Chair
The Honorable John McCain
Rankin g Member
Committee on Armed Services
United States Senate
The Honorable John F . Kerry
Chair
The Honorable Richard G. Lugar
Ranking Member
Committee on Foreign Relations
United States Senate

The Honorable Joseph I. Lieberman
Chair
Committee on Homeland Security

and Governmental Affairs
United States Senate

The Honorable Patrick J. Leahy
C hair
The Honorable Judd Gregg
Rankin g Member
Subcommittee on State, Foreign Operations, and Related Programs
Committee on Appropriations
United States Senate

The Honorable George V. Voinovich
Ranking Member
Subcommittee on Oversight of Government Management,
the Federal Workforce, and the District of Columbia
Committee on Homeland Security and Governmental Affairs
United States Senate

The Honorable Ike Skelton
Chair
The Honorable John M. McHugh
Rankin g Member
Committee on Armed Services
House of Representatives

The Honorable Howard L. Berman
Chair
The Honorable Ileana Ros-Lehtinen
Ranking Member
Committee on Foreign Affairs
House of Representatives

The Honorable Kay Granger
Ranking Member
Subcommittee on State, Foreign Operations, and Related Programs
Committee on Appropriations
House of Representatives

The Honorable John Tierney
Chair
Subcommittee on National Se curity and Foreign Affairs
Committee on Oversight and Government Reform
House of Representatives

ENCLOSURE I. BACKGROUND

The overall goal of U.S. strategic communication efforts is to understand, engage, inform, and influence the attitudes and behaviors of global audiences in support of U.S. strategic interests. U.S. strategic communication efforts are distributed across several entities, including State, BBG, USAID, and DOD, and function under the broad guidance of the White House and National Security Council. Within the U.S. government, State's Under Secretary for Public Diplomacy and Public Affairs has the lead for U.S. strategic communication efforts.

Agency Programs

State's public diplomacy efforts are managed by the Under Secretary for Public Diplomacy and Public Affairs, who oversees the Bureaus of Educational and Cultural Affairs (ECA), International Information Programs, and Public Affairs. ECA aims to foster mutual understanding between the United States and other countries through International Visitor, Fulbright, and other academic and professional exchange programs. The Bureau of International Information Programs communicates with foreign publics about U.S. policy, society, and values through speaker programs, print and electronic publications, and Internet outreach. The Bureau of Public Affairs informs audiences about U.S. foreign policy through activities such as media outreach and news management. State's workforce of over 1,000 public diplomacy officers is divided between Washington and overseas posts, where public diplomacy staff report through the ambassador to their respective regional bureaus in Washington. State embassy officers engage in information dissemination, media relations, cultural affairs, and other efforts.

The BBG, as the overseer of U.S. international broadcasting efforts, aims to support U.S. strategic communication objectives by broadcasting fair and accurate information, while maintaining its journalistic independence as a news organization. The BBG operates 75 language services divided among its five broadcast entities—Voice of America (VOA), the Middle East Broadcasting Networks, Radio Free Europe/Radio Liberty, Radio Free Asia, and the Office of Cuba Broadcasting.

USAID's communication mission is to inform host country audiences about U.S. assistance. To fulfill this role, USAID maintains a public affairs office in Washington, D.C., and a network of 111 communication specialists at USAID missions worldwide. The communications specialists' outreach functions include responding to inquiries about USAID programs, collaborating with the embassy public affairs office, speech writing for the USAID mission director and others, preparing press releases, and coordinating Web site updates.

DOD's Office of the Deputy Assistant Secretary of Defense for Joint Communication is responsible for overseeing DOD activities directed at shaping departmentwide communications doctrine, organization, and training for the joint force; but this office has not issued formal policy regarding its strategic communication operations. Among other efforts, DOD has developed a predoctrinal document called the "Commander's Handbook," which provides strategic communications principles, techniques, and procedures, and has launched some strategic communication education and training initiatives to help institutionalize strategic communication. DOD's strategic communication operations are divided among public affairs activities, information operations (which includes psychological operations), and defense support to public diplomacy offices.

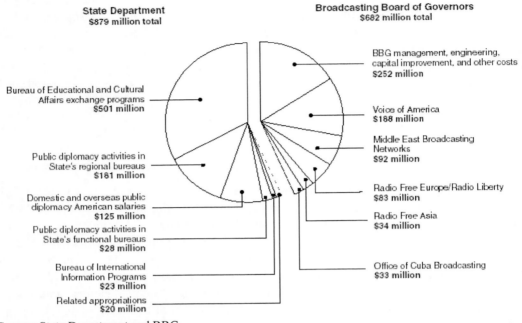

State Department
$879 million total

Bureau of Educational and Cultural Affairs exchange programs
$501 million

Public diplomacy activities in State's regional bureaus
$181 million

Domestic and overseas public diplomacy American salaries
$125 million

Public diplomacy activities in State's functional bureaus
$28 million

Bureau of International Information Programs
$23 million

Related appropriations
$20 million

Broadcasting Board of Governors
$682 million total

BBG management, engineering, capital improvement, and other costs
$252 million

Voice of America
$188 million

Middle East Broadcasting Networks
$92 million

Radio Free Europe/Radio Liberty
$83 million

Radio Free Asia
$34 million

Office of Cuba Broadcasting
$33 million

Source: State Department and BBG.
Note: Totals may not add due to rounding.

Figure 1. Key Uses of U.S. Strategic Communication Budget Resources for the State Department and the Broadcasting Board of Governors, Fiscal Year 2008

Agency Funding

As shown in figure 1, State and the BBG shared a total strategic communication budget of about $1.6 billion in fiscal year 2008, with $501 million going to State's exchange and cultural affairs programs, $378 million going to State's nonexchange programs, and the balance of $682 million going to the BBG to support its global broadcasting efforts.USAID funds all domestic and some foreign audience communications out of limited agency operating expenses. There is no stand-alone budget for agency communications other than the operational budget amount allotted to USAID's headquarters public affairs bureau through the annual budget process.[4] USAID's main resource for communicating to foreign audiences is its worldwide network of communications specialists, most of whom are Foreign Service Nationals. USAID missions usually establish a program budget for mission or country communications based on amounts left over within the mission budget or through use of hard-to-utilize local currency accounts maintained by the embassy or mission, or both.

DOD does not have a separate budget covering its strategic communication activities. DOD officials said that they consider strategic communication to be a process instead of a discrete set of programs, and as a result, cannot identify DOD's spending on its strategic communication efforts. Nonetheless, DOD officials acknowledge the department spends hundreds of millions of dollars each year to support its outreach efforts, and DOD has identified strategic communication as a critical capability it intends to develop and support with related policy and doctrinal guidance, training, and staff and program resources.

ENCLOSURE II. STRATEGIC AND OPERATIONAL PLANNING

Issue

A national strategy is a critical planning tool that provides policymakers and implementing agencies with direction and guidance on goals, resource allocations, program implementation, and evaluation and ensures effective oversight and accountability. Beginning in 2003, we reported on the importance of a national communication strategy to ensure agency efforts are properly coordinated, convey consistent messages to target audiences, focus on achieving concrete and measurable objectives, and lead to mutually reinforcing benefits overseas.[5] In 2005, we specifically recommended such a strategy be developed.[6] In June 2007, the previous administration released a national communication strategy, which established three objectives: (1) offer a positive vision of hope and opportunity, (2) nurture common interests and values, and (3) help isolate and marginalize violent extremists. The strategy also provided guidance on such topics as target audiences, public diplomacy priorities, and interagency coordination, and outlined implementation plans for each communication objective. However, the strategy failed to include a clear definition of the problem, desired results, and a delineation of agency roles and responsibilities. Moreover, the strategy is not adequately supported by agency-specific plans and country-level plans modeled on private-sector best practices that could help increase the coordination and effectiveness of U.S. communication efforts that are distributed across four major agencies, dozens of discrete programs, a diverse range of communication objectives, and assorted target audiences around the world. The National Defense Authorization Act for Fiscal Year 2009 requires that the President issue a new comprehensive strategy by December 2009 to guide interagency strategic communication efforts.[7] It is important that the President and Congress, in devising this new strategy, incorporate the need to (1) address key planning elements such as a desired end-state with clear outcome and subordinate goals, and (2) develop plans and policies regarding the need for supporting department and country-level planning efforts that incorporate private-sector best practices. Absent the development of such a detailed strategy, the U.S. government runs the risk that its communication efforts will lack coordination and focus, and fail to achieve strategic objectives.

Key Findings

2007 National Strategy Only Partially Addressed Key Planning Elements

In 2004, GAO identified a set of desirable characteristics to aid in the development and implementation of national strategies, enhance their usefulness as tools to help make policy and program decisions, guide resource allocations, and assure better accountability for results.[8] However, the June 2007 communication strategy did not address or only partially addressed such key characteristics as defining the purpose of the document, describing the nature and scope of the problem, developing a hierarchy of strategic goals and performance objectives, describing future costs and needed resources, and delineating U.S. government roles and responsibilities. Table 1 lists all six characteristics identified by GAO and our assessment of whether the June 2007 strategy generally addresses, partially addresses, or does not address the key elements that support each characteristic.

The new administration needs to fully consider these characteristics in drafting the new strategy called for by the National Defense Authorization Act to ensure the strategy more extensively guides key planning, decision- making, and oversight processes in line with strategic communication objectives.

Table 1. June 2007 National Strategy's Conformance with GAO's Desirable Characteristics

Characteristics	Extent of conformance	Examples of missing or incomplete elements
Clear purpose, scope, and methodology	Partially addresses	• Purpose • Methodology
Detailed discussion of problems, risks, and threats	Does not address	• Problem definition • Risk assessment
Desired goals, objectives, activities, and outcome-related performance measures	Partially addresses	• Overall desired results, or "end- state" • Hierarchy of strategic goals and subordinate objectives • Milestones and outcome-related performance measures
Resources, investments, and risk management	Does not address	• Resources and investments a ssociated with the strategy • Sources of resources • Risk management principles
Delineation of U.S. government roles, responsibilities, and coordination mechanisms	Partially addresses	• Lead, support, and partner roles and responsibilities of specific federal agencies, departments, or offices • Discussion of how conflicts will be resolved
Description of strategy's integration among and with other entities	Partially addresses	• Addresses integration with relevant documents from other agencies and subordinate levels

Source: GAO analysis.

Supporting Agency Plans Have Generally Not Been Developed

Beginning in 2003, GAO recommended that State develop an agency-level plan to integrate its diverse public diplomacy activities and direct them towards common objectives. We noted that the absence of a strategy may hinder the department's ability to guide its programs towards the achievement of concrete and measurable results. State responded to this recommendation with improvements to its strategic planning process; however, the department still lacks an agency-level plan that specifically supports the current national strategy. Significantly, the June 2007 national communication strategy calls for the development of such agency-level plans. The strategy indicates agency plans should identify key programs and policies that support the national strategy's objectives, identify key audiences, assign agency responsibility, outline specific implementation plans, and develop criteria to evaluate effectiveness. Among the four nonintelligence agencies (State, USAID, BBG, and DOD) involved in U.S. strategic communication efforts, only DOD responded to this call for an agency-specific plan. However, DOD's plan only lists programs and policies that support the national strategy's objectives, while omitting any details on target audiences, DOD's role in relation to other agencies, implementation plans, and performance measures. In the absence of supporting agency plans, no clear link can be established between national communication objectives, agency programs, and results, raising doubts about whether agency programs have been strategically designed to support a common purpose in the most efficient and effective manner possible. The new administration should require the development of supporting agency plans as it drafts the new strategy called for by the National Defense Authorization Act.

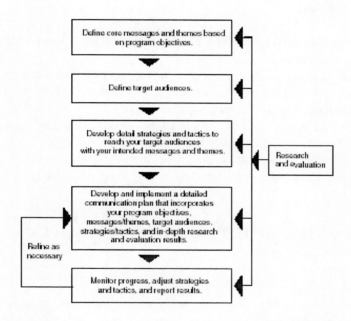

Source: GAO.

Figure 2. Key Elements of the Campaign-Style Approach

State Department Lacks Country-Level Plans

We have recommended that State develop detailed country-level plans that incorporate strategic communication best practices—which we refer to as the "campaign-style approach."[9] As shown in figure 2, the campaign-style approach includes defining a core message, identifying target audiences, developing detailed communication strategies and tactics, and using research and evaluation to inform and redirect efforts as needed.

Though we have reported that both USAID and DOD have sought to develop country-level communication plans that generally adhere to the campaign-style approach, State has not yet developed such plans. Our 2006 review of public diplomacy operations in Nigeria, Pakistan, and Egypt found that this approach and corresponding communication plans were absent, and that in-country public diplomacy planning efforts represented top-level statements of intent with little detailed planning to support post communication goals. In 2007, we reported that State's attempt to improve country-level planning through a pilot effort at 18 posts served as a useful exercise, but the country plans lacked key elements of the campaign-style approach. State officials told us a new initiative will be launched this year requiring embassies to develop "public diplomacy implementation plans" that address post outreach efforts. State intends to pilot test these plans in 12 countries. It remains to be determined whether these new plans will fully incorporate the campaign-style approach to strategic communication.

The new administration should require the development of supporting country-level plans as part of its new strategy. In the absence of such plans, program officials will likely fail to effectively harness available resources towards explicit communication goals and objectives.

Oversight Questions

1. What is the status of current agency efforts to meet the December 2009 deadline for a new national communication strategy?
2. To what extent will the President's new communication strategy incorporate key planning elements such as a clear definition of the problem, desired results, and a delineation of agency roles and responsibilities?
3. What is the status of developing agency-level plans that support the national strategy's communication goals and objectives?
4. To what extent does State plan to develop country-level communication plans that adhere to the campaign-style approach recommended by GAO?

ENCLOSURE III. PERFORMANCE MEASUREMENT

Issue

It is critical that agencies comprehensively measure the performance of their strategic communication efforts to understand which efforts are most effective and, in turn, determine how to make most efficient use of limited resources. However, U.S. agencies have not fully demonstrated the effect of their strategic communication efforts on the national communication goals, such as countering ideological support for violent extremism. Since 2003, GAO and other organizations have called on agencies to fully embrace a "culture of measurement" for their strategic communication efforts, beginning with a comprehensive communication strategy that would better enable agencies to direct their multifaceted efforts towards concrete and measurable progress. While agencies have made some progress in this area, including evaluating some programs, such as exchanges, the United States still lacks a national strategy that includes desired results, performance objectives, and outcome-related indicators.

Key Findings

Limitations of Prior National-Level Performance Planning

The 2007 national communication strategy identifies three key strategic goals—(1) offer a positive vision of hope and opportunity, rooted in the most basic values of the American people; (2) nurture common interests and values; and (3) marginalize extremism. However, this strategy does not identify target "end-states," which are the desired results of such efforts, nor are the strategic goals supported by subordinate performance objectives and indicators that would allow agencies and others to gauge progress. In addition, agencies have adopted varying performance management systems that do not link back to the national communication strategy.

- BBG's performance measurement system is not explicitly linked to the national strategy. According to BBG officials, the board's statutory mandate of broadcasting accurate and objective news and information sets it apart from other strategic communication efforts. BBG officials told us BBG supports the national strategic communications goals when they are consistent with BBG's mandate and strategic plan. BBG has a standard set of performance indicators it uses to measure progress towards its overarching strategic goal to "deliver accurate news and information to significant audiences in support of U.S. strategic interests."

- USAID has not established a standard set of performance indicators for measuring progress towards the national strategic communications goals. USAID officials noted that their strategic communications do not constitute a separate program or budget line item; thus these efforts are generally not monitored or evaluated separately. However, USAID's field- based communications specialists are expected to develop communication strategies that include goals and objectives as well as performance monitoring plans for their outreach activities.

- While DOD strategic communication has a substantial role in marginalizing extremism, DOD has not established standard performance indicators to assess its effectiveness in contributing to this key strategic goal. DOD officials said this is because the department considers strategic communications to be a process instead of a discrete program, thus they are not separately monitored. However, DOD has measured the effectiveness of its communications at the project level.

- In contrast to the other three agencies, State's performance measurement system provides a set of outcome-oriented performance indicators linked to the national strategy's goals as shown in table 2. However, State has not established subordinate objectives in support of the national goals that could better illustrate the linkages between the broad strategic goals and its performance indicators.

Agencies' Ability to Measure Results Limited by Inherent Challenges and Varying Use of Research

Agencies cite three inherent challenges in measuring the effectiveness of their strategic communication efforts. First, strategic communications may only produce long-term, rather than immediate, effect. Second, it is difficult to isolate the effect of strategic communications from other influences, such as policy. Third, strategic communications often target audiences' perceptions, which are intangible and complex and thus difficult to measure. GAO and others have identified some potential best practices for assessing strategic communications programs that address some of the inherent difficulties in measuring these programs' effect on attitudes and behaviors. For example, in 2007, we reported that in-depth actionable research at every step of the communications process is critical to monitoring and evaluating progress.[10] Common private-sector measurement techniques that are used to measure results include the use of surveys and polling to develop baseline data, immediate follow-up research, and additional tracking polls to identify long-term changes over time.

In addition, agencies' funding and use of research to measure performance varies. We reported in 2007 that State has generally not adopted a research-focused approach to evaluate the effect of its thematic communications efforts. State conducts and contracts for audience research, including broad public opinion polling and focus groups, in over 50 countries each year through its Office of Research, which has an annual research budget of about $5.5 million. However, such generic research is not used to evaluate the effectiveness of public diplomacy programs. By contrast, BBG uses research to help its broadcast services plan and evaluate their programs. BBG has a research budget of about $10 million per year, which funds audience surveys, focus groups, in-depth interviews, and listener and monitor panels to support its broadcasting activities throughout the world. In our prior work, we identified shortcomings with BBG's audience research methodology. In our August 2006 report on the Middle East Broadcasting Networks, we recommended that several steps be taken to correct methodological concerns that could affect the accuracy of its research data regarding Alhurra's viewing rates and Radio Sawa's listening rates.[11] BBG has since taken steps to address some of these methodological concerns, including identifying significant methodological limitations. While USAID does not have a central research office that conducts audience research, staff at some missions contract for polling and focus groups to support specific, targeted public awareness campaigns. Finally, some of DOD's combatant commands have recently initiated their own polling and focus group efforts.

Limited Evaluation of State Public Diplomacy Programs

State has evaluated its public diplomacy programs to varying degrees. The Bureau of Educational and Cultural Affairs (ECA) has its own staffed and resourced internal evaluation unit and has been a leader in performance measurement and evaluation for several years. While this bureau has extensively evaluated its programs using its annual evaluation budget of $1.8 million, State has sponsored limited evaluation of the rest of its public diplomacy programs. For example, the Bureau of International Information Programs' Speakers Program, which it describes as its "largest and single most powerful instrument for engaging foreign publics on a person-to-person basis," has not yet been evaluated, although State is planning an evaluation of the program later in 2009. Further, embassy public affairs officers generally do not conduct systematic program evaluations and receive only limited audience polling data to help measure progress. The lack of a comprehensive system for evaluating public diplomacy performance hinders State's ability to correct its course of action or direct resources toward activities that offer a greater likelihood of success.

In order to bring measurement and evaluation for the rest of public diplomacy up to the ECA bureau's high standard, State recently established an Evaluation and Measurement Unit within State's Office of Policy, Planning and Resources for Public Diplomacy and Public Affairs. The unit is charged with developing performance measurement instruments and conducting independent evaluations of the effectiveness of all State public diplomacy programs. This unit has established a core set of public diplomacy performance indicators and launched a global public diplomacy tracking system as well as a pilot study to attempt to quantify the aggregate effect of public diplomacy programs and products.

State Department Country- Level Reporting on Results Is Inconsistent

State has inconsistent reporting requirements for its public diplomacy activities undertaken at the country-level and therefore does not ensure these efforts are measured by comparable standards, or at all. State mission performance planning guidance allows public diplomacy staff in the field to focus on public diplomacy as a stand-alone strategic goal aimed at promoting mutual understanding, to integrate public diplomacy into another strategic goal, such as counterterrorism, or do both. When treated as a stand-alone goal, posts are expected to generate related performance indicators and targets. When public diplomacy efforts are integrated with other strategic goals, posts are not required to develop related performance targets and indicators. In 2003, we administered a survey to the heads of public affairs sections at U.S. embassies worldwide covering a range of issues.[12] Survey results indicated that about 87 percent of respondents integrated public diplomacy into the missions' other strategic goals, which means that the majority of missions were not required to measure the performance of their public diplomacy programs.

Table 2. State Department's Linked Performance Indicators

National strategic goals	State's outcome-oriented performance indicators
Offer a positive vision of hope and opportunity, rooted in the most basic values of the American people	Increased understanding of U.S. policy, society, and values.
Nurture common interests and values	Percentage of exchange program participants who increased or changed their understanding of the United States immediately following their program.
Marginalize extremism	Reduction in the level of anti-American sentiment among participants of State information programs.

Source: State's Fiscal Year 2008 Performance Report.

Oversight Questions

1. How do agencies track their contributions towards common communication goals such as marginalizing extremism?
2. To what extent have agencies incorporated in-depth, actionable research into their performance evaluation efforts?
3. To what extent do available resources meet agency needs for in-depth, actionable research?
4. What effect do embassy communications efforts have beyond supporting the traditional goal of promoting mutual understanding, and how is this measured?

ENCLOSURE IV. COORDINATION OF U.S. COMMUNICATIONS EFFORTS

Issue

When agencies conduct communications programs in a fragmented, uncoordinated way, it can result in a patchwork of programs that can waste funds, lead to inconsistent messaging, and limit the overall effectiveness of the effort. Interagency coordination of U.S. strategic communication efforts is limited by several challenges, including unclear agency roles and responsibilities, a lack of sustained leadership to direct agencies' efforts, minimal interagency sharing of research, and the lack of a strategy to engage the private sector. Due, in part, to concerns about the lack of effective interagency coordination, several reports have questioned whether new leadership mechanisms and organizational structures are needed to improve U.S. strategic communication efforts. Several reports have proposed creating an independent or semi-independent organization to support the government in achieving its communications goals, while other reports propose establishing a new government agency to consolidate U.S. government communications.

Key Findings

Roles and Responsibilities Have Not Been Defined

The national communications strategy identifies the principal mechanism for the coordination of U.S. government strategic communication activities, namely the Policy Coordinating Committee (PCC) on Public Diplomacy and Strategic Communication led by State's Under Secretary for Public Diplomacy and Public Affairs, but does not address which agencies, departments, and offices will implement the strategy and their roles and responsibilities. The lack of guidance on DOD's and State's respective roles and responsibilities is of particular concern. Both departments have made marginalizing extremism—one of the three national communication goals—their top communications priority and are undertaking activities in this area. While State has been formally designated as the lead for all U.S. government strategic communications, DOD has more resources than State to apply to the strategic communications goal of marginalizing extremism. In 2006, DOD established the Office of the Deputy Assistant Secretary of Defense for Support to Public Diplomacy to support and coordinate public diplomacy efforts, and serve as the lead for developing policy within DOD on countering ideological support for terrorism. DOD officials said this office was disbanded in early 2009 and it is unclear what existing or new mechanisms, if any, will conduct its functions. Further, despite internal planning initiatives that began in 2006, DOD has not defined the roles, responsibilities, and relationships of its internal military capabilities that support strategic communications, such as public affairs, information operations, and defense support for public diplomacy.

Lack of Leadership

We reported in 2005 that a lack of leadership has contributed to agencies independently defining and coordinating strategic communications programs.[13] Some reports note that a unifying vision of strategic communications starts with sustained senior leadership from the White House focusing exclusively on global communication. In January 2003, the then-President established an Office of Global Communications to facilitate the strategic direction and coordination of U.S. public diplomacy efforts. However, this office was ineffectual in fulfilling its intended role and no longer exists. In addition, State officials told us the lack of sustained leadership at the under secretary level has also hindered interagency coordination. These officials estimate the position of the Under Secretary for Public Diplomacy and Public Affairs has been vacant about 40 percent of the time since 2001, and said the PCC did not meet when the position was vacant. A recent report on this issue notes that neither a lead organization nor lead individual has the authority to command independent departments or agencies, and the PCC structure is incapable of fostering coordination and strategic planning.[14] The report recommends alternative options to integrate government efforts, such as the creation of decentralized interagency teams made up of a small full- time staff to formulate and implement policy and support collaboration.

Minimal Interagency Sharing of Research

Several U.S. agencies conduct and sponsor audience research and media monitoring; however, they have not yet developed interagency protocols or a central clearinghouse for sharing such research as recommended by GAO in 2007.[15] Agency officials told us that barriers to sharing research include classification of documents and concerns about the release of sensitive and proprietary information. A PCC subcommittee on "Metrics and Polling," the main interagency forum for research staff to discuss issues of concern, has recently taken steps to encourage greater sharing of research information, particularly through conducting two applied research seminars in which various U.S. government agencies shared and analyzed audience, market, and opinion data with the aim of informing communication strategies for Afghanistan and Pakistan. The BBG has also recently provided other U.S. agencies with access to its audience research.

Lack of a Comprehensive Strategy to Engage the Private Sector

In 2003 and 2005, we recommended the Secretary of State develop a strategy to engage with the private sector in pursuit of common public diplomacy objectives to help ensure private-sector resources, talents, and ideas are effectively utilized in support of U.S. strategic communications. In 2005 we reported that State had engaged the private sector in the area of international exchange programs, but other efforts led by State's Under Secretaries for Public Diplomacy and Public Affairs had not yielded significant results. Since then, a former under secretary established an Office of Private Sector Outreach for Public Diplomacy and Public Affairs, which has partnered with the private sector on various projects, hosted a Private Sector Summit on Public Diplomacy in January 2007, invited private-sector experts to assist U.S. government officials in marketing public diplomacy programs, and identified action steps the private sector can take to support and improve U.S. public diplomacy. However, the office has not worked with the private sector to implement those additional action steps. While State's efforts thus far have merit, their effect may be limited if not backed by the type of comprehensive strategy to engage the private sector we have recommended.[16]

Oversight Questions

1. What is the appropriate role of DOD in relation to State in strategic communication? What are DOD's and State's respective authorities, comparative advantages, and capabilities in conducting strategic communication?
2. Given the disbanding of DOD's Office of the Deputy Assistant Secretary of Defense for Support to Public Diplomacy, what mechanisms, if any, will be instituted to carry out its functions?
3. When will DOD issue policy guidance regarding its internal strategic communication structure?
4. What are State's plans for future engagement with the private sector? When will State develop a strategy for engagement as recommended by GAO?
5. What criteria can be used to evaluate the advantages and disadvantages of creating new organizational structures for conducting strategic communication?

ENCLOSURE V. STATE'S PUBLIC DIPLOMACY WORKFORCE

Issue

Having the right people, with the right skills, in the right place is essential to the effective management of any government program. Beginning in 2003, GAO has reported that State's public diplomacy operations have been hampered by insufficient numbers and types of staff, administrative burdens and time constraints, and language proficiency shortfalls. These problems have compromised State's ability to fully execute its public diplomacy mission, led to minimal coverage at certain posts, placed a strain on more-junior staff filling positions above their pay grade, and diminished effectiveness where target language proficiency levels have not been met. The department has sought to respond to these challenges by instituting a number of initiatives including a requested increase of 2,400 in American and Foreign Service National staff over the next 2 years, various financial incentives to attract and motivate staff, and increased training opportunities. It remains to be determined whether these assorted initiatives will fully address the human capital challenges identified by GAO; a failure to do so by State will compromise the effectiveness of its public diplomacy operations for the foreseeable future.

Key Findings

Staffing Shortages and Lack of Mid-Level Officers Hinder U.S. Outreach Efforts

State has experienced a shortage of public diplomacy staff since 1999 when the United States Information Agency was merged into the department. In 2003, GAO reported that State experienced a 13 percent vacancy rate in its public diplomacy positions. Similar findings were reported by GAO in May 2006, and data from November 2007 show a vacancy rate of over 13 percent. In our 2003 report, we noted that more than 50 percent of those responding to our survey of public diplomacy officers felt the number of Foreign Service officers available to perform public diplomacy duties was inadequate. Our May 2006 report noted that while several recent reports on public diplomacy had recommended increased spending on U.S. public diplomacy programs, several embassy officials told us that, given current staffing levels, they lacked the capacity to effectively utilize increased funds.

In August 2006, we reported that State's consular and public diplomacy positions were the hardest to fill, with 91 percent of the vacancies in these two tracks at the mid-level. We noted this staffing gap placed pressure on State to appoint junior officers to so-called "stretch positions"—whereby they serve in a position above their pay grade—to fill as many of these vacancies as possible. For example, at the time of our visit in 2006 the U.S. Ambassador to Nigeria—which had the third largest mission in Africa with nearly 800 employees—told us the embassy had only three senior officers, and public affairs were handled entirely by first-tour junior officers. Ambassadors at posts GAO visited stated that junior officers, while generally highly qualified when entering the Foreign Service, lack sufficient training to handle some of the high-stress situations they encounter and therefore often end up making mistakes. A January 2008 analysis by State's Human Resources Bureau indicates that mid-level shortages continue. The report notes the public diplomacy cone has the highest mid-level deficit among the five generalist cones, and public diplomacy officers are being promoted through the mid-levels at higher rates than other cones. State officials expect it will take several years before the mid-level deficit is erased. One senior State official noted accelerated rates of promotion have led to concern that some public diplomacy officers may not have the requisite experience and expertise to perform effectively at their current levels.

Administrative Burden and Lack of Time Cited as Limiting Factors

In 2003, we reported public diplomacy officers at posts were burdened with administrative tasks, and thus had less time to conduct public diplomacy outreach activities than they did when the United States Information Agency was responsible for U.S. public diplomacy efforts. More than 40 percent of the 118 public affairs officers responding to our survey reported the amount of time they had to devote exclusively to executing public diplomacy tasks was insufficient. During our overseas fieldwork, officers told us that, while they managed to attend U.S. and other foreign embassy receptions and functions within their host country capitals, it was particularly difficult to find time or staff resources to travel outside the capitals to interact with ordinary citizens. In May 2006, we noted one senior State official overseas told us administrative duties, such as budget, personnel, and internal reporting, compete with officers' public diplomacy responsibilities. Another official in Egypt told us she rarely had enough time to strategize, plan, or evaluate programs.

This challenge is compounded at posts with short tours of duty, including many posts of strategic importance in the Muslim world, as officials stated it is difficult to establish the type of close working relationships essential to effective public diplomacy when in the country for only a short time. In May 2006, we reported the average length of tour at posts with significant Muslim populations was 2.1 years, compared with 2.7 years in the non- Muslim world. Noting the prevalence of 1-year tours at such posts, a senior official at State said public affairs officers who have shorter tours tend to produce less effective work than officers with longer tours.

Language Proficiency Shortfalls Remain

Beginning in July 2003, GAO reported that 21 percent of officers in public diplomacy language-designated positions did not meet the language requirements for their position. We reported similar findings in May 2006, and as of October 2008 this figure stood at 25 percent. Our May 2006 report noted this problem was particularly acute at posts where Arabic—classified as a "superhard" language by State—predominates. In countries with significant Muslim populations, we reported 30 percent of language- designated public diplomacy positions were filled by officers without the requisite proficiency in those languages, compared with 24 percent elsewhere. In Arabic language posts, about 36 percent of language-designated public diplomacy positions were filled by staff unable to speak Arabic at the designated level. In addition, State officials said there are even fewer officers willing or able to speak on television or engage in public debate in Arabic. The information officer in Cairo stated his office does not have enough Arabic speakers to engage the Egyptian media effectively.

Effect of Several Recent Initiatives Remains to Be Determined

State is seeking to increase its total staffing by over 2,400 individuals over the next 2 years to, in part, create the "personnel float" needed to allow staff to take language and other forms of training, fill vacant positions, and ease the burden on existing staff. State has also repositioned several public diplomacy officers as part of its transformational diplomacy initiative, and is increasing its overall amount of language training and providing supplemental training for more difficult languages at overseas locations. The department has also increased its language proficiency and hardship-post service incentives and requirements. However, it remains to be determined whether these efforts will collectively resolve State's longstanding human capital challenges.

Other groups have reported that additional human capital challenges help to explain State's long-standing difficulties filling open public diplomacy positions with fully qualified staff. For example, the United States Advisory Commission on Public Diplomacy issued a report on the status of State's human capital operations since the integration of the United States Information Agency into the department in 1999.[17] This chapter addresses a range of topics that the commission believes have significantly contributed to State's human capital problems. Discussed topics include hiring, training, promotion practices, and the degree to which the 1999 merger of the United States Information Agency into State has resulted in better integration of the public diplomacy function into the work of State—in particular as measured by the presence of public diplomacy officers in the department's decision-making ranks.

Oversight Questions

1. What is State's strategy to obtain a sufficient number of staff to create the desired training float needed to fill vacant public diplomacy positions and meet all required language training needs?
2. What is State's strategy to address the deficit in mid-level management expertise?
3. Are public affairs officers at posts overburdened with administrative duties? If so, what can be done to alleviate this situation?

ENCLOSURE VI. OUTREACH EFFORTS IN HIGH-THREAT POSTS

Issue

Conditions in high-threat posts have led to security precautions that limit public access to U.S. embassies and reduce the number of external facilities open to local populations—thereby limiting the effectiveness of U.S. outreach efforts. Beginning in the late 1990s, security concerns led to the fortification of preexisting and new embassies, which in many cases entailed increased physical barriers around the embassies, as well as the location of embassy complexes to more remote locations. These measures have had the ancillary effect of making the United States seem unapproachable and distrustful, according to State officials, leading to increased anti-American sentiments amongst local populations. Compounding this problem, security and budgetary considerations brought about the closure of publicly accessible facilities outside the embassy compound, such as American Centers and Libraries. While little has been done to change the forbidding presence associated with many embassies, State has responded to the lack of external facilities by exploring a variety of outreach mechanisms such as American Corners, which are centers that provide information about the United States, hosted in local institutions and staffed by local employees. It is important that State determine the relative effectiveness of these alternative outreach mechanisms and, in turn, find the right balance between security and mission concerns.

Key Findings

Enhanced Security Measures and the Closure of Public Facilities Have Limited Outreach Efforts

Since the 1998 bombings of the U.S. embassies in Kenya and Tanzania, Congress has provided State hundreds of millions of dollars annually for embassy construction to secure facilities around the world. Among the many embassy security-related construction requirements is that facilities be further offset from the street, leading to the building of many new embassies several miles from urban centers. Such sites tend to be in remote areas poorly served by public transportation, and these relocations have diminished the ability of local citizens and U.S. embassy personnel to interact. As we reported in May 2006, the new security architecture has created heavily-protected structures that make embassies seem less welcoming to local citizens. Congress has also mandated that sites selected for new U.S. diplomatic facilities abroad meet a colocation requirement designed to ensure all U.S. government agencies, except those under the command of a United States area military commander, be located on the same compound, complicating attempts to establish diplomatic venues outside the compound.

In addition, due to security concerns and other factors, State closed or eliminated funding for many publicly accessible facilities that provided an opportunity for local populations to interact directly with Americans with the goal of promoting mutual understanding.[18] Beginning in the late 1990s, the United States began to close its worldwide network of American Cultural Centers operated in downtown locations in capital cities around the world, which offered reading rooms; group lectures; film, music, and art series; and English language instruction.[19] With the closure of these facilities, their operations were transferred to Information Resource Centers located within heavily fortified embassy compounds, many of which are now open by appointment only or have hours of operation and security policies limiting public access. In May 2006, we reported that, in Pakistan, for example, all American Centers closed for security reasons and selected operations moved to the embassy's Information Resource Center.[20] Our report noted that concrete barriers and armed escorts outside the embassy compounds contribute to a perception that visitors are not welcome, as do requirements restricting visitors' use of cell phones and pagers within the embassy. According to one official in Pakistan, the number of visitors to the embassy's Information Resource Center has declined to as few as one per day because many visitors feel humiliated by the embassy's rigorous security procedures. We also reported the Information Resource Center in Abuja, Nigeria, is open only to students and other specific demographic groups, and access is granted by appointment only. The head of the center in Abuja said accessibility was one of his primary challenges.

State Has Responded to Security Concerns and Actions by Establishing a Range of Alternate Outreach Mechanisms

Over the past two decades, State has experimented with a number of alternative outreach mechanisms designed to offset the increasingly isolated nature of U.S. diplomatic operations. These alternative mechanisms generally consist of small outposts with no or few U.S. staff, or virtual, internet-based efforts supported by in-person travel to a city or region. Specific alternate outreach mechanisms include the following:

- *American Presence Posts*: Headed by an American officer, these posts provide citizen, commercial, and public diplomacy outreach services to a major city or region. There are currently nine such posts worldwide. While plans to create additional posts are on hold for budgetary and other reasons, State would like to add more American Presence Posts over the next few years.

- *American Corners*: These provide the United States with a physical public diplomacy outpost, which includes internet access, a small reference collection, and a discussion forum. Sponsored by a host country's municipal or national government, the U.S. government is only required to fund the equipment and materials used. Staff are provided by the host institution. There are approximately 410 American Corners throughout the world, and State plans to develop up to 30 more corners over the next 2 years.

- *American Discovery Centers*: These are small kiosks that provide information on America. The prime example of the use of these kiosks is Pakistan. In May 2006, we reported there were over 180 such kiosks, primarily in schools. State is considering the expanded use of such kiosks.

- *Virtual Presence Posts*: Virtual Presence Posts are generally designed to combine virtual presence through an embassy-hosted Web site with coordinated outreach, programming, and travel targeted at a particular city or region.

- *Other outreach mechanisms*: In our May 2006 report on outreach to the Muslim world, we noted that in Nigeria several embassy staff, including the Ambassador, often travel together to cities lacking a permanent American presence; according to embassy officials, these "embassy on the road" tours typically last 3 or 4 days and can involve dozens of individuals. A variation on this theme are embassy "circuit riders," who are staff who travel from the embassy on a scheduled basis to cover an assigned city or territory.

To date, only American Corners have been formally evaluated by State. State's evaluation was generally favorable; however, in May 2006, we reported that, while one State official told us American Corners are the best solution given the current security environment, others have described them as public diplomacy "on the cheap." The American Corner we visited in Nigeria was confined to a single small room housing a limited reference library and a small selection of donated books. At a meeting with a focus group of Nigerians in Abuja who had participated in U.S.- sponsored exchanges, no one present was familiar with the American Corner. Other posts we visited have had difficulty finding hosts for American Corners, as local institutions fear becoming terrorist targets.

The Center for Strategic and International Studies (CSIS) has recommended that State systematically determine and coordinate how and where to locate alternative outreach mechanisms on a country by country basis.[21] According to CSIS, each country mission should conduct this assessment, in coordination with the relevant State regional bureau, and integrate it into the post's strategic planning process. To support the effective development of these country-level strategies, CSIS recommended that State establish a federally-funded research center to assist with a number of related data analysis tasks.

Oversight Questions

1. To what extent has State evaluated the effectiveness of alternative outreach mechanisms such as American Corners, American Presence Posts, and Virtual Presence Posts?
2. What process guides post decisions on the need to establish outreach mechanisms and how are decisions made regarding the mix, number, and placement of these facilities? How is this process linked to post efforts to reach specific target audiences?
3. How would reestablishing American Centers contribute to fulfilling U.S. strategic communication goals?

ENCLOSURE VII. INTERAGENCY EFFORTS TO ADOPT A NEW APPROACH TO PUBLIC DIPLOMACY

Issue

The United States needs to consider new approaches to conducting its strategic communication efforts in response to dynamic changes in the ways people around the world receive and use information. In particular, the rise of social networking, namely through Internet sites such as Facebook and Twitter, has transformed the nature of communications globally. State's prior Under Secretary for Public Diplomacy and Public Affairs recently endorsed a new public diplomacy approach, referred to as Public Diplomacy 2.0, that could more fully engage these new and evolving communication trends. Key issues that remain to be addressed include the level of resources the United States should devote to this new approach, how agency operations will be guided when there is limited knowledge or agreement on how to operate in this new information environment, and how results will be measured when message control is partly or completely ceded to other groups that can distribute information through hundreds or thousands of diverse communication channels. These and other considerations should be incorporated in the President's new communication strategy, which could provide the best means for outlining a vision for Public Diplomacy 2.0 efforts. While GAO has not previously assessed this issue, current information suggests a failure to adapt in this dynamic communications environment could significantly raise the risk that U.S. public diplomacy efforts could become increasingly irrelevant, particularly among younger audiences that represent a key focus of U.S. strategic communication efforts.

Key Findings

Public Diplomacy 2.0 Initiatives Are Underway

The most recent Under Secretary for Public Diplomacy and Public Affairs noted in December 2008 that the United States should place a greater reliance on dialogue and collaboration, enabled by emerging social networks, in addition to the traditional model of public diplomacy that has focused on building a positive image of the United States, mainly through long-term programs like cultural and educational exchanges and efforts to tell America's story.[22] State, the BBG, and DOD have begun to respond to this and earlier calls for change. State has been most active in this new approach, and the BBG's international broadcasting has the potential to help form social networks of like-minded people who listen to services such as the Voice of America (VOA) and Radio Free Asia and then pass along this information through word of mouth, blogs, Internet sites, and other means. DOD has chosen to engage in this new approach to a certain degree; however, DOD officials said it would represent a "sea change" in the department's culture to allow its staff to fully engage in Public Diplomacy 2.0–style activities.

Specific examples of agency Public Diplomacy 2.0 initiatives include the following:

- In December 2008, State joined with major new media companies and the Columbia University School of Law to bring together a number of youth movements from around the world to New York City to launch an Internet- based global network to mobilize people against violence and oppression. (See http://www.gao.gov/media for an independently produced, State-endorsed video clip of the event that was edited by GAO.)
- State has also held blogger-only press conferences, started its own blog, established a page on Facebook and a social networking site called Exchanges Connect, created a digital outreach team to participate in blogs and Web chat rooms with the goal of countering ideological support for terrorism, and hosted YouTube video contests on such topics as "what is democracy."
- VOA maintains pages on YouTube, Facebook, and Twitter in multiple languages. According to BBG officials, there have been 4 million views of VOA-produced videos in the past year. VOA also distributes its content through podcasts, syndicated feeds to users' desktops, and mobile phones. For example, VOA has an agreement with Nokia to distribute English language content on mobile phones sold in China.
- VOA created a special U.S. election Web site in 2008 that attracted traffic from more than 200 countries and resulted in thousands of users joining an online VOA community, where they were able to share photos, ask questions, and comment about the U.S. electoral process.
- DOD plans to hold a conference on emerging Web technologies in July 2009 to gain a better awareness and understanding of these tools, identify barriers to their

adoption (such as restrictions due to policy, organizational culture, and other factors), and determine implementation strategies. Many DOD commands now have their own official blog sites and use tools such as Twitter and Facebook. The U.S. Army has also had success using online games and a variety of mechanisms to reach out to younger audiences.

Challenges and Practical Considerations

Agencies seeking to implement this new approach to public diplomacy face several key challenges. First, there is a general lack of adequate research and understanding of how government entities can and should operate in a social network environment. Second, agencies will generally lose control over content since participants in a dialogue or collaborative project are free to voice their own opinions and distribute information as they choose. As noted by one senior State official, however, a difference in opinions is one of the core strengths of the approach and the underlying basis for its effectiveness. Third, views expressed by U.S. officials on, for example, social networking sites or blogs, become part of the permanent discussion record, which raises practical questions about how best to mitigate potential instances of miscommunication. Fourth, the level of available resources is small compared to the magnitude of the global communications environment. For example, State's Digital Outreach team consists of eight individuals seeking to provide a U.S. point of view into a communication environment consisting of millions of personal blogs and discussion forums on thousands of Web sites. Finally, this approach is likely to pose technical challenges, as agency efforts to plan, coordinate, fund, implement, and evaluate their Public Diplomacy 2.0 efforts could strain systems and capabilities that have had difficulty operating smoothly in the less complex environment of traditional public diplomacy efforts.

Oversight Questions

1. To what extent will the Public Diplomacy 2.0 approach be included in the President's December 2009 national communication strategy?
2. What criteria should be used to guide strategic investment decisions regarding this new approach to public diplomacy?
3. How do agencies intend to address the challenges identified by GAO such as the lack of in-depth research on social networking and resource constraint issues?
4. Are there other challenges and practical considerations that should be considered in adopting this new approach?

APPENDIX I. EXTENT TO WHICH THE JUNE 2007 NATIONAL STRATEGY ADDRESSES GAO'S DESIRABLE CHARACTERISTICS

In a 2004 GAO testimony, we identified six desirable characteristics of an effective national strategy that would enable its implementers to effectively shape policies, programs, priorities, resource allocations, and standards that would enable federal departments and other stakeholders to achieve the identified results.[23] We further determined in that testimony that national strategies with the six characteristics can provide policymakers and implementing agencies with a planning tool that can help ensure accountability and more effective results. To develop these six desirable characteristics of an effective national strategy, we reviewed several sources of information. First, we gathered statutory requirements pertaining to national strategies, as well as legislative and executive branch guidance. We also consulted the Government Performance and Results Act of 1993, general literature on strategic planning and performance, and guidance from the Office of Management and Budget on the President's Management Agenda. In addition, among other things, we studied past reports and testimonies for findings and recommendations pertaining to the desirable elements of a national strategy. Furthermore, we consulted widely within GAO to obtain updated information on strategic planning, integration across and between the government and its partners, implementation, and other related subjects. We developed these six desirable characteristics based on their underlying support in legislative or executive guidance and the frequency with which they were cited in other sources. We then grouped similar items together in a logical sequence, from conception to implementation. Table 3 provides these desirable characteristics and examples of their elements.

Table 3. Summary of Desirable Characteristics of an Effective National Strategy

Desirable characteristic	Brief description
Purpose, scope, and methodology	Addresses why the strategy was produced, the scope of its coverage, and the process by which it was developed.
Problems, risks, and threats	Addresses the particular national problems and threats the strategy is directed toward.
Desired goals, objectives, activities, and performance measures	Addresses what the strategy is trying to achieve; steps to achieve those results; as well as the priorities, milestones, and performance measures to gauge results.
Resources, investments, and risk management	Addresses what the strategy will cost, the sources and types of resources and investments needed, and where resources and investments should be targeted by balancing risk reductions and costs.
U.S. government roles, responsibilities, and coordination mechanism	Addresses who will be implementing the strategy, what their roles will be compared to those of others, and mechanisms for them to coordinate their efforts.
Integration among and with other entities	Addresses how a national strategy relates to other strategies' goals, objectives, and activities—and to subordinate levels of government and their plans to implement the strategy.

Source: GAO.

To assess U.S. strategic communication planning efforts, we examined the *June 2007 U.S. National Strategy for Public Diplomacy and Strategic Communication*. To determine whether this national strategy contains all six desirable characteristics of an effective national strategy that we developed and used in our prior work, we first developed a checklist of these characteristics, along with their 27 component elements. Two GAO staff members then independently assessed the national strategy for its inclusion of the 27 elements, recorded their findings on separate checklists, and met to reconcile any differences in their assessments. Once these assessments were reconciled, one additional GAO staff member reviewed this analysis for completeness and accuracy. To determine the extent to which the national strategy addressed GAO's six characteristics of an effective national strategy, we developed the following three categories: the strategy (1) generally addresses a characteristic when it explicitly cites all elements related to that characteristic; (2) partially addresses a characteristic when it explicitly cites at least one, but not all, of the elements related to that characteristic; and (3) does not address a characteristic when it does not explicitly cite any of the elements related to that characteristic. By applying these categories to our checklists of the 27 elements, we developed a consolidated summary of the extent to which the strategy addressed the six characteristics of an effective national strategy. Figure 3 shows the results of our assessment of the national communication strategy.

	Characteristic	Element
1. Clear purpose, scope, and methodology	◐	
Purpose		
1a. Identifies the impetus that led to the strategy being written, such as a statutory requirement, mandate, or key event.		○
1b. Discusses the strategy's purpose.		○
Scope		
1c. Defines or discusses key terms, major functions, mission areas, or activities the strategy covers.		●
Methodology		
1d. Discusses the process that produced the strategy (e.g., what organizations or offices drafted the document, whether it was the result of a working group, or which parties were consulted in its development).		○
1e. Discusses assumptions or the principles and theories that guided the strategy's development.		◐
2. Detailed discussion of problems, risks, and threats	○	
Problem definition		
2a. Includes a detailed discussion or definition of the problems the strategy intends to address.		○
2b. Includes a detailed discussion of the causes of the problems.		○
2c. Includes a detailed discussion of the operating environment.		○
Risk assessment		
2d. Addresses a detailed discussion of the threats at which the strategy is directed.		○
2e. Discusses the quality of data available (e.g., constraints, deficiencies, and "unknowns").		◐
3. Desired goals, objectives, activities, and outcome-related performance measures	◐	
Goals and subordinate objectives		
3a. Addresses the overall results desired (i.e., an "end state").		○
3b. Identifies strategic goals and subordinate objectives.		◐
Activities		
3c. Identifies specific activities to achieve results.		●
Performance measures		
3d. Addresses priorities, milestones, and outcome-related performance measures.		◐
3e. Identifies process to monitor and report on progress.		●
3f. Identifies limitations on progress indicators.		●
4. Resources, investments, and risk management	○	
Resources and investments		
4a. Identifies what the strategy will cost.		○
4b. Identifies the sources (e.g., federal, international, and private, and types of resources or investments needed, e.g., budgetary, human capital, information technology, research and development, and contracts).		◐
Risk management		
4c. Addresses where resources or investments should be targeted to balance risks and costs.		○
4d. Addresses resource allocation mechanisms.		○
4e. Identifies risk management principles and how they help implementing parties prioritize and allocate resources.		○
5. Delineation of U.S. government roles, responsibilities, and coordination mechanism	◐	
Organizational roles and responsibilities		
5a. Addresses who will implement the strategy.		◐
5b. Addresses lead, support, and partner roles and responsibilities of specific federal agencies, departments, or offices (e.g., who is in charge during all phases of the strategy's implementation).		○
Coordination		
5c. Addresses mechanisms or processes for parties to coordinate efforts within agencies and with other agencies.		●
5d. Identifies process for resolving conflicts.		○
6. Description of strategy's integration among and with other entities	◐	
6a. Addresses how the strategy relates to the strategies of other institutions and organizations and their goals, objectives, and activities (horizontal).		●
6b. Addresses integration with relevant documents from other agencies and subordinate levels (vertical).		◐

● Generally addresses
◐ Partially addresses
○ Does not address

Source: GAO analysis.

Figure 3. Extent to Which the June 2007 National Strategy for Public Diplomacy and Strategic Communication Addresses the 27 Elements of the Desirable Characteristics of a National Strategy

APPENDIX II. GAO CONTACT AND STAFF ACKNOWLEDGMENTS

Staff Acknowledgments

In addition to the individual named above, Audrey Solis (Assistant Director), Michael ten Kate, and Emily Gupta made key contributions to this chapter. Technical assistance was provided by Robert Alarapon, Martin de Alteriis, Jeffrey Baldwin-Bott, Joseph Carney, Marcus Corbin, and Leah DeWolf.

Related GAO Products

Broadcasting to Cuba: Actions Are Needed to Improve Strategy and Operations. GAO-09-127. Washington, D.C.: January 22, 2009.

U.S. Public Diplomacy: Actions Needed to Improve Strategic Use and Coordination of Research. GAO-07-904. Washington, D.C.: July 18, 2007.

Foreign Assistance: Actions Needed to Better Assess the Impact of Agencies' Marking and Publicizing Efforts. GAO-07-277. Washington, D.C.: March 12, 2007.

U.S. International Broadcasting: Management of Middle East Broadcasting Services Could Be Improved. GAO-06-762. Washington, D.C.: August 4, 2006.

Department of State: Staffing and Foreign Language Shortfalls Persist Despite Initiatives to Address Gaps. GAO-06-894. Washington, D.C.: August 4, 2006.

U.S. Public Diplomacy: State Department Efforts to Engage Muslim Audiences Lack Certain Communication Elements and Face Significant Challenges. GAO-06-535. Washington, D.C.: May 3, 2006.

U.S. Public Diplomacy: Interagency Coordination Efforts Hampered by the Lack of a National Communication Strategy. GAO-05-323. Washington, D.C.: April 4, 2005.

U.S. International Broadcasting: Enhanced Measure of Local Media Conditions Would Facilitate Decisions to Terminate Language Services. GAO-04-374. Washington, D.C.: February 26, 2004.

U.S. Public Diplomacy: State Department Expands Efforts but Faces Significant Challenges. GAO-03-951. Washington, D.C.: September 4, 2003.

U.S. International Broadcasting: New Strategic Approach Focuses on Reaching Large Audiences but Lacks Measurable Program Objectives. GAO-03-772. Washington, D.C.: July 15, 2003.

GAO's Mission

The Government Accountability Office, the audit, evaluation, and investigative arm of Congress, exists to support Congress in meeting its constitutional responsibilities and to help improve the performance and accountability of the federal government for the American people. GAO examines the use of public funds; evaluates federal programs and policies; and provides analyses, recommendations, and other assistance to help Congress make informed oversight, policy, and funding decisions. GAO's commitment to good government is reflected in its core values of accountability, integrity, and reliability.

End Notes

[1] We use the terms "public diplomacy," "outreach," and "strategic communication" interchangeably in this chapter.

[2] This chapter expands on issues discussed on GAO's transition Web site, http://www.gao.gov/media

[3] These papers are based on the continuing work of GAO, the 10 related reports we have issued since July 2003 (see list of related GAO products), and select studies conducted by outside groups.

[4] In 2008, this amounted to $1.7 million.

[5] GAO, *U.S. Public Diplomacy: State Department Expands Efforts but Faces Significant Challenges*, GAO-03-951 (Washington, D.C.: Sept. 4, 2003).

[6] GAO, *U.S. Public Diplomacy: Interagency Coordination Efforts Hampered by the Lack of a National Communication Strategy*, GAO-05-323 (Washington, D.C.: Apr. 4, 2005).

[7] Pub. L. No. 110-417, Sec. 1055(a).

[8] GAO, *Combating Terrorism: Evaluation of Selected Characteristics in National Strategies Related to Terrorism*, GAO-04-408T (Washington, D.C.: Feb. 3, 2004).

[9] GAO has also discussed the use of a "program logic model" to further improve planning efforts at the interagency, department, and country level. A logic model systematically outlines program activities, inputs, outputs, outcomes, and program effect in a direct relational path.

[10] GAO, *U.S. Public Diplomacy: Actions Needed to Improve Strategic Use and Coordination of Research*, GAO-07-904 (Washington, D.C.: July 18, 2007).

[11] GAO, *U.S. International Broadcasting: Management of Middle East Broadcasting Services Could Be Improved*, GAO-06-762 (Washington, D.C.: Aug. 4, 2006).

[12] GAO, *U.S. Public Diplomacy: State Department Expands Efforts but Faces Significant Challenges*, GAO-03-951 (Washington, D.C.: Sept. 4, 2003).

[13] GAO, *U.S. Public Diplomacy: Interagency Coordination Efforts Hampered by the Lack of a National Communication Strategy*, GAO-05-323 (Washington, D.C.: Apr. 4, 2005).

[14] Project on National Security Reform, *Forging a New Shield* (Arlington, Va., Nov. 26, 2008).

[15] GAO, *U.S. Public Diplomacy: Actions Needed to Improve Strategic Use and Coordination of Research*, GAO-07-904 (Washington, D.C.: July 18, 2007).

[16] GAO, *U.S. Public Diplomacy: State Department Expands Efforts but Faces Significant Challenges*, GAO-03-951 (Washington, D.C.: Sept. 4, 2003); and GAO-05-323.

[17] United States Advisory Commission on Public Diplomacy, *Getting the People Part Right: A Report on the Human Resources Dimension of U.S. Public Diplomacy* (Washington, D.C., June 25, 2008).

[18] According to State, only about 30 American Cultural Centers remain open today. U.S. funding for binational outreach centers in Latin America was also eliminated; however, about 110 centers remain open with other revenue sources. Congress is now considering the option of reopening American Cultural Centers where security conditions permit and resuming some level of funding for binational centers where appropriate. See Committee on Foreign Relations, United States Senate, *U.S. Public Diplomacy—Time to Get Back in the Game*, 2009.

[19] As we noted in our May 2006 report, in 1990 the majority of posts had such publicly accessible facilities; now, however, few do.

[20] We reported in May 2006, that State's Bureau of International Information Programs operates more than 170 such centers worldwide.

[21] Center for Strategic and International Studies, *The Embassy of the Future* (Washington, D.C., Oct. 15, 2007).

[22] In articulating his support for Public Diplomacy 2.0, State's most recent Under Secretary for Public Diplomacy and Public Affairs highlighted the example of a social movement directed against rebel forces in Colombia, which illustrates the power of the collaborative, social networking approach in action. In this instance, according to the Under Secretary, an unemployed computer technician in Colombia started a Facebook page that grew quickly to more than 400,000 members. The group, called One Million Voices against the FARC, was able to mobilize 12 million people to engage in street protests on a single day in 190 cities around the world, just 2 months after it was set up.

[23] GAO, *Combating Terrorism: Evaluation of Selected Characteristics in National Strategies Related to Terrorism*, GAO-04-408T (Washington, D.C.: Feb. 3, 2004).

In: U.S. Public Diplomacy: Background and Issues
Editor: Matthew B. Morrison

ISBN: 978-1-61728-888-3
© 2010 Nova Science Publishers, Inc.

Chapter 3

U.S. PUBLIC DIPLOMACY: TIME TO GET BACK IN THE GAME[*]

John F. Kerry

LETTER OF TRANSMITTAL

UNITED STATES SENATE,
COMMITTEE ON FOREIGN RELATIONS,
Washington, DC, February 13, 2009.

Dear Colleague: Recent polling suggests that support for the United States throughout the world is on a slight increase but remains well below the fifty percent mark in many countries, even among those nations normally considered strong allies. This less- than-positive attitude towards our nation has impacts ranging from national security threats, to lost trade opportunities, to a significant drop in tourism, to parents overseas refusing to allow their children to be educated in U.S. universities.

The sources of this problem are many. Some of these include honest disagreements with our policies and our actions. But many are based on misrepresentations of our goals, values and motives targeted at those prepared to believe the worst about us. Yet, in spite of recent actions to counter these misperceptions, our efforts to present our point of view have not been getting through. It is time to re-think how we conduct our Public Diplomacy.

With this in mind, I sent Paul Foldi of my Senate Foreign Relations Committee staff to travel to the Middle East and Latin America in December 2008 to discuss U.S. Public Diplomacy efforts with our Embassy and local officials. His report focuses on the need for greater direct U.S. engagement with average citizens overseas who now have virtually no contact with Americans. In order to overcome years of mistrust, this re-engagement should be on the same scope and scale as currently conducted by the British, French and German

---

[*] This is an edited, reformatted and augmented version of a U. S. Government Printing Office publication dated May 2009.

governments, all of which currently offer language instruction and information about their countries in their own government-run facilities throughout the world. Iran is also dramatically increasing its outreach efforts through its network of Cultural Centers in Africa, Asia and the Middle East, many of which are located in the very locations where we are reducing our public presence.

The United States used to have a similar worldwide program through its "American Centers," which taught English, housed libraries and hosted U.S. film series, and featured exhibitions and lectures by visiting American authors, scientists, human rights lawyers, and other speakers. The consolidation of the United States Information Agency into the State Department along with security concerns resulted in the demise of almost all the Centers (the excellent American Centers in Alexandria, New Delhi and Rangoon are among the few exceptions) and led to their rebirth as Information Resource Centers (or "IRCs") most often housed *inside* our new Embassies. These Embassy compounds place a premium on protecting our diplomats and often convey an atmosphere ill-suited to encouraging the casual visitor, with almost half of the 177 IRCs operating on a "by appointment only" basis. Additionally, usage figures demonstrate that our IRCs in the Middle East which are located *inside* our Embassies receive six times *fewer* visitors than similar facilities in the region located outside our compounds.

This lack of easily accessible facilities, where foreigners can read about United States history and government and access newspapers and the Internet in an environment free from their own government's censorship has hurt us—particularly when over 80% of the world's population is listed by Freedom House as having a press that is either "Not Free" or only "Partly Free."

Where once we were seen as the world's leader in intellectual discourse and debate, we are now viewed as withdrawn and unconcerned with any views other than our own. While the re-creation of the U.S. Information Agency (USIA) is not realistic, a program to re-establish the American Centers that uses the teaching of English to offset operating costs would go far to demonstrate that we are committed to re-engaging in a dialogue with the world.

Such a program would entail re-locating a small number of Embassy officials outside our diplomatic compounds in those locations where the security climate permits and where we are able to provide them with appropriately secure facilities. If we hope to change opinions towards us, we must be able to interact with the world. We have learned much in recent years about keeping our personnel overseas safe; as such, increased accessibility need not come at the cost of security.

Mr. Foldi's report provides important insights into the current state of our Public Diplomacy and offers valuable recommendations based on his travels and years of work in the field. As the title of his report suggests, we have been too long on the sidelines of Public Diplomacy in recent years, and it is indeed time for the United States to "Get Back In The Game." I hope that you find this chapter helpful as Congress works with the new administration to strengthen our Public Diplomacy efforts and look forward to continuing to work with you on these issues.

Sincerely,

RICHARD G. LUGAR,
Ranking Member.

On behalf of the Senate Committee on Foreign Relations, minority staff traveled to Egypt, Jordan, Mexico and the Dominican Republic from December 1–12, 2008. The purpose of the trip was to examine U.S. Public Diplomacy facilities as platforms for engagement with foreign audiences, including the role of English language instruction as a vehicle to facilitate greater access to information about the United States and interaction with core American values.

Executive Summary

It is no secret that support for the United States has dropped precipitously throughout the world in recent years.[1] Many experts believe this is due not only to various U.S. foreign policy developments but also to the method in which we conduct our Public Diplomacy. Public Diplomacy requires our diplomats to interact not only with Foreign Ministry officials but with local journalists, authors, scientists, artists, athletes, experts and academics as well the average citizen.

The entity created within the U.S. government to deal with Public Diplomacy and to communicate with the rest of the world—the United States Information Agency (USIA)—was abolished in 1999. While the Department of State absorbed USIA's personnel and maintained some of its programs, most agree that U.S. focus on Public Diplomacy began to diminish from this point on. (Nonetheless, re-creating USIA, or something similar, is neither feasible nor affordable in today's budgetary environment.)

This lack of focus was also partly due to the belief that, with the collapse of the Soviet Union, we had won the "War of Ideas"—a belief that 9/11 quickly shattered. We now find ourselves having to focus our Public Diplomacy efforts not only on those who "hate us," but also on many former friends and allies who now mistrust our motives and actions.

In order to improve the situation we must address the difficulties we now face in conducting people-to-people interactions and providing access to information about the United States—the core of U.S. Public Diplomacy policy. Both aspects of this policy served as the foundations of our best Public Diplomacy platforms—the "American Center"—which housed libraries, reading rooms, taught English and conducted countless outreach programs, book groups, film series, and lectures that enabled foreigners to meet with Americans of all walks of life and vocations and hold conversations on issues of mutual interest.

These free-standing American Centers were drastically down-sized and re-cast as "Information Resource Centers" (IRCs), most of which were then removed from easily accessible downtown locations due to security concerns following the attacks on our embassies in Kenya and Tanzania in 1998. Those IRCs that were relocated to our Embassy compounds have seen significant reductions in visitors—IRCs in the Middle East that are located *off* our compounds receive six times *fewer* visitors per month as those located *on* our compounds. Thus we have created a vicious cycle: frustrated by our inability to connect with audiences overseas who no longer trust us, we have in fact *weakened* our efforts at Public Diplomacy by denying them access to both American officials as well as uncensored information about us.

The State Department—working with Congress and host governments—needs to re-create the American Center system in secure facilities outside our Embassy compounds from which we can provide foreign audiences with greater access to information about the United States through libraries, periodicals and an uncensored Internet. At the same time, much as the British, French and Germans all offer classes overseas in their mother tongues, we must use the teaching English both as a draw to bring individuals back into our Centers and as a source of funding by using tuition fees to offset the costs of running them.

RECOMMENDATIONS

- Congressional support is needed for the Department of State to create more accessible Public Diplomacy platforms by pushing Information Resource Centers (IRCs) out of remote Embassy compounds and allowing them to be re-built as stand-alone American Centers in more centrally located areas. In order to accomplish this, the so-called "co-location requirement" should be re-visited to allow these new Centers to be established as well as to permit those few facilities still off-compound to remain as such, as long as appropriate security measures are in place.
- IRCs and American Centers should operate six days a week and ensure that hours of operation maximize usage by local publics.
- The Department of State should engage in the teaching of English using American or American-trained teachers hired directly by the Embassy, not sub-contractors, and using standardized techs appropriate for each region/culture. This will ensure that the Department has full control over the content and quality of the education, and will go far to advancing our Public Diplomacy efforts.
- Charging for this English instruction is appropriate and logical in these budgetary times.
- If the security situation in an area deteriorates to the point that a stand-alone American Center must be closed for a prolonged period of time, the facility should be preserved, perhaps re-cast for other use, but not permanently closed. These Centers serve as high-profile symbols of America's desire for direct engagement with local populations as well as our commitment to education and access to uncensored information; abandoning them indicates we have given up on advancing these ideals.
- In Latin America, rather than create competing institutions that offer English language and cultural programming, the State Department should examine cost and policy implications of formally re-establishing U.S. government links with the network of Bi-National Centers (BNCs) in the region. BNCs were originally created by the United States but are now wholly run by independent local boards.
- American *Corners*—smaller versions of IRC s—are housed in local university or public office buildings. At a cost of $35,000 each, and with over 400 already established worldwide, the Department of State should take a careful look at any requests for additional American Corners to ensure the need is truly justified. American Corners are appropriate for remote locations that lack any other U.S. presence but should not be used as substitutes in capitals for American *Centers*, particularly as American Corners are run by local staffs who are neither employed

nor managed by U.S. Embassy officials and thus represent a literal out-sourcing of American Public Diplomacy.

- In those capitals where an American Corner does exist, its collection should be combined with the Embassy's IRC to form the nucleus of the new American Center's resources.
- The State Department's Arabic book translation program is crucial to providing information in local texts and should be strongly supported until free-market forces step in. The Department should examine potential cost savings by consolidating Cairo and Amman operations as long as both are able to continue to provide input into the translation selection process.
- The term Information Resource Center is cumbersome and, for most foreigners, confusing. A return to the simpler "Library" seems appropriate for those IRCs that must remain on embassy compounds.
- Given the disparity between the 11,000 graduates of the English language focused Access Microscholarships targeted mainly at under-served Muslim youth, and the 300 slots available for the State Department's YES exchange program which sends Muslim youth to spend a year in American High Schools, the State Department needs to ensure that adequate funding is available for follow- on programming to keep the vast majority Access graduates engaged and using the skills that have been invested in them, even if this requires a reduction of the portion of the Access program's budget and fewer annual graduates.
- The State Department should re-engage with the U.S. Motion Picture Licensing Corporation to allow greater public awareness of Embassy-run American film series than permitted under the current, overly restrictive, Licensing Agreement negotiated between the two.

INTRODUCTION

Public Diplomacy is the conduct of diplomacy beyond the boundaries and venues of traditional foreign ministries and halls of power of a nation and requires interacting directly with the citizens, community leaders, journalists and policy experts who are the future leaders and current opinion shapers of their country. Public Diplomacy also seeks to create a better understanding of our nation with a foreign populace as a whole by providing them access to American culture, history, law, society, art and music that might not otherwise be available through standard local media outlets that often provide biased reporting about the United States and our involvement in the world.

Visitor exchange programs are an important component of Public Diplomacy. These State Department exchanges send experts from the U.S. to countries throughout the world and, equally important, bring foreigners to the United States to meet with their counterparts here. The contacts and professional relationships fostered in these programs are one of the hallmarks of our people-to-people diplomacy, but they are not alone. The Peace Corps and Fulbright Scholarships are equally vital to providing long-term access to Americans and America. The Voice of America and its affiliates are also a crucial element in our policy.

In spite of these efforts, the fact that U.S. Public Diplomacy policy is in disarray is neither a secret nor a surprise. The U.S. Government Accountability Office, in its November 6, 2008 list of thirteen urgent issues demanding the next administration's attention to ensure the nation's security, placed "improving the U.S. image abroad" fifth.[2] Study after study[3] points to our difficulties in explaining our foreign policy to skeptical publics overseas. In short, the U.S. "brand" has not been doing well in the marketplace of world ideas.

This is partly a result of honest disagreements that some audiences have with our policies. It is also due to a skewed vision that many in the world receive about the U.S. either from biased reporting and/or because they are denied access to Internet sites that are blocked or heavily filtered.[4] Denied this information, even with our excellent exchange programs, the average citizen also has limited or no contact with Americans. Offering greater access to our ideas, citizens and officials will provide an important antidote to these ills.

THE AMERICAN CENTER—PUBLIC DIPLOMACY PLATFORMS PAR EXCELLENCE

For years, our premier overseas Public Diplomacy platforms were the American Centers, operated by the United States Information Agency as stand-alone facilities located downtown in capital cities. The Centers offered reading rooms with the latest American and foreign newspapers and housed libraries with collections of American history, economics, legal, scientific and classic literature.[5] Center staff coordinated book discussion groups, lectures by visiting American experts, and model United Nations and American Congress programs with local youth. Centers ran American film series programs and served as venues for visiting American artists and musicians. English language instruction was also a staple of most Centers. Importantly, access to these facilities was free of charge and buildings were situated in the most vibrant part of city centers. All of these services are critical in countries either too poor or too repressive to provide any such institutions to their own publics.

Americans long accustomed to our daily newspapers, 24-hour television news cycle and unfettered access to the Internet sometimes forget that many societies still live with state control of radio and TV, Internet censorship and no right to freedom of speech.[6] At the same time, many of these same governments use their control of the media to espouse distorted stories and unbalanced images of the United States. American Centers offered a neutral[7] space for foreigners to access information without interference or oversight from repressive host governments as well as a welcoming environment more conducive to engagement with American officials. Yet, despite the significant Public Diplomacy value of these Centers to project America's ideas and images, several events occurred that led to the rapid demise of all but a handful.

FROM "AMERICAN CENTERS" TO "IRCS"

The American Centers program closed as a result of a confluence of several events, including: the end of the Cold War, the rise of the Internet, and the absorption of the U.S. Information Agency (USIA) into the Department of State. The first created the false impression that the great debate was over regarding the primacy of democratically elected governments. The second created the false belief that we could conduct Public Diplomacy primarily through an electronic medium. The third resulted in Public Diplomacy officers more focused on localized issues related to their Embassy and Ambassador rather than global U.S. Public Diplomacy policy. As a result, most Centers were significantly downsized in terms of material and staff and relocated into Embassies in their truncated forms as Information Resource Center (IRCs), many of which are now open only by appointment or have hours of operation that limit public use. (See chart below.)

The collapse of the Soviet Union and the end of the Cold War suggested to many policy makers that the continued need to make the case for American democratic values was finally over. As a result of this "victory," funding cuts in Public Diplomacy efforts were considered part of a logical "peace dividend," and Centers began to see their programming budgets reduced and funding for book programs slashed. The attacks of 9/11 and subsequent events demonstrate that work in this field is far from over, as even in Europe many "natural" allies now regard the United States with distrust.

Information Resource Centers—Locations and Access[8]

Region	IRC total	IRCs located on embassy compound	IRCs with public access by appointment only	IRCs with no access to the public
Africa	37	21 (57%)	9 (24%)	0
East Asia	28	18 (64%)	15 (54%)	3 (Sydney, Singapore, Hong Kong)
Europe	55	43 (78%)	30 (55%)	11 (Brussels, Baku, Berlin, Copenhagen, Nicosia, Paris, Tallinn, The Hague, Moscow, Yekaterinburg, Stockholm)
Middle East	16	12 (75%)	6 (50%)	2 (Sana'a, Yemen; Beirut, Lebanon)
South and Central Asia	16	8 (50%)	8 (50%)	2 (Karachi and Lahore, Pakistan)
Latin America	25	20 (80%)	19 (76%)	1 (Bogota, Colombia)
Total	177	122 (69%)	87 (49%)	19 (11%)

The rise of the Internet led many to conclude that more and more Public Diplomacy outreach could be conducted just as easily through websites and local Internet Cafes as through more costly U.S. brick and mortar facilities. There is no question that book purchase and shipping expenses are not insignificant given the far-flung nature of many of our Embassies. Definite cost savings can be achieved through uploading information on the Internet. In fact, many IRCs now subscribe to vast legal and scientific database services which can be accessed at users' homes via many IRCs' websites. Such data is no doubt valuable for foreign researchers and generates a certain recognition of the U.S. as leader in education and freedom of information. However, if enhanced people-to- people interactions are judged to be a key component for improving our Public Diplomacy efforts, cutting out the interaction with Americans seems counterintuitive.

The 1999 dissolution[9] of the United States Information Agency (USIA), which ran the American Centers, and the absorption of USIA's personnel and some of its programs into the State Department, continued to chip away at the Centers and overall Public Diplomacy funding in light of what State viewed as Congressional pressures to continue to reduce spending overseas.[10] USIA officers were re-cast as Public Diplomacy (PD) "coned" officers in the State Department.[11] As Foreign Service Officers, PD officials in the field report not to the Under Secretary for Public Diplomacy in Washington but to their Ambassador at post. Quite naturally, many PD officers are more concerned with supporting his or her Ambassador's immediate press needs rather than worrying if their Ambassador's initiatives track with overall U.S. Public Diplomacy priorities.

In the ten years since the Foreign Affairs Reform and Restructuring Act took effect, it is clear that the abolishment of USIA failed to improve our Public Diplomacy efforts significantly. In spite of the wishes of many, however, there is neither the political will nor budgetary outlays available to recreate USIA, or any other similar stand-alone entity.[12]

IMPACT OF SECURITY CONCERNS ON PUBLIC DIPLOMACY

At the same time that budgetary and bureaucratic pressures were impinging on public diplomacy efforts, the Department of State was reeling from the 1998 bombings of our Embassies in Kenya and Tanzania. Responding quickly, Congress provided, and continues to provide, the Department of State hundreds of millions of dollars annually for Embassy construction to replace chancery buildings.[13] In order to build facilities that can withstand blasts such as those that struck Nairobi and Dar es Salaam, new embassy buildings must have a one hundred foot set-back from the perimeter fence in order to dissipate the shock waves of an explosion.

Sites with sufficient acreage to meet these new set-back requirements can only be found miles away from the previously convenient downtown locations of our original Embassies. Such sites by definition tend to be in remote areas poorly served by public transportation. These relocations have resulted in decreases in both the ease and frequency of locals visiting American officials and vice versa—creating a veritable diplomatic lethargy in many locations. Equally impacted has been the foot-traffic in IRCs that are located on Embassy compounds. At the same time, new security architecture has created structures that project a Fortress America environment that seems to say anything but ''Welcome''[14] which has led to a similar inertia in our Public Diplomacy efforts in many of these locations.

The same Act that creates these new Embassy construction standards also requires that, ''In selecting sites for new United States diplomatic facilities abroad, all personnel of United States Government agencies except those under the command of a United States area military commander shall be located on the same compound.'' This portion of the Act is known as the "co-location" requirement and is most often cited as the mandate for the closure of stand-alone American Centers and their subsequent absorption into Embassy facilities as truncated

IRCs. There is a waiver for this requirement, but it has rarely been adopted and only on a case-by-case basis. The only blanket exception is for the Peace Corps, which was given a Congressional exemption (see Appendix).

According to data provided by the State Department, those IRCs located off the compound receive significantly *more* visitors than those located on the compound. As the chart below illustrates, in the Middle East—perhaps our area most in need of outreach—with 12 IRCs on Embassy compounds and 4 located off, those off the compound received almost six times as many visitors per month (843) as those on the compound (139). IRCs in Latin America, East Asia, South Central Asia have even greater disparities.

Average Number of Visitors/IRC On/Off Embassy Compound

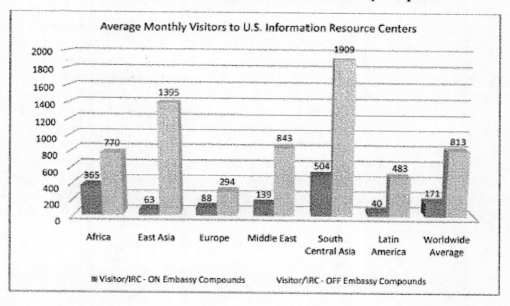

Average Monthly Visitors to U.S. Information Resource Centers

THE COMPETITION

Where is the best place to learn French?
The Alliance Franc̦aise run by the French Embassy.
Where is the best place to learn English?
The British Council.[15]

As American Centers began to disappear, our involvement in the direct teaching of English declined at the same time, and the British have been more than willing to step into the breach. Just as American college graduates are often fiercely loyal to their alma maters, graduates of the Alliance or British Councils form a bond with those nations that lasts a lifetime based on their years of exposure to those countries through the educational advantages they gained through study in each. Having virtually ceased to offer the same educational opportunities, the United States is missing out on creating similarly supportive lifelong linkages.

The British Council has locations in some 110 countries with over 7,900 staff. A standard British Council facility will have 15 or more classrooms that teach English from the morning to night. While some funding comes directly from the British government, much of their operating budget must come from fees generated locally through teaching as well as providing space and proctoring of international testing such as the UK equivalent of the U.S. "TOEFL" (Test of English as a Foreign Language) exam that is required of all potential immigrants to Great Britain. Additionally, local multinational firms either contract with the Council for special training sessions on site, or bring instructors to their institutions. To date, tuition for British Council language instruction is considered prohibitively expensive by most locals, resulting in a clientele of primarily the economic and social elite.

As with American Centers, British Councils house library facilities with computers hooked to the Internet. The Councils are modern, spacious, well-staffed and, importantly, open six days a week to maximize attendance and outreach opportunities. Additionally, and uniquely, they provide a well-stocked section of children's books which starts the "bonding" experience with the UK at an even earlier age. Like France's Alliance Franc̜aise centers, British Councils routinely contract with a local caterer to establish a cafeteria which not only adds to students' convenience, and therefore market share, but in some countries provides the only common area where members of different social groups can interact without fear of arousing the suspicions of local political or religious authorities. Both French and British facilities maintain sufficient public space to host their own cultural events or art shows— some even act as galleries and retain a certain percentage of each sale. Their facilities also offer sufficient multipurpose rooms/auditoriums for film showings or lectures. Except for the oldest and most established of our Centers, American IRCs rarely have either large conference rooms or dedicated auditoriums due to the constant pressure within Embassies for the limited chancery space available.

British Council Cairo, Egypt—complete with Henry Moore sculpture.

Entrance to library portion of the building above, including latest pop CDs to draw in local youths.

BI-NATIONAL CENTERS

Latin America is the one exception to British Council dominance in English language instruction. In this region, Bi-National Centers (BNCs) are considered the premiere institution in this field. BNCs are, however, a legacy of earlier, closer bilateral engagement be¬tween those nations and the United States. A typical BNC was very similar in structure to current British Councils—English Language programs were used to fund programmatic and library activities and were initially U.S. government facilities run by USIA officers.

However, as budgetary constraints took hold and later, as USIA was absorbed into the State Department, the U.S. government began to disengage from day-to-day operations to the point that, now, BNCs are *completely independent* of U.S. operational and budgetary support, oversight, and programmatic direction. Few locals, however, seem to realize this and still consider BNCs to be part of our Embassies. Fortunately, most BNCs are well-funded because of their tuition base, and many put the local Department of State IRC to shame.

IRANIAN CULTURAL CENTERS[16]

Not only are our allies engaged in expansive Public Diplomacy efforts. Tellingly, Iran is now conducting an active outreach program particularly in those predominantly Muslim African and Asian countries. Iranian Cultural Centers offer Persian language classes and extensive library resources. These Centers serve Iran as a mouthpiece to promote anti-

American propaganda and have been alleged in local media to be extremist recruitment centers and covers for intelligence operatives. In over half of the locations listed below, the American Embassy's Information Resource Center is either not open to the public or open by appointment only, which begs the question, how can we possibly expect our ideas to compete in these critical marketplaces if the average citizen cannot easily access them?

OTHER U.S. GOVERNMENT EFFORTS[17]

The United States has not been completely idle in Public Diplomacy or in the use of English language instruction to further those goals:

- Some 20 *Regional English Language Officers* are sprinkled throughout American Embassies, but travel is expensive and many RELOs are too constrained by duties at their home embassies to engage in sufficient regional visits and thus have limited impact.
- There are currently 136 *English Language Fellows* in 76 countries. Fellows work with specific institutions on issues ranging from teacher training classes for English instructors to teaching English directly. These initiatives provide unprecedented pedagogical opportunities for the United States to impact Education Ministry policies throughout the world, but they are largely invisible to the general population of each country.
- The *Peace Corps* is also heavily involved in this area as almost 20% of Peace Corps Volunteers (PCVs) have "Teaching English" as their primary task in the field. PCVs are one of the most effective examples of people-to- people Public Diplomacy, and they invariably depart after their two years leaving nothing but a positive impression. PCVs are, however, are only in some 60 countries throughout the world and generally located in more remote locations in their countries.
- As part of a reaction to the closing of American Centers, the Bush Administration began a program of establishing *American Corners* throughout the world. To date there are over 400 Corners in municipal buildings, university libraries or other public buildings in regions that often have no other U.S. diplomatic presence. Books related to the United States and computers are supplied to each location, but the operation, maintenance and programming offered by each Corner is in the hands of a foreign national who is neither paid nor overseen by U.S. Embassy officials and thus amount to nothing less than an outsourcing of U.S. Public Diplomacy. The results in terms of U.S. Public Diplomacy are therefore mixed; some Corners are vital hubs of information, others dusty relics that offered little more than a photo-op for an ambassador at their opening. None offers direct access to Americans. While appropriate for remote regions where the U.S. has no diplomatic presence, Corners are too small to take the place of American Centers in a capital city.

Iranian Cultural Centers

Asia	Africa	Europe	Middle East	South Central Asia
Bangladesh	Ethiopia	Armenia	Egypt	Afghanistan
China	Ghana	Austria	Kuwait	India (2 Centers)
Indonesia	Kenya	Azerbaijan	Lebanon	Kazakhstan Pakistan (8 Centers)
Japan	Nigeria	Bosnia & Herzegovina	Qatar	
Thailand	Sierra Leone	Bulgaria	Saudi Arabia	Sri Lanka
	South Africa	Croatia	Syria	Tajikistan
	Sudan	France	Tunis	Turkmenistan
	Tanzania	Germany	United Arab Emirates	Uzbekistan
	Uganda	Greece	Yemen	
	Zambia	Italy		
	Zimbabwe	Russia		
		Serbia		
		Spain		
		Turkey (2 Centers)		

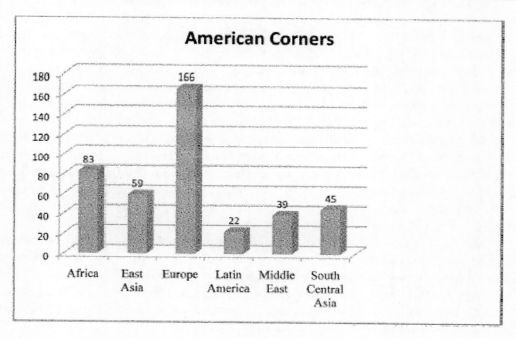

- *Access Microscholarship* grants are awarded primarily in the Muslim world to lower-income youth to provide access to U.S.-sponsored English classes. The classes are run by local contractors and vary according to local markets. Some offer not only English lessons but research on the United States in English on computers at their facilities and emphasize critical thinking as part of their curriculum. The intent of the scholarships is not only to reach the best and brightest of a non-traditional audience, but to provide them with sufficient language skills so they may successfully compete in the State Department's Youth Exchange and Study (YES) program that brings Muslim high school age students to the U.S. for a year of study. (Prior to Access scholarships, too many YES participants were from the elite strata of society, most of whom already had exposure to the U.S. through tourist visits.) Some 11,000 Access students graduate each year, but many are concerned that there is no further follow-up programming to keep them engaged.[18]

None of these options has the Public Diplomacy impact of a stand-alone American Center located in the heart of a nation's capital. Such Centers are true flagships not only of American outreach but also represent our vital and *visible* commitment to the freedom of information, thought and discussion. As such, occasionally, they can even play a direct role in the democratic aspirations of a repressed nation.

THE AMERICAN CENTER IN BURMA

A recent article in The New Yorker magazine[19] provides ample evidence of the role a U.S.-run facility in fostering democratic ideas and actions. As discussed in his well-documented August 25, 2008 piece, journalist George Packer describes the vital role the U.S. American Center in Rangoon[20]—with its James Baldwin Library and Ella Fitzgerald Auditorium—played in the cultural and political lives of the Burmese people. Mr. Packer discusses how U.S. diplomatic officials used the facility to meet with average citizens to discuss everything from literature and performing arts to both local and U.S. politics.

Embassy Public Diplomacy personnel who ran the Center purchased thousands of new books for the Library, and now have over 13,000 titles. As a result of outreach efforts, membership for the Center tripled. Book clubs sprang up that enabled older Burmese dissidents to discuss their past activities with younger activists bent on reform. Operating six days a week provided additional opportunities for average citizens to use the Center and take part in the discussions. Twelve Internet stations offered access to information unavailable to even those few non-government Burmese who have a computer at home. The Center became one of the main focal points for dissidents and organizers of the fall 2007 protests against the Burmese military dictatorship.

Portraying our Centers as potential instruments for democratic regime change is perhaps the shortest way to ensure their closure, but, to date, the Center in Rangoon remains open and active. With well over 10,000 visitors a month—making it easily our most visited Public Diplomacy facility in the world—our Center in Rangoon demonstrates that if people are given the opportunity to access ideas and information about democracy, the desire for freedom can thrive in even the most repressive of regimes.

CONCLUSION

There is no question that our standing in the world is nowhere near where it should be. This may change in the short term as the new administration pursues alternative foreign policy practices, but what may prove more difficult to overcome in the long term is the lingering suspicion that we no longer seek to collaborate and cooperate.

Such doubts about our motives and intentions peaked just as America was seen as closing itself off, which only added to this climate of mistrust. It mattered little to the world that much of this was the result of terrorist attacks against the United States, nor that these attacks produced in our own country a similar degree of mistrust towards much of the world. This led to a foreign policy environment which seemed to put security above all other considerations.

These security concerns, in turn, brought about the closure of many American Centers with English classes terminated and truncated remains of their library collections brought inside our new Embassy compounds as Information Resources Centers. At the same time foreign audiences, used to convenience and the freedom of access to American Centers, were loathe to submit to what they believe are cumbersome appointment schedule requirements, hostile security environments and reduced resources. As such, not surprisingly, IRC foot-traffic is significantly lower for those situated inside our chancery compounds.

Thus, we have succeeded in sidelining some of the greatest assets we have in the field of Public Diplomacy by restricting access to the very information and individuals needed to educate international audiences about who we really are as a nation, rather than the images that our detractors continue to use to portray us. It is, indeed, time for us to get back in the game.

A new Public Diplomacy approach designed to re-engage with the rest of the world is crucial to improving our standing in the world. Care must be taken to ensure that any new programs are viewed not as mere short-term public relations campaigns designed to "sell" the image of the United States. Sophisticated foreign publics have become suspicious of recent attempts to paint the United States in too rosy a picture—what some would argue is a classic case of confusing "Public Relations" with "Public Diplomacy." True Public Diplomacy changes will involve long-range efforts to demonstrate a renewed willingness on our part to discuss rather than to dictate.

Reinvigorating the American Centers will go far to providing this by offering a more neutral location for our diplomats and visiting scholars to begin to repair the breach that has been created. Ambassadors continue to hear from foreign leaders and opinion makers who fondly recall learning about the United States and the world outside in our Centers. They equally loudly lament the closure of our facilities and ask how we can be surprised by down-turns in public opinion towards us when their citizens have nowhere to go to obtain unbiased information. It is now time to turn this argument on its head and work with these same governments to provide us with appropriate, secure, and hopefully donated space in order to re-establish American Centers in centrally located areas, using the literary and staffing resources of the Embassy's IRC along with the books and computers from any existing American Corner in that capital to form the nucleus of the new American Center's offerings.

In the years that have elapsed since the tragic bombings of our Embassies, we have developed the security technologies needed to keep our diplomats safe and must ensure as many measures as possible are properly in place before moving forward. To assist in this,

Congress needs to provide the State Department a clear signal of support for such actions modeled on the legislation (see Appendix) used to allow the Peace Corps to maintain its offices off U.S. Embassy compounds.

Equally important in these tight budget times, the Department should immediately begin to explore how to recommence the teaching of English in order to create the needed "pull" to bring skeptics of the United States into the Centers as well as use the revenues generated to partially offset operating costs. English has become the common language of not only commerce, but science, industry, and most importantly—the Internet. Teaching English will not only provide a marketable skill required for advancement in our international marketplace, but it will also allow us to re-introduce America and American values to much of a world that still views us with suspicion.

None of this offers a quick-fix; rather it portends a long-term reorientation of Public Diplomacy requiring years of dedication, funding and oversight. But if the United States hopes to regain the trust of the world as the leader in freedom of information, education excellence, and democratic values, such a commitment is essential.

SITE VISITS

Egypt

The United States has two major Public Diplomacy resources in Egypt, the free-standing American Center in Alexandria and the IRC inside the Embassy in Cairo.

Of the two, the American Center is by far the more impressive for reasons of access, scale, programming space, and overall facilities. A former American Consulate, the Center in Alexandria is in some respects a true jewel, with a library stocked with books in English and Arabic as well as a computer center with a dozen stations used for Internet research. English instruction is provided by the NGO AmidEast in classrooms situated on third floor. Visitors to the Center are screened by local guards first at the gate and then through a second metal detector at the door of the Center; however, AmidEast students are directed up an exterior staircase to the third floor and never enter the Center.

Interior views of the exceptional American Center in Alexandria.

Embassy Cairo's IRC is housed inside our well-guarded Embassy which is part of a diplomatic enclave that is blocked off to vehicular traffic. Walk-ins are welcome during the Embassy workweek Sunday thru Thursday 10 am–4 pm, with late closing at 7 pm on Mondays and Wednesdays. The IRC is well stocked with books on the United States and has an extensive audio and visual library for use on site but acknowledges that its location on the compound serves as deterrence to attracting more visitors. Data provided by the Department of State notes that the American Center in Alexandria, a city of some 4 million, receives on average 1,600 visitors a month while Cairo—a city of at least twice that size—receives less than an 1,000. Embassy officials who recognize the need to provide a more accessible outreach program have begun to look at various properties outside the compound but still within the enclave that provide both appropriate space and security.

Jordan

Our embassy in Amman boasts what could easily be mistaken for an American Center. The Embassy's American Language Center (ALC) has been in operation since 1989. It currently teaches some 2,400 students per year in 14 classrooms, but unlike the American Center in Alexandria which out-sources the teaching to a contractor—AmidEast—ALC instructors are contracted directly by the Embassy, thus saving on the "middle man" overhead costs implicit in all sub-contracting arrangement.

The ALC[21] is a stand-alone building located off a major street in downtown Amman, and students are screened twice before entering. As pictured below, there is no American flag on the front nor a great seal of the Department of State; in fact the word "American" is not even displayed, only the initials "ALC." Also illustrated below is the excellent library located in the basement of the building which houses several thousand volumes, computer terminals, serves as a Wi-Fi hot-spot, and boasts a flat screen TV with Digital Video Conference capability. This modern, state-of-the-art facility, however, is virtually unused as Embassy security officials will not allow general public access; only students registered with the ALC may use the facility.

The top photo above shows the very discreet American Language Center (ALC); its completely empty and unused library is shown in the photo below it.

Mexico

The Ben Franklin Library[22] has been in operation in downtown Mexico City since 1942 and is a mainstay of our Public Diplomacy efforts. In addition to providing an impressive collection of 23,000 books on America, U.S. law and economics (primarily in English but also Spanish), it boasts 130 periodicals and over 600 videos on American history and culture. It is one of the better-known landmarks in the city and projects an impressive image of the United States. A significant draw to the library is the "Education USA"[23] section that counsels Mexican students on selecting and applying to American universities. This service is a function of the Department of State and is contracted out to different NGOs; the Institute of International Education runs the program in Mexico while AmidEast does so in Egypt. Some contend that this represents another example of "out-sourcing" Public Diplomacy, while others argue that such activities are peripheral activities that would distract or dilute PD officers' attention from more "core" programmatic activities.

An active conference schedule included discussions of recently published books, films about American history and lectures on the American political process and the recent election. The library itself occupies the ground floor of a building shared with the U.S. Foreign Commercial Service on a busy downtown street. The State Department estimates that some 1,200 users visit the library every month.

Santo Domingo

The Dominican Republic presents a more typical situation in the Western Hemisphere. The Embassy runs a small IRC known as the "Ben Franklin Center," which offers limited resources (some 2,400 titles) and is housed in a single room in a small, off the beaten path, bungalow that serves as the Embassy's Public Affairs Section. To address their small size, the staff has aggressively compiled an impressive list of on-line databases[24] that members of the IRC—which have included Dominican Presidents and Cabinet members—use with great frequency. The push to more and more on-line services is understandable as overall costs are minimal when compared to publications. However, from a Public Diplomacy perspective, this trend is troubling. If true Public Diplomacy work most effectively involves interactions between Americans and foreign nationals, then relegating "contact" to a mere Internet portal to U.S. government documents, however useful, eliminates the "public" in Public Diplomacy.

At the same time, the IRC must compete with Santo Domingo's well-established Bi-National Center[25] which offers both a private K–12 school as well as separate English classes for ages 5 to adult. The BNC's library offers a collection of 13,000 titles in English and Spanish, and boasts a gallery and auditorium that seats 300. The BNC is located on a major thoroughfare and a few blocks from a major university.

View of the landmark Ben Franklin Library in Mexico City before opening hours.

In the first photo above, Embassy Santo Domingo IRC's library of 2,400 titles; in the bottom photo, a small portion of Santo Domingo's Bi-national Center's 13,000 titles.

The ViewSpace exhibit in Santo Domingo's Museum of Natural History. The flat-screen TV in the darkened room depicts photos and video of outer space courtesy of NASA. Underneath the NASA insignia a sign in Spanish reads "Courtesy of the Franklin Center of the United States Embassy."

An excellent example of low-cost, high impact Public Diplomacy is the Public Affairs Section's partnership with the National Museum of Natural History.

Using a service provided by NASA and for less than $200 a year, the Embassy provides a "ViewSpace" exhibit which offers museum visitors a constant stream of recent and historic images from American space missions and from satellites such as the Hubble Space Telescope. This demonstration of U.S. technology, scientific education and space exploration is one of the most popular exhibits in the museum.

APPENDIX

American Corners

In part to counter the restricted access of IRCs located on Embassy compounds, the Bush Administration established the "American Corners" program. Corners are created in partnership with local municipalities or universities to provide space, sometimes literally a *corner* in a room, in which the Embassy supplies, at a start-up cost of $35,000, half a dozen computers connected to the Internet and a collection of some 800 books. Approximately a third of the titles are American fiction with the rest distributed between reference, How-To-For-Dummies type guidebooks, biographies, and English teaching material.

If viewed not as a *substitute* for a formal American Center facility but rather as a *supplement,* the Corners do in fact provide Public Diplomacy platforms for U.S. programming to have a home— particularly in the more remote areas of larger countries where the U.S. lacks any formal diplomatic facility. For example in Russia, outside of our Embassy in Moscow, the U.S. has consulates in only St. Petersburg, Yekaterinburg, and Vladivostok, but there are 33 Corners throughout the country. Belarus has 12 Corners; Indonesia has 11 Corners, the Philippines—14, Afghanistan—7.

American Corners

Country	City
AFRICA: 83 In Operation 6 Underway	
Angola	Luanda
Benin	Abomey-Calavi
Benin	Grand-Popo
Benin	Parakou
Benin	Porto-Novo
Botswana	Gaborone
Burkina Faso	Bobo-Dioulasso
Burkina Faso	Fada N'gourma
Burkina Faso	Zorgho
Cameroon	Bertoua
Cameroon	Buea
Cameroon	Garoua

(Continued)

Country	City
Cape Verde	Fogo Island
Comoros	Moroni
Congo	Pointe-Noire
Democratic Republic Congo	Kinshasa
Democratic Republic Congo	Lumbumbashi
Cote d'lvoire	Abidjan
Cote d'lvoire	Tiassale
Cote d'lvoire	Yamoussoukro
Equatorial Guinea	Bata (Underway)
Equatorial Guinea	Malabo (Underway)
Eritrea	Dekemhare
Eritrea	Keren
Eritrea	Massawa
Ethiopia	Bahir Dar
Ethiopia	Dire Dawa
Ethiopia	Harar
Ethiopia	Jimma
Gambia, The	Banjul
Ghana	Accra
Ghana	Tamale
Guinea	Kankan
Kenya	Lamu
Kenya	Mombasa
Kenya	Nairobi (Underway)
Liberia	Buchanan
Liberia	Kakata
Liberia	Monrovia
Liberia	Virginia Township
Liberia	Zwedru
Madagascar	Antananarivo
Madagascar	Antsiranana
Madagascar	Mahajanga (Underway)
Malawi	Blantyre
Malawi	Mzuzu
Malawi	Zomba
Mali	Gao
Mauritania	Nouakchott
Mauritania	Nouakchott (ISERI)
Mozambique	Maputo
Mozambique	Nampula
Namibia	Keetmanshoop
Namibia	Oshakati (MOU not renewed in 2008)

(Continued)

Country	City
Namibia	Walvis Bay
Niger	Agadez
Niger	Maradi
Niger	Zinder
Nigeria	Abeokuta
Nigeria	Abuja
Nigeria	Bauchi
Nigeria	Calabar
Nigeria	Enugu
Nigeria	Ibadan
Nigeria	Jos
Nigeria	Kaduna
Nigeria	Kano
Nigeria	Maiduguri
Nigeria	Port Harcourt
Nigeria	Sokoto
Rwanda	Butare
Rwanda	Kigali
Rwanda	Kigali
Senegal	Louga
Senegal	Ziguinchor
Somalia	Mogadishu (Underway)
Sierra Leone	Bo
South Africa	Bloemfontain
South Africa	Pietermaritzburg
Sudan	Juba (Underway)
Swaziland	Nhlangano
Tanzania	Pemba
Tanzania	Zanzibar
Togo	Lome
Uganda	Fort Portal
Uganda	Mbale
Zambia	Kitwe
Zimbabwe	Bulawayo
Zimbabwe	Mutare
EAST ASIA: 59 In Operation	
Burma	Rangoon
Cambodia	Battambang
Cambodian	Kampong Cham Town
Cambodia	Phnom Penh
Fiji	Lautoka
Hong Kong	Macau, Hong Kong

(Continued)

Country	City
Indonesia	Bandung
Indonesia	Depok
Indonesia	Jakarta
Indonesia	Makassar
Indonesia	Malang
Indonesia	Medan (at IAIN)
Indonesia	Medan (at USU)
Indonesia	Semarang
Indonesia	Surabaya
Indonesia	Yogyakarta (at UGM)
Indonesia	Yogyakarta (at UMY)
Japan	Nago, Okinawa
Japan	Urasoe, Okinawa
Laos	Luang Prabang
Laos	Vientiane
Malaysia	Alor Setar, Kedah
Malaysia	Kota Bahru
Malaysia	Kuala Lumpur
Malaysia	Kuala Terengganu, Terengganu
Malaysia	Melaka
Malaysia	Sabah
Malaysia	Sarawak
Mongolia	Khovd
Mongolia	Ulaanbaatar
Philippines	Bacolod City
Philippines	Baguio
Philippines	Batac
Philippines	Cagayan De Oro
Philippines	Cebu
Philippines	Cotabato
Philippines	Davao City
Philippines	Dumaguete
Philippines	Iloilo City
Philippines	Jolo
Philippines	Manila
Philippines	Marawi City
Philippines	Tawi-Tawi
Philippines	Zamboanga
Singapore	Singapore
Singapore	Singapore
Singapore	Singapore
South Korea	Busan

(Continued)

Country	City
South Korea	Daegu
South Korea	Gwangju
Taiwan	Taichung
Thailand	Chiang Mai
Thailand	Khon Kaen
Thailand	Nakhon Si Thammarat
Thailand	Pattani
Thailand	Yala
Vietnam	Can Tho
Vietnam	Danang
Vietnam	Haiphong
EUROPE: 166 in Operation: 1 Underway	
Albania	Kukes
Albania	Tirana
Albania	Vlora
Armenia	Gyumri
Armenia	Kapan
Armenia	Vanadzor
Armenia	Yerevan
Austria	Innsbruck
Azerbaijan	Baku
Azerbaijan	Ganja
Azerbaijan	Khachmaz
Azerbaijan	Kurdemir
Azerbaijan	Lenkoran
Azerbaijan	Salyan
Belarus	Baranovichi
Belarus	Bobruisk
Belarus	Brest
Belarus	Gomel
Belarus	Grodno
Belarus	Minsk
Belarus	Mogilev
Belarus	Molodechno
Belarus	Mozyr
Belarus	Pinsk
Belarus	Polotsk
Belarus	Vitebsk
Bosnia & Herzegovina	Banja Luka
Bosnia & Herzegovina	Bihac
Bosnia & Herzegovina	Doboj
Bosnia & Herzegovina	Mostar

(Continued)

Country	City
Bosnia & Herzegovina	Sarajevo
Bosnia & Herzegovina	Tuzla
Bosnia & Herzegovina	Zenica
Bulgaria	Sofia
Bulgaria	Varna
Bulgaria	Veliko Turnovo
Croatia	Osijek
Croatia	Rijeka
Croatia	Zadar
Croatia	Zagreb
Cyprus	Famagusta
Cyprus	Nicosia
Czech Republic	Brno
Czech Republic	Pilzen
Denmark (Greenland)	Nuuk
Estonia	Kuressaaare
Estonia	Narva
Estonia	Viljandi
Georgia	Akhaltsikhe
Georgia	Batumi
Georgia	Gori
Georgia	Khashuri
Georgia	Rustavi
Georgia	Tblisi (at State Univ.)
Georgia	Tblisi
Georgia	Telavi
Georgia	Zugdidi
Greece	Athens
Greece	Corfu
Greece	Nea Philadelphia
Greece	Sparta
Greece	Veroia
Greece	Xanthi
Hungary	Debrecen
Hungary	Pecs
Hungary	Veszprem
Italy	Trieste
Kosovo	Mitrovica
Kosovo	Pristina
Kosovo	Prizren
Latvia	Daugavpils
Latvia	Liepaja

(Continued)

Country	City
Lithuania	Siauliai
Macedonia	Bitola
Macedonia	Skopje
Macedonia	Tetovo
Moldova	Balti
Moldova	Ceadir Lunga
Moldova	Ungheni
Montenegro	Podgorica
Norway	Stavanger
Poland	Gdansk (Underway)
Poland	Lodz
Poland	Wroclaw
Romania	Bacau
Romania	Baia Mare
Romania	Bucharest
Romania	Cluj Napoca
Romania	Constanta
Romania	Craiova
Romania	Iasi
Romania	Timosoara
Russia	Arkhangelsk
Russia	Bryansk
Russia	Chelyabinsk
Russia	Irkutsk
Russia	Kaliningrad
Russia	Kazan
Russia	Khabarovsk
Russia	Moscow (Library of Foreign Literature)
Russia	Moscow (Parliamentary Library)
Russia	Moscow (State Children's Library)
Russia	Murmansk
Russia	Nizhniy Novgorod
Russia	Novgorod Velikiy
Russia	Novosibirsk
Russia	Omsk
Russia	Perm
Russia	Petropavlovsk-Kamchatskiy
Russia	Petrozavodsk
Russia	Pskov
Russia	Rostov-on-Don
Russia	Samara

(Continued)

Country	City
Russia	Saratov
Russia	St. Petersburg (City Library)
Russia	St. Petersburg (Youth Library)
Russia	Togliatti
Russia	Tomsk
Russia	Tyumen
Russia	Ufa
Russia	Vladivostok
Russia	Volgograd
Russia	Vologda
Russia	Yekaterinburg
Russia	Yuzhno-Sakhalinsk
Serbia	Belgrade
Serbia	Bujanovac
Serbia	Kragujevac
Serbia	Nis
Serbia	Novi Sad
Serbia	Subotica
Serbia	Vranje
Slovakia	Banska Bystrica
Slovakia	Bratislava
Slovakia	Kosice
Slovenia	Koper
Turkey	Bursa
Turkey	Gaziantep
Turkey	Izmir
Turkey	Kayseri
Ukraine	Chernihiv
Ukraine	Chernivtsi
Ukraine	Dnipropetrovsk
Ukraine	Donetsk
Ukraine	Ivano-Frankivsk
Ukraine	Kharkiv
Ukraine	Kherson (Children's Library)
Ukraine	Kherson (Research Library)
Ukraine	Kirovohrad
Ukraine	Kyiv (Mohyla Academy)
Ukraine	Kyiv (Public Library)
Ukraine	Luhansk
Ukraine	Lutsk
Ukraine	Lviv
Ukraine	Mykolaiv (Children's Library)

(Continued)

Country	City
Ukraine	Mykolaiv (Research Library)
Ukraine	Odessa
Ukraine	Poltava
Ukraine	Rivne
Ukraine	Sevastopol
Ukraine	Simferopol
Ukraine	Sumy
Ukraine	Ternopil (Research Library)
Ukraine	Ternopil (Youth Library)
Ukraine	Uzhgorod
Ukraine	Vinnytsya
Ukraine	Zhytomyr
LATIN AMERICA: 22 in Operation; 2 Underway	
Brazil	Brasilia
Brazil	Fortaleza
Brazil	Salvador, Bahia
Chile	Arica
Chile	Punta Arenas
Chile	Santiago (at University)
Chile	Santiago (University of Talca)
Chile	Valdivia
Costa Rica	Limon
Ecuador	Quito
Haiti	Port-au-Prince (Underway)
Honduras	Puerto Lempira
Honduras	Tegucigalpa
Nicaragua	Managua
Panama	Panama City
Paraguay	Asuncion
Suriname	Paramaribo
Trinidad and Tobago	Scarborough
Venezuela	Barquisimeto
Venezuela	La Asuncion
Venezuela	Lecheria
Venezuela	Maracay
Venezuela	Maturin
Venezuela	Valera (Underway)
MIDDLE EAST: 39 in Operation; 3 Underway	
Algeria	Algiers
Algeria	Constantine (Underway)
Algeria	Oran (Underway)
Iraq	6 ACs

(Continued)

Country	City
Israel	Beersheva
Israel	Karmiel
Israel	Nazareth (Underway)
Israel	Yaffo
Jordan	Amman
Jordan	Zarqa
Kuwait	Kuwait City (at University)
Kuwait	Kuwait City (Gulf University)
Kuwait	Kuwait City (American University)
Lebanon	Baakleen
Lebanon	Nabatiyeh
Lebanon	Rashaya
Lebanon	Zahle
Morocco	Marrakech
Morocco	Oujda
Oman	Bureimi
Oman	Muscat (College of Bus & Sci)
Oman	Muscat (College of Technology)
Oman	Rustaq
Oman	Salalah
Oman	Sohar
Palestinian Territories	Gaza City
Palestinian Territories	Jericho
Qatar	Doha
Saudi Arabia	Jeddah
Syria	Damascus
Syria	Suweida
Tunisia	Tunis
United Arab Emirates	Al Ain
United Arab Emirates	Fujairah
Yemen	Dhamar
Yemen	Hadhramout
Yemen	Sana'a
SOUTH CENTRAL ASIA: 45 in Operation 4 Underway	
Afghanistan	Bamyan
Afghanistan	Gandez (Underway)
Afghanistan	Herat
Afghanistan	Jalalabad
Afghanistan	Kabul (at University)
Afghanistan	Kabul (Institute of Diplomacy)
Afghanistan	Khost (Underway)
Afghanistan	Kunduz (Underway)

(Continued)

Country	City
Afghanistan	Mazar-E-Sharif
Bangladesh	Chittagong
Bangladesh	Jessore
Bangladesh	Sylhet
India	Ahmedabad
India	Bhubaneswar
India	Bangalore
India	Chandigarh
India	Patna, Bihar
Kazakhstan	Aktobe
Kazakhstan	Almaty
Kazakhstan	Atyrau
Kazakhstan	Karaganda
Kazakhstan	Kostanai
Kazakhstan	Petropavlovsk
Kazakhstan	Shymkent
Kazakhstan	Uralsk
Kazakhstan	Ust'-Kamenogorsk
Kyrgyzstan	Batken
Kyrgyzstan	Jalalabat
Kyrgyzstan	Kant
Kyrgyzstan	Karakol
Kyrgyzstan	Talas
Maldives	Male'
Nepal	Bhairahawa
Nepal	Biratnagar
Nepal	Birgunj
Nepal	Pokhara
Pakistan	Islamabad
Pakistan	Karachi
Pakistan	Lahore (Underway)
Pakistan	Muzaffarabad
Pakistan	Peshawar
Sri Lanka	Kandy
Sri Lanka	Oluvil
Tajikistan	Dushanbe
Tajikistan	Khujand
Tajikistan	Kulob
Turkmenistan	Dashoguz
Turkmenistan	Mary
Turkmenistan	Turkmenabat

However, because the Corners are not staffed with nor overseen by U.S. officials, they lack the same Public Diplomacy impact of a dedicated, stand-alone brick and mortar facility in a country's capital. Some are excellent projections of American Public Diplomacy with dedicated and motivated staffs, others, can wither on the vine depending on the level of local interest and resources in providing staff willing to push the programming boundaries that may be at odds with officials in more remote locations. Again, without direct Embassy oversight and financial backing, Corners can be too inconsistent in their operations. As of February 2009, American Corners can be found in the following 414 locations.

ARABIC BOOK TRANSLATION PROGRAM

"The figures for translated books are also discouraging. The Arab world translates about 330 books annually, one fifth of the number that Greece translates. The cumulative total of translated books since the Caliph Maa'moun's time (the ninth century) is about 100,000, almost the average that Spain translates in one year." (UNDP 2002 Arab Human Development Report[26])

The 2003 Congressionally-mandated report "Changing Minds and Winning Peace—A New Direction for U.S. Public Diplomacy in the Arab and Muslim World"[27] referenced the UNDP's translation statistics and called for a massive increase in our translation efforts— up to 1,000 titles a year. This effort was viewed as part of an "American Knowledge Library Initiative" that would locate the translations in American Corners and local libraries throughout the Muslim world; however, funding constraints have prevented any such a large-scale Initiative. Instead, the U.S. government has relied on translation programs run out of the U.S. Embassies in Cairo, Egypt and Amman, Jordan.

The Cairo Arabic Book Program[28] has existed at the U.S Embassy in Cairo since the 1950s and currently translates 8–10 books a year using a budget of approximately $50,000 from the International Information Programs (IIP) section of the bureau of Educational and Cultural Affairs. This funding covers the costs of copyrights fees, translation and purchased copies.

The Program works with local publishers to select American books across a broad range of topics that are of mutual interest. Some 3,000 copies per title are published, of which the Program purchases 1,000–1,500 copies for local and regional distribution while the publisher sells the remaining copies in commercial outlets and regional book fairs. The publisher submits a draft of the translation which is reviewed by translators contracted by the Embassy. The Program and the Embassy's IRC send free copies of the books to public and university libraries, key contacts, NGOs, and other institutions. The Program does not regularly provide copies to local school libraries; however, when the Ambassador or other high level dignitaries visit a school, they take a quantity of age-appropriate books. Until two years ago the program received an extra $7,500 for shipping fees but currently regional posts either fully pay or split the shipping fees with the Program. This loss of shipping funds affects some posts' ability to procure books.

The program sends an annual e-mail within the mission and to regional posts to solicit suggestions for new titles. The e-mail also contains a tentative list of titles compiled by the program officers asking for further recommendation or comments. Based on these recommendations the Public Affairs Officer and Cultural Affairs Officer and their staffs meet to decide on the list of titles to be translated. After securing necessary copyrights, the program and the local publisher agree to go ahead on the translation of the book. The process of acquiring the copyrights, translating, editing and printing one book takes between 8–18 months.

The translation program run by the U.S. Embassy in Amman, Jordan[29] is very similar in scope and $50,000 budget, but with slightly smaller print runs of some six books annually, usually printed in Amman or Beirut. The publisher sells 1,750 copies of the 2,500 printed to the public throughout its retail shops in the region and the regional and international book fairs they attend. 750 copies are retained by the embassy for its own distribution to universities, schools, local institutions, American Corners and posts in the region.

Cairo has organized Digital Video Conferences for Joyce Hanson, author of the Captive and collaborated with Embassy Amman to program Amy Tan, the author of the Joy Luck Club. Cairo also brought the following authors for speaking events in Egypt: Walter Russell Mead, author of *Special Providence: How American Foreign Policy Has Changed the World*, Robert Putnam, author of *Making Democracy Work*, and Geneive Abdo, author of *Mecca and Main Street* whose Arabic version is due shortly. Embassy Amman also hosted a DVC with Mohamed Nimer, author of the book *Nonviolence and Peace Building in Islam*.

ENGLISH LANGUAGE FELLOW PROGRAM[30]

The State Department's bureau of Educational and Cultural Affairs (ECA) English Language Fellow Program currently supports 136 U.S. fellows on exchanges in 76 counties worldwide. The EL Fellow Program provides foreign academic institutions with American professional expertise in Teaching English as a Foreign Language (TEFL) by sending highly trained American educators abroad on ten-month fellowships. The program also affords American TEFL professionals a unique professional development opportunity that contributes to their knowledge as educators upon their return to the U.S. Fellows work on projects and provide training in areas such as the English Access Microscholarship Program, TEFL classroom teaching, teacher training, in-service and pre-service training, curriculum development, workshop and seminar design, testing, program evaluation, needs assessment, and English for Specific Purposes.

U.S. government translations of Walter Isaacson's 2003 biography of Benjamin Franklin and The Future of Freedom by Fareed Zakaria from the American Center library in Alexandria, Egypt.

Regional English Language Offices

Region	Post	Countries Covered
Africa	Dakar	Benin, Burkina-Faso, Cameroon, Republic of Cape Verde, Central African Republic, Chad, Cote D'Ivoire, Equatorial Guinea, Gabon, Gambia, Ghana, Guinea, Guinea-Bissau, Liberia, Mali, Mauritania, Niger, Nigeria, Sao Tome and Principe, Senegal, Sierra Leone, Togo
	Pretoria	Angola, Botswana, Burundi, Comoros, Democratic Republic of Congo, Republic of Congo, Republic of Djibouti, Eritrea, Ethiopia, Kenya, Lesotho, Madagascar, Malawi, Mauritius, Mozambique, Namibia, Rwanda, Seychelles, Somalia, Republic of South Africa, Swaziland, Tanzania, Uganda, Zambia, Zimbabwe
East Asia	Beijing Bangkok Jakarta	People's Republic of China, Hong Kong, Mongolia Burma, Cambodia, Laos, Taiwan, Thailand, Vietnam Brunei, Fiji, Indonesia, Japan, Korea, Malaysia, Papua New Guinea, Philippines, Singapore, Timor-Leste
Europe	Ankara Budapest Kyiv Moscow	Turkey Albania, Bosnia and Herzegovina, Bulgaria, Croatia, Czech Republic, Estonia, Hungary, Kosovo, Latvia, Macedonia, Montenegro, Poland, Romania, Serbia, Slovakia, Slovenia Armenia, Azerbaijan, Republic of Belarus, Georgia, Moldova, Ukraine Russia
Middle East	Amman Cairo Manama Rabat	Iraq, Israel, Jordan, Lebanon, Syria, West Bank/Gaza Egypt, Saudi Arabia, Sudan, Yemen Bahrain, State of Kuwait, State of Oman, Qatar, United Arab Emirates Algeria, Libya, Morocco, Tunisia
South Central Asia	New Delhi Astana	Afghanistan, Bangladesh, Bhutan, India, Maldives, Nepal, Sri Lanka, Pakistan Kazakhstan, Kyrgyz Republic, Tajikistan, Turkmenistan, Uzbekistan
Latin America	Mexico City Lima Santiago Branch Chief DC Branch Chief DC	Belize, Costa Rica, El Salvador, Guatemala, Honduras, Mexico, Nicaragua, Panama Bolivia, Colombia, Ecuador, Peru, Venezuela Argentina, Brazil, Chile, Paraguay, Uruguay Bahamas, Barbados, Cuba, Denmark/Greenland, Dominican Republic, French Guiana, Grenada, Guyana, Haiti, Italy, Jam-aica, Netherlands Antilles, Suriname, Trinidad and Tobago Materials Development

If the goal is to maximize the number of English speakers throughout the world, then this is an excellent program as the multiplier effect of American education specialists assisting in the preparation of another country's English curriculum should result in vastly more students learning English, at much less cost, than our Access scholarships. The long-term public diplomacy value for such efforts, however, is debatable. Some say that the teachers who receive the attention, skills, materials and respect from their American counterparts will result in these same teachers acting as good- will ambassadors for the United States for years to come, with the number of students they are able to influence and reach vastly outpacing direct, U.S.-sponsored classes.

Others note that the Program amounts to almost "invisible" Public Diplomacy as few in the public ever hear of these efforts due to the fact that the fellows work from *within* foreign educational systems. If a core component of public diplomacy is for a nation to "get the credit" for its efforts, this may not be the most effective program, but as a low-cost pedagogical tool, it is invaluable.

REGIONAL ENGLISH LANGUAGE OFFICES

In addition to English Language Fellows, the Department of State also supports a network of 18 Regional English Language Offices (RELOs) located in Embassies around the world that operate under the supervision of ECA's Office of English Language Programs in Washington. Each RELO is a specialist Foreign Service Officer with an advanced degree in Teaching English as a Foreign Language (TEFL)—many, in fact are former English Language Fellows.

In collaboration with U.S. Embassies, RELOs oversee the English Access Microscholarship Program, organize teacher training seminars and workshops; consult with host-country ministry, university, and teacher-training officials. They also oversee ECA's other English language activities, such as the English Language Specialists, English Language Fellow, and E-Teacher Scholarship Programs. As the attached table of Regional English Language Offices and the countries they cover suggests, RELOs are over-burdened in the extreme.

ACCESS MICROSCHOLARSHIPS

The Department of State has developed a two-year scholarship intended to provide English language skills primarily to Muslim youths aged 14 to 18 who would otherwise have little access to such classes. These so-called Access Microscholarships grew out of the difficulty the Department had in finding non-elite Muslim youths with sufficient English language proficiency to participate successfully in its Youth Exchange and Study (YES) Program. (YES students spend a full high school year in the United States living with a host family.)

According to the Department, since 2004, some 44,000 students have participated in the Access program in 55 countries. Funding for Access comes from both the State Department's bureau of Educational and Cultural Affairs (ECA) and Middle East Peace Partnership Initiative (MEPI) and has consistently risen:

FY2006	$8.75 million
FY2007	$13.5 million
FY2008	$17.4 million

According to the State Department, more than 22,000 English Access Micro-scholarship students in over 55 countries are currently studying under the Program. Approximately half of the students are in their first year. Access students can be found in the following:

- *Africa* (1,841 students): Benin, Burkina Faso, Chad, Democratic Republic of the Congo, Ethiopia, Kenya, Mauritania, Mozambique, Niger, Nigeria, Senegal, South Africa, Tanzania, Togo
- *East Asia* (2,077 students): Burma, Cambodia, China, East Timor, Indonesia, Malaysia, Mongolia, Philippines, Thailand
- *Europe* (1,606 students): Albania, Azerbaijan, Bosnia- Herzegovina, Cyprus, Kosovo, Russia, Turkey, Ukraine
- *Middle East* (11,070 students): Algeria, Bahrain, Egypt, Gaza, Iraq, Israel, Jordan, Kuwait, Lebanon, Libya, Morocco, Oman, Saudi Arabia, Syria (suspended in FY06), Tunisia, United Arab Emirates, West Bank, Yemen
- *South Central Asia* (4,813 students): Afghanistan, Bangladesh, India, Kazakhstan, Kyrgyzstan, Pakistan, Sri Lanka, Tajikistan, Turkmenistan, Uzbekistan
- *Latin America* (749 students): Argentina, Brazil, Chile, Mexico, Peru, Uruguay

Public Diplomacy officials offer high praise for the Access program as it gives the United States inroads into communities that have often been traditionally hostile towards the United States. However, comments from Access parents such as "our own government doesn't care about educating our children, but the United States does" are not unusual as children with normally very little hope of advancement in their societies are suddenly offered a language which will greatly enhance their future employment opportunities. In addition, many receive computer training, intellectual discipline, and research skills that their other schoolmates will likely never receive.

In Alexandria, Egypt Access classes are co-educational and students are encouraged to question and challenge far beyond the boundaries for normal Egyptian students. In spite of concerns of parental backlash against traditional teaching methods, only one student has been withdrawn by her parents to date. Rather, parents are clamoring for their children to be enrolled in the program because they appreciate the benefits offered.

Valid concerns about the program abound, however. In Alexandria, the NGO AmidEast (which runs Access in Egypt) runs the program for approximately $2,000 per student for the full two years. Classrooms are modern, computers are plentiful, and English instruction is conducted by American expatriates living in the city. However, this is not always the case as in other locations, locally hired instructors lack sufficient English skills and are not always sufficiently familiar with American culture and teaching methodologies to impart effectively these crucial aspects of the program.

Of equal concern is the lack of follow-on programming for Access graduates. With only 300 YES slots available each year and some 11,000 Access graduates, failure to keep the majority of Access graduates engaged with programs related to the their studies risks losing the ground gained, particularly as many will return to educational systems likely hostile to these new-found ideas of academic freedom. Failure to keep Access graduates engaged through low- cost, follow-on local U.S. programs risks seeing our investments in the education of so many wither on the vine and could even create a backlash as students once selected for their intellectual abilities and achievements feel abandoned by our government.

PEACE CORPS EXEMPTION TO CO-LOCATION REQUIREMENT[31]

SEC. 691. SENSE OF CONGRESS REGARDING THE LOCATION OF PEACE CORPS OFFICES ABROAD.

It is the sense of the Congress that, to the degree permitted by security considerations, the Secretary should give favorable consideration to requests by the Director of the Peace Corps that the Secretary exercise his authority under section 606(a)(2)(B) of the Secure Embassy Construction and Counterterrorism Act of 1999 (22 U.S.C. 4865(a)(2)(B)) to waive certain requirements of that Act in order to permit the Peace Corps to maintain offices in foreign countries at locations separate from the United States Embassy.

FILM SERIES RESTRICTIONS

One of the strongest assets in U.S. Public Diplomacy is the use of films to tell America's story to the rest of the world. Particularly, films with historical and political themes and plots are often the best demonstrations of America's values of freedom of expression. They also demonstrate a willingness to debate sensitive topics through such a public medium. As such American Centers and IRCs typically run film series with follow-on discussions.

However, rather than encourage the widest possible broadcast of such showings to the largest audience possible, the Licensing Agreement recently negotiated between the State Department and the Motion Picture Licensing Corporation suggests otherwise. Paragraph 20 of the State Department's message regarding the MOU to Embassies worldwide expressly notes the following were agreed to:

> "The films may be screened for audiences of up to 100 people per screening. They may not be screened for larger audiences.
> "No advertising is permitted. No specific titles or characters from such titles or producers' names may be advertised or publicized to the general public."

Embassy officials report they have been contacted by the MPLC when films are announced on the Internet. To avoid this, many now simply post the movie showing on a bulletin board in their facilities—a perfectly painful example of how, in the age of text messaging, our government is forced to operate in methods no different from the 19th century.

In keeping with the MOU that prohibits advertising, the American Center in Alexandria, Egypt is
    forced to restrict the announcement of upcoming film viewings and discussions to its outdoor
    bulletin board—in this case the 1994 film "Little Women" in the upper right.

STATE DEPARTMENT CABLE OF AGREEMENT WITH MOTION PICTURE LICENSING CORPORATION

UNCLASSIFIED STATE 00046191

P 011508Z MAY 08
FM SECSTATE WASHDC
TO ALL DIPLOMATIC AND CONSULAR POSTS COLLECTIVE PRIORITY

FOR PAS

E.O. 12958: N/A
TAGS: KPAO, OEXC, SCUL
SUBJECT: THEMATIC FEATURE FILM PROGRAMMING FOR EXPANDED MPLC-LICENSED PUBLIC PERFORMANCE SCREENINGS

     1. SUMMARY: ECA IS PLEASED TO ANNOUNCE IT HAS DEVELOPED THEMATIC FEATURE FILM CATEGORIES WITH SUGGESTED FILM TITLES TO ASSIST POSTS WITH ELECTION YEAR AND OTHER SUBJECT AND CONTENT-BASED PROGRAMMING OF FEATURE FILMS ON DVD OR VIDEOTAPE FORMATS. AMONG OTHERS, THE CATEGORIES INCLUDE POLITICS AND THE PRESIDENCY, THE ENVIRONMENT, WOMEN'S RIGHTS, IMMIGRATION, AND DIVERSITY. ALL FILMS LISTED HERE ARE APPROVED FOR USE UNDER THE GUIDELINES OF THE EXPANDED MPLC LICENSE ON PUBLIC PERFORMANCE SCREENING RIGHTS NEGOTIATED BY ECA AND FUNDED BY THE "R" BUREAU. THE NEWLY EXPANDED LICENSE PERMITS CONDITIONAL, NON-THEATRICAL OFF-SITE SCREENINGS IN ADDITION TO SCREENINGS AT U.S. EMBASSIES, CONSULATES AND AMERICAN CORNERS. END SUMMARY.

     THEMATIC FILM CATEGORIES AND SUBJECTS
     ----

     2. THEMATIC CATEGORIES WERE SELECTED BASED ON TOPICS RECURRINGLY REQUESTED BY POSTS AND/OR AN ASSESSMENT OF THE THEMES AND FILMS SUITABLE FOR PROGRAMMING TO ADDRESS CURRENT EVENTS [U.S. AND WORLDWIDE] AND/OR TO PROVIDE AN INSIGHT INTO U.S. SOCIETY AND CULTURE. STILL OTHERS PROVIDE A WINDOW INTO A PARTICULAR ERA IN U.S. HISTORY.
     THE FILMS RUN THE GAMUT FROM OLDER CLASSIC TITLES TO MOVIES OF MORE RECENT VINTAGE.

     TOPICS INCLUDED HERE ARE: POLITICS AND THE PRESIDENCY; THE ENVIRONMENT; FREEDOM OF THE PRESS/MEDIA; INDEPENDENT JUDICIARY/RULE OF LAW; THE POWER OF THE INDIVIDUAL IN A FREE SOCIETY; IMMIGRATION AND CULTURAL DIVERSITY; WOMEN'S ISSUES; WESTERNS WITH A MORAL; THE AMERICAN DREAM FROM RAGS TO RICHES; AMERICAN VALUES; FAMILY LIFE; THE IMPORTANCE OF EDUCATION, AND; OVERCOMING DISABILITIES.

     ADDITIONAL THEMES OR PROGRAM CATEGORIES SUCH AS SCIENCE AND TECHNOLOGY, MEDICINE, BLACK HISTORY MONTH, BIOGRAPHIES, MUSICALS, FILM NOIR, CLASSIC COMEDIES, ANIMATION, AND CHILDREN'S FILMS WILL BE AVAILABLE SHORTLY IN THE PD BEST PRACTICES SITE OF THE INTRANET, AS WILL A FULL TITLE LIST IN PDF FORMAT.

3. AUDIENCES WILL BENEFIT TREMENDOUSLY IF POSTS PROVIDE SUBJECT AND HISTORICAL CONTEXT FOR THE FILMS. WHILE SYNOPSES CAN BE FOUND AT MANY WEBSITES, ECA SUGGESTS TWO IN PARTICULAR WHICH ALSO OFFER RUNNING TIMES AND FILM RATINGS: WWW.IMDB.COM AND WWW.AMAZON.COM.

IF A FILM POST SEEKS IS NOT LISTED HERE, PLEASE CONTACT ECA/PE/C/CU-SUSAN COHEN AT COHENSL@STATE.GOV TO DETERMINE IF IT IS COVERED BY THE MPLC LICENSE.

4. POSTS MAY ORDER DVDS AND VIDEOTAPES DIRECTLY ON-LINE AT ONE OF THE FOLLOWING WEBSITES:

-- HTTP://WWW.AMAZON.COM/ <HTTP://WWW.AMAZON.COM/-->
-- <HTTP://WWW.AMAZON.COM/--> HTTP://WWW.SUNCOAST.COM/ <HTTP://WWW.SUNCOAST.COM/-->
-- <HTTP://WWW.SUNCOAST.COM/--> HTTP://WWW.DVALIBRARY.COM//ABOUTUS.ASPX <HTTP://WWW.DVALIBRARY.COM/ABOUTUS.ASPX-->
-- <HTTP://WWW.DVALIBRARY.COM/ABOUTUS.ASPX--> HTTP://WWW.MOVIESUNLIMITED.COM/MUSITE/DEFAULT.ASP? <HTTP://WWW.MOVIESUNLIMITED.COM/MUSITE/DEFAULT.ASP?-->
-- <HTTP://WWW.MOVIESUNLIMITED.COM/MUSITE/DEFAULT.ASP?--> HTTP://WWW.CDUNIVERSE.COM/DEFAULT.ASP?STYLE=MOVIE

MPLC LICENSE - BRIEF GUIDELINES
----

5. ALL FILMS LISTED BELOW ARE ON THE MPLC APPROVED SCREENING LIST. UNDER THE RENEWED AND EXPANDED COLLECTIVE LICENSING AGREEMENT WITH THE MOTION PICTURE LICENSING CORPORATION, POSTS MAY:

-- HOLD PUBLIC PERFORMANCE SCREENINGS OF FEATURE FILMS ON VIDEOTAPE AND DVD FOR AUDIENCES UP TO 100 PEOPLE AT U.S. EMBASSIES, CONSULATES AND AMERICAN CORNERS.

-- HOLD PUBLIC PERFORMANCE SCREENINGS OF FEATURE FILMS ON VIDEOTAPE AND DVD FOR AUDIENCES UP TO 100 PEOPLE AT OFF-SITE VENUES SUCH AS UNIVERSITIES, MUSEUMS, ETC. ON CONDITION THAT THE SCREENINGS BE HELD UNDER THE SPONSORSHIP, OPERATION AND DIRECT CONTROL OF U.S. EMBASSY OR CONSULAR OFFICER, OR OFFICIAL U.S. MISSION POST. THIS INCLUDES SCREENINGS AT BINATIONAL CENTERS AND OTHER LOCAL INSTITUTIONS OVERSEAS THAT HAVE ARRANGEMENTS AND/OR UNDERSTANDINGS WITH U.S. MISSIONS GOVERNING COOPERATIVE CULTURAL PROGRAMS.

-- NO ADMISSION MAY BE CHARGED AND ADVERTISING IS NOT/NOT PERMITTED.

-- FEATURE FILMS ON VIDEOTAPE OR DVD CANNOT BE SHOWN AT THEATRICAL VENUES, NON-STATE DEPARTMENT SPONSORED/ORGANIZED FILM FESTIVALS, OR AT NOON-USG SPONSORED UNIVERSITY EXHIBITIONS.

PLEASE SEE PARA. 19 FOR COMPLETE DETAILS ON THE MPLC LICENSE. FULLER DETAILS, INCLUDING INFORMATION ON HOW TO LEGALLY PROMOTE YOUR FILM SCREENING WILL BE AVAILABLE SOON ON THE PD BEST PRACTICES INTRANET SITE.

FILM THEME: POLITICS AND THE PRESIDENCY
----

6. SUB-THEME: THE CAMPAIGN, DEAL-MAKING, POLITICAL MACHINES:
-
"THE GREAT MCGINTY" 1940
"ALL THE KING'S MEN" 1949
"ADVICE AND CONSENT" 1962
"THE BEST MAN" 1964
"THE CANDIDATE" 1972
"ALL THE PRESIDENT'S MEN" 1976
"THE SEDUCTION OF JOE TYNAN" 1979
"PRIMARY COLORS" 1992
"THE CONTENDER" 2000
"ALL THE KING'S MEN" 2006
--
SUB-THEME: THE POWER OF THE MEDIA:
"A FACE IN THE CROWD" 1957
"THE LAST HURRAH" 1958
"ALL THE PRESIDENT'S MEN" 1976
"NETWORK" 1976
"GOOD NIGHT AND GOOD LUCK" 2005
--
SUB-THEME - POLITICS AND INTEGRITY:
"GABRIEL OVER THE WHITE HOUSE" 1933
"MR. SMITH GOES TO WASHINGTON" 1939
"MEET JOHN DOE" 1941
"STATE OF THE UNION" 1948
"BORN YESTERDAY" 1950
"BORN YESTERDAY" 1993
"DAVE" 1993
--
SUB-THEME - SATIRES:
"THE GREAT MCGINTY" 1940
"KISSES FOR MY PRESIDENT" 1964
"WRONG IS RIGHT" 1982
"BOB ROBERTS" 1992
"DISTINGUISHED GENTLEMAN" 1992
"DAVE"   1993
"BULWORTH" 1998
"WAG THE DOG" 1997
"ELECTION" 1999
"MAN OF THE YEAR" 2006
--
SUB-THEME - ABOUT THE PRESIDENT:
"YOUNG MR. LINCOLN" 1939
"ABE LINCOLN IN ILLINOIS" 1940
"WILSON" 1944
"THE PRESIDENT'S LADY" 1953
"SUNRISE AT CAMPOBELLO" 1960
"JFK"   1991
"NIXON" 1995
"JEFFERSON IN PARIS" 1995
"THIRTEEN DAYS" 2000
--
SUB-THEME- CAUTIONERY TALES:
"THE MANCHURIAN CANDIDATE" 1962
"DR. STRANGELOVE" 1963
"SEVEN DAYS IN MAY" 1964

"FAIL SAFE"   1964
"THE PARALLAX VIEW"   1974
"THIRTEEN DAYS"   2000
--
FICTICIOUS PRESIDENTS:
"THE AMERICAN PRESIDENT" 1995
"INDEPENDENCE DAY" 1996
"AIR FORCE ONE" 1997
--
MISC:
"CITIZEN KANE" 1941
"MEDIUM COOL" 1969

THEME: THE ENVIRONMENT
----

7. SUB-THEMES: GLOBAL WARMING, NUCLEAR POWER, POLLUTION:
"SILENT RUNNING" 1972
"SOYLENT GREEN" 1973
"THE CHINA SYNDROME" 1979
"KOYAANISQATSI" 1982
"SILKWOOD" 1983
"POWAQQATSI"   1988
"ANIMA MUNDI" 1992
"FERNGULLY:THE LAST RAINFOREST" 1992
"ON DEADLY GROUND" 1994
"WATERWORLD" 1995
"FIRE DOWN BELOW" 1997
"A CIVIL ACTION"   1998
"ERIN BROCKOVICH" 2000
"THE DAY AFTER TOMORROW" 2004
"AN INCONVENIENT TRUTH" 2006
--
SUB-THEME : ANIMALS
"BORN FREE" 1966
"NEVER CRY WOLF" 1983
"GORILLAS IN THE MIST" 1988
"FREE WILLY"   1993
"FLY AWAY HOME" 1996
"MARCH OF THE PENGUINS" 2005
--
SUB-THEME: ECO-HORROR
"THEM" 1954
"THE INCREDIBLE SHRINKING MAN" 1957
"THE BEGINNING OF THE END" 1957
"THE BIRDS" 1963
"FROGS"   1972

THEME: FREEDOM OF THE PRESS/THE MEDIA
----

8. "HIS GIRL FRIDAY" 1940
"CITIZEN KANE" 1941
"THE PAPER"   1964

"MEDIUM COOL" 1969
"ALL THE PRESIDENT'S MEN" 1976
"NETWORK" 1976
"BEING THERE" 1979
"ABSENCE OF MALICE" 1981
"BROADCAST NEWS" 1987
"THE INSIDER" 1999
"GOOD NIGHT AND GOOD LUCK" 2005

THEME: INDEPENDENT JUDICIARY / RULE OF LAW

---

9. "TWELVE ANGRY MEN" 1957
"ANATOMY OF A MURDER"   1959
"INHERIT THE WIND" 1960
"TO KILL A MOCKINGBIRD" 1962
"AND JUSTICE FOR ALL" 1979
"THE VERDICT"   1982
"CLASS ACTION"   1991
"PHILADELPHIA"   1993
"AMISTAD"   1997
"A CIVIL ACTION" 1998
"ERIN BROCKOVICH" 2000

THEME: THE POWER OF THE INDIVIDUAL IN A FREE SOCIETY

---

10. "MR. SMITH GOES TO WASHINGTON" 1939
"THE GRAPES OF WRATH" 1940
"IT'S A WONDERFUL LIFE" 1946
"HIGH NOON" 1952
"ON THE WATERFRONT" 1954
"THE SPIRIT OF ST.LOUIS" 1957
"ROCKY" 1976
"NORMA RAE" 1979
"FORREST GUMP" 1994
"ERIN BROCKOVICH" 2000
"NORTH COUNTRY" 2005
"ROCKEY BALBOA" 2006

THEME: IMMIGRATION AND CULTURAL DIVERSITY

---

11. "GENTLEMAN'S AGREEMENT" 1947
"THE FARMER'S DAUGHTER" 1947
"WEST SIDE STORY" 1961
"NOTHING BUT A MAN" 1964
"THE LEARNING TREE" 1969
"THE MOLLY MAGUIRES"1970
"THE GODFATHER" 1972
"SOUNDER" 1972
"HESTER STREET" 1975
"EL NORTE" 1983

"MOSCOW ON THE HUDSON" 1984
"WITNESS" 1985
"LA BAMBA" 1987
"MATEWAN" 1987
"MOONSTRUCK" 1987
"MILAGRO BEANFIELD WAR" 1988
"STAND AND DELIVER" 1988
"POWWOW HIGHWAY" 1989
"DO THE RIGHT THING" 1989
"AVALON" 1990
"GREEN CARD" 1990
"MISSISSIPPI MASALA" 1991
"BOYZ 'N THE HOOD" 1991
"FAR AND AWAY" 1992
"THE JOY LUCK CLUB" 1993
"CROOKLYN" 1994
"THE BROTHERS MCMULLEN" 1995
"LONE STAR" 1996
"SOUL FOOD" 1997
"SELENA" 1997
"SMOKE SIGNALS" 1998
"BARBERSHOP" 2002
"GANGS OF NEW YORK" 2002
"MY BIG FAT GREEK WEDDING" 2002
"WINDTALKERS" 2002
"THE NAMESAKE" 2006

THEME: WOMEN'S ISSUES
----

12. "CHRISTOPHER STRONG" 1933
"JEZEBEL" 1938
"THE WOMEN" 1939
"NOW VOYAGER" 1942
"WOMAN OF THE YEAR" 1942
"DOUBLE INDEMNITY" 1944
"SPELLBOUND" 1945
"MILDRED PIERCE" 1945
"ADAM'S RIB" 1949
"ALL ABOUT EVE" 1950
"THE COUNTRY GIRL" 1954
"OKLAHOMA CRUDE" 1973
"ALICE DOESN'T LIVE HERE ANYMORE" 1974
"HESTER STREET" 1975
"THE TURNING POINT" 1977
"NORMA RAE" 1979
"KRAMER VS KRAMER" 1979
"ALIEN" 1979
"BODY HEAT" 1981
"TOOTSIE" 1982
"SILKWOOD" 1983
"TERMS OF ENDEARMENT" 1983
"BABY BOOM" 1987
"BULL DURHAM" 1988
"THE ACCUSED" 1988

"WORKING GIRL" 1988
"STEEL MAGNOLIAS" 1989
"WHITE PALACE" 1990
"FRIED GREEN TOMATOES" 1991
"THELMA AND LOUISE" 1991
"A LEAGUE OF THEIR OWN" 1992
"THE BALLAD OF LITTLE JO" 1993
"SLEEPLESS IN SEATTLE" 1993
"JOY LUCK CLUB" 1993
"LITTLE WOMEN" 1994
"THE BRIDGES OF MADISON COUNTY" 1995
"BOYS ON THE SIDE" 1995
"WAITING TO EXHALE" 1995
"COURAGE UNDER FIRE" 1996
"THE FIRST WIVES CLUB" 1996
"FARGO" 1996
"THE ASSOCIATE" 1996
"JACKIE BROWN" 1997
"PARADISE ROAD" 1997
"G.I. JANE" 1997
"ONE TRUE THING" 1998
"GIRL INTERRUPTED" 1999
"YOU CAN COUNT ON ME" 2000
"MILLION DOLLAR BABY" 2004
"MARIA FULL OF GRACE" 2004
"NORTH COUNTRY" 2005
"A MIGHTY HEART" 2007

THEME: CLASSIC WESTERNS WITH A MORAL
----

13. "THE OX-BOW INCIDENT" 1943
"MY DARLING CLEMENTINE" 1946
"RED RIVER" 1948
"TREASURE OF THE SIERRA MADRE" 1948
"SHE WORE A YELLOW RIBBON" 1949
"HIGH NOON" 1952
"SHANE" 1953
"THE SEARCHERS" 1956
"GUNFIGHT AT OK CORRAL" 1957
"3:10 TO YUMA" 1957
"THE MAGNIFICANT SEVEN" 1960
"THE MAN WHO SHOT LIBERTY VALANCE" 1962

THEME: THE AMERICAN DREAM FROM RAGS TO RICHES
----

14. "BOUND FOR GLORY" 1976
"LEADBELLY" 1976
"COAL MINER'S DAUGHTER" 1980
"LA BAMBA" 1987
"TENDER MERCIES" 1983
"WALK THE LINE" 2005

----

17. "THE MIRACLE WORKER" 1962
"STAND AND DELIVER"   1988
"LEAN ON ME"   1989
"DEAD POET'S SOCIETY" 1989
"MR. HOLLAND'S OPUS" 1995
"MUSIC OF THE HEART"   1999
"PAY IT FORWARD"   2000
"COACH CARTER" 2005
"THE PURSUIT OF HAPPYNESS"   2006
"FREEDOM WRITERS   2007

THEME: OVERCOMING ADVERSITY
----

18. "BEST YEARS OF OUR LIVES" 1946
"JOHNNY BELINDA" 1948
"BRIGHT VICTORY"   1951
"THREE FACES OF EVE"   1957
"SUNRISE AT CAMPOBELLO" 1960
"DAVID AND LISA" 1962
"THE MIRACLE WORKER"   1962
"WAIT UNTIL DARK"   1967
"BANG THE DRUM SLOWLY" 1973
"THE OTHER SIDE OF THE MOUNTAIN" 1975
"ORDINARY PEOPLE"   1980
"CHILDREN OF A LESSER GOD" 1986
"RAIN MAN"   1988
"THE WATERDANCE" 1992
"PHILADELPHIA"   1993
"FORREST GUMP" 1994
"THE SHAWSHANK REDEMPTION" 1994
"SLING BLADE"   1996
"GOOD WILL HUNTING" 1997
"GIRL INTERRUPTED" 1999
"REMEMBER THE TITANS" 2000
"I AM SAM"   2001
"ANTWONE FISHER" 2002
"WE ARE MARSHALL" 2006
"GLORY ROAD" 2006

DETAILS OF 2008 EXPANDED COLLECTIVE LICENSING AGREEMENT WITH THE MOTION
PICTURE LICENSING CORPORATION [MPLC]
----

19. THE RENEWED AND EXPANDED LICENSING AGREEMENT THAT ECA NEGOTIATED
WITH THE MPLC PERMITS WIDER FLEXIBILITY IN THE USE OF FILM AS A MAJOR POST
PROGRAMMING TOOL. THE LICENSE IS FUNDED FOR THE SECOND YEAR BY THE OFFICE OF THE
UNDER SECRETARY FOR PUBLIC DIPLOMACY AND PUBLIC AFFAIRS. IT PERMITS CONTINUED
PUBLIC PERFORMANCE SCREENINGS OF FEATURE FILMS ON VIDEOTAPE AND DVD AT U.S.
EMBASSIES, CONSULATES AND AMERICAN CORNERS.

THIS YEAR'S EXPANDED RIGHTS ALSO PERMIT NON-THEATRICAL OFF-SITE SCREENINGS ON CONDITION THAT THOSE SCREENINGS MUST ALWAYS BE HELD UNDER THE SPONSORSHIP, OPERATION, AND DIRECT CONTROL OF U.S. EMBASSY OR CONSULAR OFFICIALS.

THUS, SCREENINGS MAY NOW BE HELD AT BINATIONAL CENTERS, SCHOOLS, COLLEGES AND UNIVERSITIES IF IN CONNECTION WITH A USG-ORGANIZED CULTURAL PROGRAM AND UNDER THE SPONSORSHIP, OPERATION AND DIRECT CONTROL OF U.S. EMBASSY OR CONSULAR OFFICIALS.

20. OTHER MPLC REGULATIONS:

- THE FILMS MAY BE SCREENED FOR AUDIENCES OF UP TO 100 PEOPLE PER SCREENING. THEY MAY NOT BE SCREENED FOR LARGER AUDIENCES.

- NO ADMISSION MAY BE CHARGED.

- NO ADVERTISING IS PERMITTED. NO SPECIFIC TITLES, OR CHARACTERS FROM SUCH TITLES, OR PRODUCERS' NAMES MAY BE ADVERTISED OR PUBLICIZED TO THE GENERAL PUBLIC.

- THE TAPES OR DVDS MUST BE LEGALLY OBTAINED FROM A LEGITIMATE SOURCE.

- USG MISSIONS AND AMERICAN CORNERS ARE RESPONSIBLE FOR OBTAINING THEIR OWN VIDEOCASSETTES AND DVDS.

- USG MISSIONS AND AMERICAN CORNERS MAY NOT DUPLICATE, EDIT OR IN ANY WAY MODIFY THE VIDEOTAPES AND DVDS OBTAINED FOR PUBLIC PERFORMANCE USE.

- IMPORTANT: BECAUSE OF RIGHTS RESTRICTIONS, COPYRIGHT AND ROYALTY ISSUES, FEATURE FILMS ON VIDEOTAPE OR DVD CANNOT/CANNOT BE SHOWN AT THEATRICAL VENUES, NON-STATE DEPARTMENT SPONSORED OR ORGANIZED FILM FESTIVALS, OR AT NON-USG SPONSORED UNIVERSITY EXHIBITIONS.

21. THE COLLECTIVE MPLC LICENSE HAS LONG BEEN A PROGRAM TOOL TO AUGMENT ECA/PE/C/CU'S 35MM FEATURE FILM PROGRAM.
DETAILS OF THAT PROGRAM WILL BE ANNOUNCED VIA SEPTEL.
PLEASE ADDRESS ANY QUESTIONS ABOUT THE 35MM FILM PROGRAM OR ABOUT THE PUBLIC PERFORMANCE COLLECTIVE LICENSE TO ECA/PE/C/CU-SUSAN COHEN, COPY TO LAFAYE PROCTOR.

FILMS COVERED UNDER THE MPLC
----

22. THE TITLES THAT MAY BE PUBLICLY PRESENTED UNDER THIS LICENSE ARE MOTION PICTURES THAT HAVE BEEN PRODUCED AND/OR DISTRIBUTED BY THE MOTION PICTURE COMPANIES LISTED BELOW, PROVIDED THAT THE SPECIFIC TITLES COVERED UNDER THIS AGREEMENT ARE EITHER:

[A] AVAILABLE IN HOME VIDEO OR DVD RELEASE IN THE COUNTRY IN WHICH THE EXHIBITION WILL OCCUR; OR

[B] AT LEAST SIX [6] MONTHS OR NINE [9] MONTHS HAVE PASSED SINCE THE U.S. THEATRICAL RELEASE; WHICHEVER IS EARLIER [SEE BELOW]

THE MOTION PICTURE COMPANIES COVERED UNDER THE MPLC ARE THE FOLLOWING: ALLEY CAT FILMS, AMERICAN PORTRAIT FILMS, BEDFORD ENTERTAINMENT,BEST FILM & VIDEO,

BIG IDEA, INC., BILLY GRAHAM EVANGELISTIC ASSOCIATION/WORLD WIDE PICTURES,
BRIDGESTONE MULTIMEDIA/ALPHA OMEGA PUBLISHING, BRITISH AND FOREIGN BIBLE SOCIETY,
BRUDER RELEASING, INC., BUENA VISTA PICTURES*, CANNON PICTURES, CAREY FILMS LTD.,
CASTLE HILL PRODUCTIONS, CDR COMMUNICATIONS, CENTRAL PARK MEDIA, CHOICES, INC.,
CHRISTIAN CINEMA.COM, CHRISTIAN TELEVISION ASSOCIATION, CINEMATHEQUE COLLECTION,
CLASSIC MEDIA/GOLDEN BOOKS ENTERTAINMENT, COLUMBIA PICTURES*, CROWN VIDEO, DAVE
CHRISTIANO FILMS, DREAM, LLC, DREAMWORKS ANIMATION SKG*, DREAMWORKS PICTURES*,
EO INTERNATIONAL, ERF CHRISTIAN RADIO & TELEVISION, ERIC VELU PRODUCTIONS, FAMILY
ENTERTAINMENT LIBRARY, FANGORIA VIDEO, FOCUS FEATURES*, FOX 2000 FILMS*, FOX
SEARCHLIGHT PICTURES*, GATEWAY FILMS/VISION VIDEO, GOSPEL COMMUNICATIONS
INTERNATIONAL/GOSPEL FILMS, GRACE PRODUCTS/EVANGELICAL FILMS, GRIZZLY ADAMS
PRODUCTIONS, GRIZZLY ADAMS/TOTAL LIVING PRODUCTIONS, HANNA-BARBERA**, HARBINGER
COMMUNICATIONS, HARVEST PRODUCTIONS, HARVEY ENTERTAINMENT, HOLLYWOOD
PICTURES*, INSPIRED STUDIOS, INSPIRED WELLNESS VIDEO, INTERCOMM, INC., INTERNATIONAL
CHRISTIAN COMMUNICATIONS [ICC], INTERNATIONAL FILM FORUM, INTERNATIONAL FILMS,
JEREMIAH FILMS, KALON MEDIA, INC., LANTERN FILM AND VIDEO, LEARNING CORPORATION OF
AMERICA**, LINN PRODUCTIONS, LORIMAR TELEPICTURES**, MAHONEY MEDIA GROUP, INC.,
MARALEE DAWN MINISTRIES, MC DOUGAL FILMS, MC GRAW-HILL, MEDIASERF GERMANY,
MESSENGER FILMS, METRO-GOLDWYN-MAYER [PRE-1986 TITLES]**, METRO-GOLDWYN-MAYER
[MGM] STUDIOS, MILLENNIUM FILMS, NEW WORLD PICTURES, NU IMAGE, INC., OCTOBER FILMS*,
OPEN DOOR INTERNATIONAL, ORION PICTURES, PARAMOUNT CLASSICS*, PARAMOUNT
PICTURES*, PARAMOUNT VANTAGE, PEACE ARCH ENTERTAINMENT GROUP, INC., PETER PAN
VIDEO, POLYGRAM FILMED ENTERTAINMENT*, PRAISE HOME VIDEO, PROVIDENCE
ENTERTAINMENT, REPUBLIC PICTURES*, RKO PICTURES**, RUSS DOUGHTEN FILMS, SCHOLASTIC
ENTERTAINMENT, SCREEN GEMS*, SIDE BY SIDE FILMS, SIGNAL HILL PICTURES, SONY PICTURES
CLASSICS*, SONY PICTURES ENTERTAINMENT*, SPARK PRODUCTIONS, LTD., STUDIO CANAL,
TEENERGY PRODUCTIONS, THINKFILM COMPANY, INC., TOMMY NELSON, TOTAL LIVING VIDEO
CURRICULUM, TOUCHSTONE PICTURES*, TRANS ATLANTIC PICTURES, TRISTAR PICTURES*,
TRIUMPH FILMS**, TURNER HOME ENTERTAINMENT**, TVA/QUIGLEY'S VILLAGE, TWENTIETH
CENTURY FOX FILM CORP.*, UNITED ARTISTS PICTURES, UNIVERSAL PICTURES*, USA FILMS*,
VIDA ENTERTAINMENT, WALT DISNEY PICTURES*, WARNER BROS.**, WARNER INDEPENDENT
PICTURES**, WORLD ALMANAC VIDEO, AND XENON HOME VIDEO.

      *   SIX [6] MONTHS
     ** NINE [9] MONTHS

      RICE

    UNCLASSIFIED STATE 00046191

                     O

End Notes

[1] A February 6, 2009 BBC World Service Poll of more than 13,000 respondents in 21 countries still showed the United States with a 40% positive-43% negative rating. http://news.bbc.co.uk/ 2/hi/ 7873050.stm.

[2] http://www.gao.gov/transitionl2009/urgent/.

[3] These include: Arndt, Richard. The First Resort of Kings: American Cultural Diplomacy in the Twentieth Century. New York: Potomac Books, Inc., 2007; Kiesling, John Brady. Diplomacy Lessons: Realism for an Unloved Superpower. Washington, D.C. Potomac Books, Inc., 2006; Peterson, Peter G. Finding America's Voice: A Strategy for Reinvigorating US Public Diplomacy (Report of An Independent Task Force Sponsored by the Council on Foreign Relations). New York: Council On Foreign Relations, Inc., 2003; Rosen, Brian and Charles Wolf, Jr. Public Diplomacy: How to Think About and Improve It. Santa Monica: RAND Corporation,

2004; Rugh, William A. American Encounters With Arabs: The Soft Power of US Public Diplomacy in the Middle East. London: Praeger Security International, 2006.

[4] Recent revelations have surfaced that China has again begun to deny access to various Internet sites it had stopped blocking during the 2008 Olympic games (see: http://www.nytimes.com/ 2008/12/17/world/asia/17china.html?hp). U.S. facilities with filter-free Internet provide a natural magnet for the public in many locations where repressive governments try to deny information to their citizens.

[5] As a result of our extensive collections, many foreigners had their first exposure to serious research and uncensored information in an American Center's library—one reason why the Centers are most commonly referred to overseas as the "American Library," in spite of the entirety of a Center's offerings.

[6] Freedom House's 2008 Global Press Freedom report counts 66% (123) of the world's nations as having either a Not Free or only Partly Free press. These 123 countries represent over 80% of the world's population. http://www.freedomhouse.org/uploads/fop08/FOTP2008Charts.pdf.

[7] "Neutral" in the sense of a less formal setting than a U.S. Embassy, but by no means free from risk as many repressive governments, to this day, monitor and track all visitors to U.S. facilities.

[8] Figures provided by the Department of State for 2008.

[9] See the Foreign Affairs Reform and Restructuring Act of 1998 in Division G of the FY2008 Omnibus Appropriations legislation (PL105–277), which begins on p. 761. http:/ /frwebgate. ccess.gpo.gov/cgi-bin/getdoc.cgi?dbname=105_cong_public_laws f:publ277.105.pdf.

[10] See public diplomacy funding figures in CSIS Appendix to Armitage-Nye April 24, 2008 Senate testimony; http://www.csis.org/media Appendix.pdf.

[11] Foreign Service Officers are career-tracked in one of five "cones"—Consular, Economic, Management, Political or (since the absorption of USIA into the State Department in 1999)— Public Diplomacy.

[12] See for example the proposed creations of: "USA-World Trust" in the Brookings report "Voices of America" http://www.brookings.edu//media/ diplomacy_lord/11_public_diplomacy_ lord.pdf; the Defense Science Boards "Center for Global Engagement" http://www.acq.osd.mil/dsb/reports /2008-01-Strategic Communication.pdf; Meridian International Center for the Study of the Presidency's call for a "Foundation for International Understanding" http://www.thepresidency.org/FIU/fiu.html; Business for Diplomatic Action's "Corporation for Public Diplomacy" http://www.businessfordiplomaticaction.org/ action/a _business_perspective_on_public_ diplomacy _10 _2007 _approvedfinal.pdf; Heritage Foundation's "Independent Public Opinion Research Center" http://www.heritage.org/ Research/PublicDiplomacy/bg1875.cfm; Public Diplomacy Council—"U.S. Agency for Public Diplomacy" www.pdi.gwu.edu.

[13] See Secure Embassy Construction and Counterterrorism Act of 1999, found in Title VI of Division A of the FY2000 Omnibus Appropriations Act (PL106–113), starting on p. 451; http:// frwebgate.access f:publ113.106.pdf.

[14] Visiting an IRC in a new US Embassy was likened to "going to jail or getting into Fort Knox" according to one interviewee in the State Department's 2003 "Changing Minds Winning Peace: A Strategic Direction for U.S. Public Diplomacy in the Arab and Muslim World." http:// www.state.gov/documents/organization/24882.pdf.

[15] Staff conversations with several interlocutors in both Egypt and Jordan, all of which pro duced identical results.

[16] Iranian Cultural Center information can be found at http://culturebase.icro.ir/.

[17] Further discussions of each of these elements can be found in the Appendix.

[18] See a recent review of the program in the New York Times which quotes one 15 year old Egyptian girl: "We don't want it to be two years that just passed and then it's over." http:// www.nytimes.com/2009/02/06/world/middleeast/06cairo.html?_r=1&scp=2&sq= access&st=cse.

[19] http://www.newyorker.com/reporting/2008/08/25/080825fa_fact_packer/.

[20] http://burma.usembassy.gov/the_american_center.html.

[21] http://www.alc.edu.jo/web

[22] http://www.usembassy-mexico.gov/bbf/biblioteca.htm.

[23] http://www.educationusa.state.gov/.

[24] http://www.usemb.gov.do/IRC/IRCindex.htm.

[25] http://www.dominicoamericano.edu.do/english/index.asp.

[26] Found on page 78 of http://www.nakbaonline.org/download/UNDP/EnglishVersion/Ar- Human-Dev-2002.pdf.

[27] The so-called "Djerejian Report" after the former U.S. Ambassador who chaired the effort http://www.state.gov/documents/organization/24882.pdf.

[28] A list of books translated by the U.S. Embassy in Cairo: http://cairo.usembassy.gov/pa/ rbo.htm.

[29] A list of books translated by the U.S. Embassy in Amman: http://jordan.usembassy.gov/ abp_titleslin_stock.html.

[30] According to the State Department, 136 English Language Fellows are currently assigned as follows: Africa: 17; East Asia: 28; Europe: 33; Middle East 21; South Central Asia: 13; Latin America: 24.

[31] See Section 691 (page 1415) of Public Law 107–228 http://frwebgate.access getdoc.cgi?dbname=107_conglpublic_laws&docid=f:publ228.107.pdf.

In: U.S. Public Diplomacy: Background and Issues
Editor: Matthew B. Morrison

ISBN: 978-1-61728-888-3
© 2010 Nova Science Publishers, Inc.

Chapter 4

STATEMENT OF EVELYN S. LIEBERMAN, DIRECTOR OF COMMUNICATIONS, SMITHSONIAN INSTITUTE, TO THE U.S. SENATE FOREIGN RELATIONS COMMITTEE, HEARING ON "THE FUTURE OF AMERICAN PUBLIC DIPLOMACY"

Evelyn S. Lieberman

Mr. Chairman, members of the committee, thank you for inviting me here to discuss the future of American public diplomacy. Today, I would like to look back briefly at the creation of the State Department office of public diplomacy and what that experience might tell us as we work to support and better equip the foreign service professionals who represent our government, our culture and our people to the world.

I had the honor of serving as the first under secretary of State for public diplomacy and public affairs during the final year of the Clinton administration. My tenure in that job was fairly brief and I have since observed the State Department and public diplomacy from the outside vantage point of a private citizen. I do know that Secretary of State Clinton has a deep, longstanding commitment to strengthening our public diplomacy and she has assembled a superb public diplomacy team. My hope, in appearing before you, is that some of the things I learned as under secretary remain relevant today.

Prior to becoming under secretary, I had worked as deputy White House chief of staff and had served as director of the Voice of America. At VOA I learned firsthand the wisdom and power of diplomatic speech that is honest and respectful of its audience. Good news or bad news, VOA broadcasts the truth, and because of that countless millions listen, and they listen with trust. Over the years, VOA's Office of Development and Training has conducted workshops for more than 5,000 foreign journalists in 140 countries.

So when Secretary of State Madeleine Albright asked me to head the State Department's new public diplomacy office, she described its mission in words that hit home. "We are trying," she said, "to build a new diplomacy that listens more."

This was only a decade ago, but it was before 9/11, and it was medieval times in terms of where we are today with Internet and global communications. Yet although there was no Twitter, no I-phones or You Tube, it was a pivotal time in American diplomacy. New forces of global communication—the internet, cell phones, 24-hour cable news—were pulling our nation and the world together. Our planet was shrinking fast, as we crossed borders online and watched the world on TV and computer screens. It became tempting to think that the unifying wonders of technology would give us a global village—a uniformity that might sweep away old divisions rooted in national, ethnic and cultural identities. It was indeed a new world, but Secretary Albright cautioned us: "Globalization," she said, "has blurred many... national and cultural traditions, but it has by no means erased them." That was true then and it is true today.

We needed and still need to reshape our traditional diplomacy—to take it beyond the formal channels and often elite settings in which it has operated for so long. To strengthen our diplomacy in the new information age, President Clinton and Congress agreed to restructure the foreign service by merging the US Information Agency and the State Department office of public affairs, creating the Office of Public Diplomacy and Public Affairs. The reorganization aimed to give foreign service officers in USIA—the principle practitioners of public diplomacy—more equal status in the department when it came to formulating and executing foreign policy. The Office of Public Diplomacy is the only branch of the State Department that partners with independent, nongovernmental organizations and programs, and its commitment to open debate and cross-cultural understanding is essential to advancing our diplomatic mission.

As the first under secretary, I did not myself get to practice much public diplomacy—my job was to rewire the structural circuitry, meld press operations with cultural outreach, and institute an organizational framework where public diplomacy could thrive. We were combining two distinct, institutional cultures that had functioned separately in Washington and at our embassies for generations—traditional diplomats, used to working in classified settings behind closed doors and the cultural and public affairs people who engaged foreign publics, presenting American culture abroad and nurturing dialogue, largely through educational and cultural programs and exchanges. This second group brought America to other countries and other cultures home to us. As with most big ideas, implementation meant organizational sausage-making at all levels of the Department—combining payroll functions, reconfiguring office space, safe-guarding the rights and aspirations of our foreign service professionals as we reorganized, and deciding what to cut and what to keep.

To do this job, I met with hundreds of staff and employees on both sides of the merger, visited embassies to learn how they operated and observed the cultural, educational and exchange programs that now were run by the office I led. This process led me to believe even more in the goal of the merger—to infuse cultural and public diplomacy into the every day conduct of foreign affairs. It meant including public diplomacy specialists in strategic planning. It meant adding a public diplomacy voice to internal policy debates, no matter what the issue—combating terrorists, promoting the rule of law, stopping the trafficking in human beings, fighting disease, strengthening civil institutions, addressing weapons proliferation—the myriad, daunting issues that the State Department tackles every day.

In launching Public Diplomacy at the Department, we did not aim to end—or to alter too suddenly—the practices and tenets of traditional diplomacy. We wanted to encourage and enable diplomats to work in a world where foreign relations were increasingly conducted in public, instantaneously, through mass media or, just as often, through local media or targeted Internet communications. We realized that in the new world of global information, millions of people could access and observe policy making and instantly register their opinions, ideas and objections. People no longer waited to hear what diplomats had hammered out in closed rooms; they could watch leaders shape policy live and in real time, witness the decision process and, by reacting, help drive it.

Indeed, the rise of interactive, internet-based communications had changed the interests and expectations of our global audience. People no longer only wanted to hear arguments— they wanted to argue back. Audiences still would listen but they also expected to be heard. Our mission as diplomatic communicators was not simply to make presentations but to engage foreign publics in conversations, and conversations have to be two-way. Simply airing pro-American ads on Al Jazeera will not work because they are all push and no pull—they encourage attitudes toward our country that they seek to reverse. Simply put, we need communication strategies that "listen more." We must stand firm against and defeat terrorists, but it is wrong—and can be dangerously wrong— to believe that simply listening shows weakness, or that respect for other cultures naively invites exploitation.

A 2007 study by the Center for Strategic and International Studies, entitled, "The Embassy of the Future," put matters succinctly. "America's diplomats," it said, "are struggling to break free from the bureaucratic practices that keep them inside U.S. embassy buildings and that emphasize the processing of information over the personal, active, direct engagement that wins friends and supporters for America—the kind of diplomacy that inspired foreign service officers to serve their country in the first place."

Seeing the results and impact of public diplomacy programs in education and culture made it clear to me that "personal, active, direct engagement" by diplomats is one of the best foreign policy tools that we have. At one point we polled our ambassadors, who unanimously attested to the value and import of educational and cultural programs and charged us to do more to strengthen them.

When I became under secretary I was astonished to discover the extent to which these programs had to struggle for resources to survive, let alone grow. We all know that throwing money at issues does not necessarily improve things, but these programs work so powerfully for our country that I continue to advocate a great surge in their growth whenever I get the chance, just as I did as under secretary and as—I am sure—my successors have done. And with, I would bet, unfortunately consistent results.

When I was under secretary, the Fulbright Senior Scholars program sent 1,000 Americans to lecture and conduct research in 140 countries, and the Fulbright Student Program supported 800 Americans studying abroad and 3,000 foreign students studying here. These were respectable numbers, I suppose, but Fulbright participants were chosen from among many thousands more gifted applicants who would have benefited the program immensely had we had the means to accept them.

Fulbright students and scholars should be viewed as a smart investment in American security and international peace, not simply as a budget expense. Similarly, the Citizens Exchange Program in fiscal year 2000 engaged 1,000 Americans and 3,000 foreign citizens in professional and cultural exchanges, and our International Visitors Program enabled about 5,000 emerging foreign leaders to visit the United States. At the time, alumni of the Visitors program included more than 200 current or former heads of state of foreign governments— leaders who knew America, who had friends here— leaders to whom this country was a human place, not an abstraction or a piece of propaganda. As of today, more than 330 alumni of our educational and cultural programs have gone on to become heads of state or government and more than 40 are Nobel laureates. We should be investing heavily in these programs.

A singular project that we undertook in November of 2000 was The White House Conference on Culture and Diplomacy, a colloquy hosted by President and Mrs. Clinton and Secretary Albright that assembled 200 cultural leaders, artists, and diplomatic leaders from around the world, as well as congressional leaders. Organized in partnership with the Office of the First Lady, the National Security Council and the White House Millennium Council, the conference focused attention on the role of culture in U.S. foreign policy and produced recommendations for future development of American cultural diplomacy.

The event was high profile, involving a major Islamic leader, an African Nobel Laureate in Literature, two former American Poets Laureate, and some of the world's most recognized actors, artists and musicians, not to mention the President, First Lady, Secretary of State, ministers of culture from around the world and leaders of private foundations, NGO's and multinational companies. The conference received global media coverage, and large numbers of Americans heard about the connections between culture and public policy around the world—about the powerful force that public diplomacy can be in a dangerous and threatening world. Opening the conference in the East Room of The White House, Mrs. Clinton said, "It is the arts and humanities that give us roots, that foster our civil society and democracy and create a universal language so that we can understand each other better as nations and human beings."

In her remarks, Secretary Albright declared that we were assembled "for the first—but I hope not the last" such conference. As it turns out, it was the first *and* last, and I would hope that similar, cultural diplomacy summits be held at the highest level— events involving international leaders in culture, government and the arts that can reach millions though global media and the worldwide web. Too few Americans know about the importance of public diplomacy; we need to tell its story.

Conducting effective public diplomacy is more difficult today than it was prior to 9/11, when we launched the State Department program. We must, of course, ensure the safety and security of foreign service officers. In some countries, it takes exceptional fortitude and courage for a diplomat to work beyond embassy walls. An ambitious program to construct and modernize embassies, begun, I believe, under Secretary of State Powell, aims to build embassies that are safe, functional and able to advance our diplomatic mission. In some cases, however, new embassies have been relocated outside major cities, where access to them is limited. Security and cost concerns require limitations, but we must do everything we can to see that our embassies are as open to the public as they can be, and not remote from urban centers.

In some countries, our diplomatic missions have set up small, unclassified posts that consist of a single foreign service officer, who wears many hats, assisted by one or two host national staff. These American Presence Posts, or APPs, operate in cities distant from the embassy and engage in a full range of person-to-person diplomacy—public relations, trade and commercial affairs, liaisons with local government, and so on. Security is always an issue; APPs cannot operate everywhere. But they are a strong public diplomacy asset. Similarly, some embassies are establishing "American Corners," spaces that offer the public access to American books, DVDs, CDs, informational materials and the Internet. Operating in institutions such libraries or universities and staffed by a person from the host institution, American Corners are another good way to engage and serve foreign publics. Virtual Presence Posts, which offer internet connectivity to the public, also are being used increasingly as a diplomatic tool.

These programs and others like them should be replicated as much as possible, just as the cultural, educational and exchange programs sponsored by the Office of Public Diplomacy should be allowed to grow significantly. Our country needs to invest in these proven, public diplomacy programs on a major scale, and our government and its leaders should de a better job of informing the American people about the need to strengthen public diplomacy and its role in our foreign affairs.

Thank you.

In: U.S. Public Diplomacy: Background and Issues
Editor: Matthew B. Morrison

ISBN: 978-1-61728-888-3
© 2010 Nova Science Publishers, Inc.

Chapter 5

WRITTEN TESTIMONY OF AMBASSADOR KAREN HUGHES, TO THE U.S. SENATE FOREIGN RELATIONS COMMITTEE, HEARING ON "THE FUTURE OF AMERICAN PUBLIC DIPLOMACY"

Karen Hughes

Mr. Chairman, Members of the Committee, Senator Kaufman—with whom I had the great pleasure of working on the Broadcasting Board of Governors and who is a great champion of public diplomacy and particularly international broadcasting—thank you for inviting me here today.

Let me start by saying the two and a half years I spent as Under Secretary were among the most challenging and difficult, yet in the end some of the most rewarding, of my entire career.

Working with an outstanding team of career foreign and civil service officers and public diplomats around the world, we were able to make a number of significant changes. Much more needs to be done and I want to outline some thoughts about that today.

People often talk about public diplomacy in the context of the most recent opinion poll but to view public diplomacy as an international popularity contest is a fundamental misunderstanding.

America's engagement with foreign publics is actually a vital foreign policy and national security priority that seeks to promote our national ideals and interests and to undermine our enemies.

When I took office, a strategic plan for US public diplomacy did not exist. We worked in an interagency process to develop one and put in place three strategic imperative, which I believe remain vital today.

First, that America must offer a positive vision of hope and opportunity rooted in our most basic values, values which are not merely American, but universal human rights – liberty, justice, the rule of law, rights for women and other minorities, a fundamental belief in the dignity of every individual.

Second, to isolate and discredit Al Qaeda, and other violent extremists, and undermine their attempt to appropriate religion to their cause.

Third, to nurture common interests between Americans and people of different countries across the world.

You can put most US public diplomacy activities into four broad categories:

1. Communications
2. Education and exchange programs (the heart of public diplomacy)
3. The Deeds of Diplomacy (concrete things we do in areas such as education, health and economic development that make such an impact on people's lives)
4. International broadcasting (which now reaches 171 million people across the world)

COMMUNICATIONS

With the explosion of media channels across the world, today's ambassadors and public diplomats have to be trained and effective communicators and empowered to speak on behalf of our country.

I found the bilateral set-up of the State Department is often counterproductive, particularly when dealing with regional networks like Al Jazeera that reach broad audiences across an entire region. I remember meeting with an Ambassador; Al Jazeera was by far the number one source of news and information in his county yet they weren't headquartered in his country so he had no strategy or personnel to deal with them. We set up hubs and put language qualified communicators there. The daily job of those communicators was to get out and explain and advocate our policies.

We need better language training of our personnel. Most of State's training teaches officers to be able to engage in conversations, but not television interviews. We need effective spokespeople who are able to communicate on television in key languages.

Public diplomacy has to be more involved in assigning State Department personnel and have the flexibility to move people to respond to urgent needs or world events.

Communications have to be two-way. It's imperative to put in place a unit to monitor international media, listen to what they are saying about US policies, provide US government's position in response, etc. Secretary Clinton's team has kept up with that practice and I believe it's vitally important.

And I'd like to mention two other areas. One, we were more engaged on Internet and put in place a program blogging in Arabic, Farsi, Urdu to correct misrepresentations and undermine the work of extremists. Two, there was a concerted effort to communicate that Al Qaeda's attacks often killed fellow Muslims. These are vitally important communications strategies that undermine extensive communications of extremists.

EDUCATION AND EXCHANGE

Education and exchange programs are the heart of public diplomacy. During my tenure we dramatically expanded English language training; it's a skill young people across the world want because it gives them opportunities, and also gives them access to a wider body of knowledge and brings them in contact with an American. We are also allowed to reach much younger demographics (8-14 year olds) with in-country programs to learn English.

Doubled participation in exchange programs worked to make more strategic and focused on those who have a wide circle of audience and influence such as clerics and journalists, and also women who have a rippling impact on societies.

We worked with university leaders and reversed the trend of decline in student visas, that had occurred after 9/11, and the number of students has been growing and setting new records ever since.

We began using technology to expand the impact of exchanges, encouraging them to blog about their experience, giving them a camera and asking to make YouTube videos. However, much more needs to be done in this area to maximize the impact of exchanges.

Also, the act of citizen dialogue: We sent Muslim Americans overseas to engage with Muslim communities through sports diplomacy, music and culture. These are spaces where Americans can come in contact with foreign publics.

Most of these programs that build relationships and understanding over the long term are hard to fund, but they are vital and must be expanded in a world that is increasingly inter-connected.

DEEDS OF DIPLOMACY

Collaborative programs such as a breast cancer initiative with women in Middle East does more than share expertise in a way that improves women's health – it also teaches them to learn to network, to stand up for themselves, to more fully participate in their societies.

I believe there are many such ways to partner on issues of mutual interest in ways that improves people's lives and shows the heart and compassion of our country.

The USNS Comfort and the AIDS initiative in Africa are examples of things that are not just development, they are also public diplomacy that communicate who we are and we must view them that way.

INTERNATIONAL BROADCASTING

Improved television offerings: Members of the Broadcasting Board of Governors had had the foresight to start new Arabic television and radio stations before I arrived. We worked to get additional funding and provide relevant programming such as a new midday show, women's programs and others that build value. They now have a weekly audience of 35 million.

I just returned from Dubai where I announced the results of the most comprehensive survey every done with Arab youth. The survey compiled 2,000 in person interviews and was conducted by my company Burson-Marsteller. Findings from the survey showed Arab youth are increasingly connected: 3 out of 4 have mobile phones, 3 in 5 use the Internet at least once a day. The survey also highlighted the crucial importance of television in the lives of Arab youth.

78 percent said they get their news and information from television. Overwhelmingly 66 percent said their favorite leisure pastime is watching television.

Let me tell you why I worry about that for our national interests; if you see something on television, you tend to give it more credibility because you've seen it with your own eyes. Yet the view is often quite misleading. I'll close with a story from a young man I met in China, who had just returned from his first trip to America. I asked him what surprised him. He said he was surprised by how friendly Americans were, how much they cared about their families and how many of them went to church or synagogue or mosque.

I told him that if you take a survey of Americans and ask what's most important to them, not all of them, but most will say family and faith – yet he just told me that surprised him, so I asked: What's the disconnect. His reply has haunted me ever since: America, he said, is NOT the way it looks on television.

There should be calls for continued investment in international broadcasting, and additionally a lot more private sector partnerships (documentaries, etc.)

Some recommendations:

We need changes in personnel training and deployment at State, more in-depth language training of spokesmen in key languages and maybe we need to keep those people in one region of the world, rather than transferring them around. This will strengthen public diplomacy within the regional bureaus, which is the power structure at State, and give the Under Secretary greater authority to assign personnel and allocate resources.

We need more accessible spaces and expanded American corners. We need Americans staffing them; we cannot conduct public diplomacy while walled off in embassies

We have to encourage more conversations and recognize that's going to mean less control. Internet chat means someone may not like what is said, a call-in show means someone may not agree with all the opinions expressed. Al Qaeda is a one way communicator; we have to be a two-way facilitator.

We need to confirm board members at the Broadcasting Board of Governors and continue to improve international broadcasting.

Public diplomacy needs an advocate at the White House. I regularly met with, and saw, President Bush and he put me in the lead of inter-agency. I was in all of Secretary Rice's highest level policy meetings and all that was important but it was still very hard to get it done. We need someone at White House who cares and comes to work every day thinking about this and coordinating with the Under Secretary and that's hard because the White House tends to focus on the domestic audience – after all, that's who elects the President. But for our national interests we have to do a lot more thinking and planning about our conversations and interactions with publics across the world.

In: U.S. Public Diplomacy: Background and Issues
Editor: Matthew B. Morrison

ISBN: 978-1-61728-888-3
© 2010 Nova Science Publishers, Inc.

Chapter 6

TESTIMONY OF JAMES K. GLASSMAN, TO THE U.S. SENATE FOREIGN RELATIONS COMMITTEE, HEARING ON "THE FUTURE OF AMERICAN PUBLIC DIPLOMACY"

James K. Glassman

Mr. Chairman, Members of the Committee:

Senator Kaufmann, you and Vice President Biden, more than any other individuals in recent years, have advanced the cause of public diplomacy as champions of international broadcasting. Thank you for your long service to your country.

I had the unique honor myself of serving, far more briefly, in two public diplomacy positions: First as chairman of the Broadcasting Board of Governors, where I was a colleague of the future Senator Kaufmann. The BBG oversees all non-military taxpayer-funded U.S. international broadcasting, including radio, television, and Internet in 60 languages across more than 100 countries. Then, as Under Secretary of State for Public Diplomacy and Public Affairs, in charge of engagement with foreign publics.

This hearing asks four of us who have served or are serving in the latter post to address the future of public diplomacy. *That future, in my view, is in doubt.*

While the men and women who practice public diplomacy are working diligently and courageously, they lack what the Djerejian Group, a 2003 commission, called the proper "strategic direction"[1] to contribute effectively toward the achievement of the American interest.

In short, here is the problem with public diplomacy: *It is not today being taken seriously as a tool of national security by policymakers.* Will it be in the future? Perhaps only in a desperate response to a terrible crisis. Such delay is unacceptable.

In my testimony today, I will describe what a serious public diplomacy – what I call "*Strategic* Public Diplomacy" – looks like. In the second half of the last administration, President Bush and the leadership of the State Department, the Pentagon, the National Security Council, the BBG, and the intelligence community – with support from a handful of members of Congress and staffers – were succeeding in developing this new vision of public diplomacy and putting it into practice, especially to counter violent extremism.

Today, that effort needs to be sustained, renewed, and invigorated. There are areas in the world where Strategic Public Diplomacy is not merely one tool, but, in fact, the best tool, for achieving America's interests. One of those areas is Iran, which I will address today.

Public diplomacy needs to be sharp, not flaccid. It needs to focus on key foreign policy problems, not merely on vague, feel-good improvements in the far-off future. It needs to be primarily an activity of national security, not of public relations. It needs to be mobilized and sent into battle to win the ideological conflicts of our time.

During the Cold War, with institutions like Radio Free Europe, the Congress of Cultural Freedom, the publication Problems of Communism, educational and cultural exchanges, and the U.S. Information Agency, the United States became very effective at public diplomacy. Public diplomacy played an essential role in defeating communism.[2] But after the Berlin Wall came down, our arsenal of persuasion was dismantled.

"At a critical time in our nation"s history," said the report of the Advisory Group on Public Diplomacy for the Arab and Muslim World, "the apparatus of public diplomacy has proven inadequate... First and foremost, public diplomacy requires a new strategic direction, informed by a seriousness and commitment that matches the gravity of our approach to national defense and traditional state-to-state diplomacy."[3] True in 2003; still true today.

'WE CANNOT KILL OR CAPTURE OUR WAY TO VICTORY'

Here is the best definition of public diplomacy: *understanding, engaging, informing and influencing foreign publics with the goal of achieving the national interest of the United States of America.* Of the four activities, the most important is "influencing." Public diplomacy is a means, not an end. It is a particular set of tools and approaches that help us influence foreigners in order to achieve goals that the United States desires.

During the Bush Administration, the relevant ends were keeping the United States safe and promoting freedom – ends that are linked.

Today, the greatest threats to safety and freedom come from violent extremists and their supporters, mainly using terrorism to try to achieve their aims.

As Secretary of Defense Robert Gates said, "Over the long term, we cannot kill or capture our way to victory. Non-military efforts – ...tools of persuasion and inspiration – were indispensable to the outcome of the defining struggle of the 20th century. They are just as indispensable in the 21st century – and perhaps even more so."[4]

In keeping with that belief, President Bush in 2006 designated the Under Secretary of State for Public Diplomacy as the lead official across government in strategic communications – which is a rubric that includes public diplomacy as well as other activities, including covert and kinetc ones, that attempt to communicate a specific, intentional message to the rest of the world. The Secretary of State and I believed that, given my own background and the nature of the threats, this role should be my primary one. Our focus was countering violent extremism by engaging in a "war of ideas," or what we also termed "global strategic engagement."

Drawing on the work of my predecessor, Karen Hughes, I built an interagency structure that allowed visibility into the strategic communications work being done in other parts of government, including the military, the intelligence community, the foreign assistance apparatus, Treasury, and elsewhere.

Beyond visibility, we were able, working with the National Security Council, to assign specific agencies to perform specific duties in pursuit of clear strategic goals. I also created a small inter-agency group called the Global Strategic Engagement Center, or GSEC, with a State Department director and members from the Department of State and the intelligence community, to handle day-to-day operations.

By the time I left government, this structure was working well, with State at the top of it, as it should be. We received superb cooperation, both from the military and from the intelligence community. Yes, the Department of Defense had more resources for strategic communications activities, but DoD worked in concert with us and looked to us for leadership.

We tried to achieve our war-of-ideas goals in two ways: first, by pushing back and undermining the ideology behind the violent extremism while at the same time explaining and advocating free alternatives and, second, by diverting young people from following a path that leads to violent extremism.

What all terrorist groups have in common, in fact, is the exploitation of vulnerable young people, who are isolated and indoctrinated and become the shock troops.

In both of these endeavors – undermining and diverting – *Americans themselves are rarely the most credible actors and voices.* Much of what we did was encourage others. For example, we supported a global organization of female family members of victims of violent extremism and supported another network, based in Europe, of Muslim entrepreneurs.

In Afghanistan, with the most meager resources, we helped stand up an Afghan-led media center in Kabul. In October 2008, the Taliban stopped a bus at Maiwand, pulled off 50 passengers and beheaded 30 of them.[5] The media center"s leaders immediately brought together 300 Afghan religious leaders who issued a statement condemning the action and calling it anti- Islamic. The effort led to widespread anti-Taliban protests.[6]

(I am happy to note that the new Afghanistan and Pakistan Regional Stabilization Strategy calls for an expansion of the Afghan Government Media and Information Center and the establishment of 16 provincial satellite offices.[7])

We often worked in partnership with private-sector organizations, deploying small amounts of money, in the low hundreds of thousands of dollars. A good example was providing funds to the International Center for Religion and Diplomacy, a group that has been working for years to enhance education (to include academic subjects, plus the teaching of universal values such as tolerance and critical thinking) in Pakistan's madrassas, often breeding grounds of terrorists.[8] The ICRD has so far trained over 2,000 madrassa leaders.

We also funded "Life After Death," a documentary by Layalina Productions, a U.S.-based non-profit, on the journey of families of 9/11 victims as they commiserate with families of terrorism victims in Spain, Jordan, and Egypt.[9] The documentary was first aired last fall on Al Arabiya News Channel throughout Arab-speaking nations.

All of these efforts were aimed at specific goals. We wanted, for example, to show the widespread and senseless suffering caused by violent extremists, especially in their attacks against fellow Muslims. We also wanted to find ways – such as through encouraging entrepreneurship, improving madrassas, or expanding an excellent English-teaching program that teaches values as well – to divert young people from a path to terrorism.

'MUTUAL INTEREST AND MUTUAL RESPECT'

We took our direction from the National Strategy for Combating Terrorism of 2006, which stated: "In the long run, winning the War on Terror means winning the battle of ideas."[10] So our mission then and, it is my hope, today is *to use the tools of ideological engagement – words, deeds, and images – to create an environment hostile to violent extremism.*

What do these efforts in strategic public diplomacy have to do with improving America"s image abroad? Very little, in an immediate sense. The United States itself is not at the center of the war of ideas. Rather, as I will explain a bit later, the United States is being affected by conflicts within Muslim societies, which themselves are ground zero for this enormous struggle, which involves both ideology and violence.

In his inaugural address, President Obama stated, "To the Muslim world, we seek a new way forward, based on mutual interest and mutual respect."[11] He repeated this powerful phrase in speeches in Istanbul and Cairo last year. We do indeed have mutual interest, even with people who may disagree with us on such policy matters as Iraq and the Israeli-Palestinian issue.

On the threat of violent extremism, we are absolutely on the same page as Muslim societies. As a result, even in countries where vast majorities say, even today, that they view the U.S. unfavorably – Jordan, Saudi Arabia, and Egypt, to name a few – our mutual interest in defeating the terrorist threat (and, I should add, in constraining the Iranian threat) – the United States can work cooperatively, using public diplomacy methods, to reach mutual strategic goals.

Americans, for example, have a clear mutual interest with the Pakistanis, who, according to recent Pew Research surveys, view us more unfavorably than practically any other people (in fact, favorability dropped, to just 16 percent, between 2008 and 2009).[12] We both want to defeat the Taliban and Al Qaeda for the sake of a stable, free Pakistan and a safer America. That interest can be achieved even if Pakistanis harbor animus toward Americans.

The latest Pew data reinforce this notion. By a margin of 63 percent to 12 percent, Pakistanis support America's "providing intelligence and logistical support to Pakistani troops fighting extremist groups. By 47 percent to 24 percent, Pakistanis even support U.S. "missile strikes against leaders of extremist groups." What can public diplomacy do in Pakistan? Working quietly, it can help the Pakistani government reinforce the notion that the violent extremist threat is real and that "this is Pakistan's war."[13]

Still, the default position in U.S. public diplomacy – getting people to like us better – has irresistible inertia. When in doubt, policymakers and practitioners turn to brand-burnishing. But the unresolved question is whether a better-liked America is one that can more easily achieve its national security goals. Certainly, some public diplomacy activities can, over the long run, improve foreigners' understanding of the United States, our people, our values, and our policies – and we should vigorously pursue those activities. But, in addition to such activities, the tools of Strategic Public Diplomacy must be applied toward urgent goals for which likeability means little.

Much of the public diplomacy effort in the past has focused on our own image, on how we are seen by others. *But today, in the war of ideas, our core task is not how to fix foreigners' perceptions of the United States but how to isolate and reduce the threat of violent extremism.* In other words, it's not about us.

'AN OBSERVABLE BUT INTANGIBLE ATTRACTION'

In all aspects of public diplomacy – both traditional and strategic -- we require a new approach to communications, to the engaging and informing that lead to the influencing. We began to develop such an approach during my brief tenure, calling it Public Diplomacy 2.0. It is an approach that Secretary Clinton has embraced.[14]

The approach begins with research on America"s image. We found three reasons for low favorability – differences with our policies, a lack of understanding of those policies and beliefs, and a perception that the United States does not respect the views of others, does not listen to them, or take them seriously. These last two subjects – lack of understanding by foreigners and lack of respect by us – cannot be addressed by preaching or by telling the world how wonderful we are. In fact, the technique of standing in one place and spraying a message widely to others is not very effective in today's world.

A better way to communicate is through the generation of a wide and deep conversation. Our role in that conversation is as facilitator and convener. We generate this conversation in the belief that our views will be heard – even if U.S. government actors are not always the authors of those views.

This new approach takes advantage of new social networking technologies like Facebook and YouTube and Second Life, whose essence is multiple, simultaneous conversations, in words and pictures. And, in fact, *the method of communication is itself a reflection of American values.* The medium, as Marshall McLuhan said, is the message. We, as Americans, do not dictate. Rather, we believe that, in a free and open discussion, the best ideas will prevail, and we want to encourage the free expression of views, rather than drowning out words that disturb us.

Joseph Nye, former dean of the Kennedy School of Government at Harvard, has written: "If I am persuaded to go along with your purposes without any explicit threat or exchange taking place – in short, *if my behavior is determined by an observable but intangible attraction – soft power is at work.* Soft power uses a different type of currency (not force, not money) to engender cooperation – an attraction to shared values and the justness and duty of contributing to the achievement of those values."[15]

Public Diplomacy 2.0, endorsed at the highest levels of government during my tenure at the State Department, embodies Nye's description of soft power. Specifically, in 2008, our Education and Cultural Affairs Bureau, under the direction of Goli Ameri, an Iranian-American with experience as a technology executive, launched the first U.S. government social-networking website. The site, ExchangesConnect,[16] on the Ning platform, provides a forum around the topic of international exchanges.

The U.S. government cannot control everything that goes on within this forum (indeed, during the fighting in Gaza, much of the comment on the site was in opposition to U.S. policy), and the lack of control naturally produces some anxiety. But we live in a world in which we have two choices: preach and be ignored, or convene a conversation and be heard – and, if our views are persuasive, have influence. ExchangesConnect is now running its second annual video contest, this one with the theme, "Change Your Climate, Change Our World." Among the top 40 entries are videos from Egypt, Turmenistan, Cuba, and Vietnam.[17]

In 2008, the Bureau of International Information Programs – with such private sector partners as YouTube, the Tisch School at New York University, and NBC Universal -- initiated a video contest called the Democracy Video Challenge, with the theme "Democracy Is..." We wanted contestants, most of them young Internet users, to define democracy for themselves in three-minute films. There were 900 entries from around the world, with the winner chosen by a vote on the Web – which, again, we did not control.

Perhaps the best example of PD 2.0 in action is the Alliance of Youth Movements. In the fall of 2008, a young State Department official named Jared Cohen suggested that I travel to Colombia to see what that government, with U.S. help, had done to encourage young fighters to leave the FARC, the terrorist group (which started in the 1960s as the military wing of Colombia's communist party) that had been killing and kidnapping innocents. Were there lessons here for the demobilization and reintegration of violent extremists in the Middle East?

Also at Cohen's suggestion, I met with the leaders of a spontaneous civilian movement that used Facebook to bring 12 million people into the streets of cities around the world in early 2008 to oppose the FARC. That movement, One Million Voices Against the FARC, had real-life effects, demoralizing FARC fighters and causing them to demobilize. As a result of this and other efforts, the size of the FARC was cut in half and its effectiveness significantly reduced.

The dynamic young founder of the anti-FARC group, Oscar Morales,[18] worked without the support – or, even, at first, the knowledge – of the Colombian government. Morales, a young computer technician, was simply a citizen, angry at what terrorists were doing in his country. This was a model we wanted to replicate. So we decided to bring Morales together with young representatives of similar anti-violence and pro-social-change organizations using the Internet from countries like Egypt, Mexico, and the UK, as well as officials of technology companies such as Facebook, Google, Howcast, and AT&T.

The State Department provided only a small amount of seed money. We were conveners and facilitators. At a New York conference in late 2008, the young people decided to create their own network – which is now called the Alliance of Youth Movements (AYM), with a social networking site, including how-to hub, and a professional executive director.[19] With backing from Secretary Clinton, the group held a conference in Mexico in October, in part with the purpose of pushing back against narco-terrorism, and will hold another meeting next month in London.

Unfortunately, not all PD 2.0 ideas have become reality. We were on the brink of launching the contemporary analogue of "Problems of Communism," the USIA journal that confronted the Soviet ideology for 40 years during the Cold War. Our version, tentatively called "Problems of Extremism" (POE), was planned as a journal, a website, and a platform for conferences. We wanted it to become the locus of liberal thought, promoting freedom, tolerance, and women's rights, with emphasis on the conflicts (which I will explain below) that are occurring in Muslim societies. The POE venture, like AYM, would be a non-profit foundation, with a small amount of seed money provided by the U.S. government and other funding from foreign governments and private institutions.

Finally, a good example of PD 2.0 even before such a rubric existed is the Digital Outreach Team, begun under Ambassador Hughes. Team members go into chat rooms and on interactive websites, in Arabic, Farsi, and Urdu (and, we had planned, Russian), to explain U.S. policy and refute lies and distortions. They identify themselves as working for the U.S. government and provide links to easily accessible facts on the Internet.

Public Diplomacy 2.0 would be an unfulfilled idea if it were not for Web 2.0, the interactive tools now available on the Internet. Yes, Al Qaeda and other violent extremist organizations have exploited the Internet to their advantage, but that edge has diminished – and not just because the jihadist message has worn thin with Al Qaeda's penchant for slaughtering fellow Muslims.

Why? One reason, says analyst Daniel Kimmage in the New York Times, is that "the Qaeda media nexus...is old hat. If Web 1.0 was about creating the snazziest official Web resources and Web 2.0 is about letting users run wild with self-created content and interactivity, Al Qaeda and its affiliates are stuck in 1.0."[20]

The Internet world of Al Qaeda is one of direction: believe this, do that. The Internet world of today is one of interactivity and conversation: I think this, your ideas are unconvincing, I need more information to make up my mind, let's meet at 3 p.m. Thursday for a peaceful protest. In fact, the Internet itself is becoming the locus of Civil Society 2.0.

This new virtual world is democratic. It is an agora. It is not a place for a death cult that counts on keeping its ideology sealed off from criticism. The new world is a marketplace of ideas, and it is no coincidence that Al Qaeda blows up marketplaces.

U.S. INTERNATIONAL BROADCASTING

While taxpayer-funded, non-military U.S. international broadcasting is almost 70 years old, the fundamental principle that underlies it is the same as that of Public Diplomacy 2.0: rather than preaching, the BBG's entities seek to inform and to generate a conversation, also with the ultimate objective of securing American interests. The BBG's broadcasters embody President Obama's notion of mutual interest and mutual respect.

Along with the Fulbright educational exchanges, U.S. international broadcasting is almost certainly the most successful public diplomacy program. It is also the largest. The BBG budget rose from $440 million in 2001 to $758 million in fiscal 2010.

The BBG's success may be attributed in part to its clear mandate. It does one thing and does it well: as a reliable source of news, it presents an accurate, objective and comprehensive view of America and its policies and, through surrogate broadcasters like Radio Free Europe/Radio Liberty (RFE/RL), the BBG serves as a free, mature communications medium in nations lacking in such institutions.

Between 2001 and 2009, the weekly audience of the BBG increased by approximately three-fourths, to 171 million, and nearly the entire increase occurred in languages of strategic importance, such as Arabic, Farsi, and Urdu. Particularly remarkable is the Arabic service, Middle East Broadcasting Network.

Before MBN's launch, just seven years ago, the Arabic audience for BBG – through Voice of America (VOA) radio, was only two to three million. Today, the total audience – that is, listeners and viewers who tune in at least once a week on radio or TV – is 35 million. In the 14 countries where the BBG has done research (Algeria, Bahrain, Egypt, Iraq, Jordan, Kuwait, Lebanon, Morocco, Oman, Qatar, Saudi Arabia, Syria, Tunisia, and UAE), 92 million adults have access to satellite TV. Alhurra's weekly audience in these 14 countries, as measured consistent with international broadcasting standard, is 27.5 million -- almost a third of the potential audience.[21]

While Alhurra's weekly audience is less than the weekly audiences for Al Jazeera and Al Arabiya, it is greater than all other non-Arab broadcasters combined (including BBC Arabic). Alhurra and the BBG's Arabic radio network, Radio Sawa, have a weekly audience of 71 percent of Iraqis and 61 percent of Syrians. Together, Sawa and Alhurra reach an upduplicated audience of more than 35 million. In each of the 14 researched markets, Alhurra figures among the top 20 TV channels of all kinds (entertainment as well as news), except in Saudi Arabia, where it is 21st. Surveys find that Alhurra is considered "trustworthy" by at least 90 percent of its viewers in such countries as Syria, Egypt, Jordan, and Kuwait. In the past few weeks, Alhurra, with a larger audience in Iraq than Al Jazeera, has provided vigorous, objective coverage of that country's elections.

Meanwhile, two other BBG entities, RFE/RL and VOA are together broadcasting a stream in Pashto and Dari 24/7 into Afghanistan, where RFE/RL is the number-one news station in the country. Separately, last December, RFE/RL began broadcasting in local Pashto dialects to Pakistan and the border regions with Afghanistan over a new station called Radio Mashaal, offering an alternative to extremist stations in the region. Radio Deewa, a product of VOA, is now broadcasting nine hours a day in Pashto to federally administered tribal areas of Pakistan, reaching 14% of Pashtuns in this critical area.

VOA has the largest combined radio and television audience in Iran of all international broadcasters, with one in four adult Iranians tuning in to a VOA program once a week. PNN broadcasts seven hours of television daily, repeated in a 24 hour format, and five hours of radio. Programming is also available around the clock on the Internet.

At the end of December, VOA launched a new Web application that allows users in Iran to download and send content to VOA's Persian News Network with their iPhones. The application enables users of Apple iPhones and Android phones to get the latest news from PNN and, with a single click, to send links to VOA stories via Facebook and Twitter pages and email accounts. The application will be available shortly in Apple's online store, PNN's Web site (http://www1.voanews.com/persian/news/) and on PNN's Facebook and Twitter accounts.

The application also gives Iran's "citizen journalists" the opportunity to use their iPhones and Android phones to send video and still pictures taken on their devices to a secure Web site where VOA's PNN editors can download the images and review them for possible broadcast use and Web posting.

RFE/RL's Radio Farda continues to provide hard-hitting news and information in a 24/7 format that gets stories to the Iranian people that their government denies them on domestic media outlets. Radio Farda has reported the harsh crackdown in the aftermath of the flawed June election.

The BBG is focused not only on areas of conflict. It has a major presence in Africa, where it has gained a reputation for broadcasting useful information about health; in Cuba;

Russia; and in parts of Asia where freedom of the press is constrained, such as China and Burma. BBG budgets rose significantly in the seven years following the 9/11 attacks.

Because of evolving audience tastes, as well as legal, political, and technical obstacles to radio and TV in countries such as Russia, the BBG has moved more and more toward reaching audiences through the Internet.

But all is not well. The BBG's purpose and achievements need to gain greater understanding and support among policymakers.

The BBG is an independent agency of the federal government, with eight governors, four from each party, nominated by the president and confirmed by the Senate, plus the Secretary of State, who typically appoints as representative the Under Secretary of State for Public Diplomacy and Public Affairs.

Unfortunately, in recent years, the confirmation process has become fraught with difficulty. As a result, although it occurred in June 2007 – more than two and a half years ago -- my confirmation was the last voted by the Senate for a BBG governor. Natural attrition has left the BBG with only four governors plus the Secretary of State – a total of five, which is the minimum for a quorum.

The BBG is no ordinary board; its governors serve as a collective chief executive officer for this critical organization. Imagine a CEO who serves with barely half of his or her intellectual and physical strength, and you'll get an idea of the status of the BBG today. I urge the Senate to confirm a full slate of governors immediately. *The lack of action over the past few years on confirmations of governors is a sad manifestation of the overall standing of public diplomacy among too many policymakers.* We can't wait.

TRADITIONAL PUBLIC DIPLOMACY

My predecessor, Ambassador Hughes, gave me two excellent pieces of advice, and I passed them on to my successor: First, the best thing we can do for the long run in traditional public diplomacy is put Americans face to face with foreigners, and, second, we can't do enough English teaching.

We put people face to face mainly through exchanges. Ambassador Hughes's great accomplishment was expanding these programs that had been languishing. The U.S. now brings about 50,000 people from other countries to the U.S. on programs like Fulbright and YES (for high school students, mainly from Muslim-majority nations) and International Visitor Programs, whose graduates have included such figures as Hamid Karzai and Margaret Thatchter, when they were rising stars.

Education is America's greatest brand, and we have bounced back dramatically from 9/11. Today, despite tougher visa requirements, more than 600,000 foreign students are matriculating in the US – an all-time record.

Fulbright is the largest single public diplomacy program of the State Department, with federal support that has been increasing consistently for the past six years,[22] thanks to the efforts of President Bush and the U.S. Congress. In fiscal 2004, federal spending on Fulbright was $150 million; in 2010, it will be $254 million. Fulbright too has become more strategic. Exchanges for university students and scholars in both directions have increased substantially in Muslim-majority countries, including Afghanistan, Indonesia, Turkey, and Iraq. The

Fulbright program in Pakistan is the largest in the world. Globally, applications are at their highest level in history.

While the U.S. government is the top funder of Fulbright scholarships, there are substantial contributions coming now from 100 countries, including major investments from India, China, Turkey, Chile, and Indonesia. And as an example of the public-private partnerships that are so critical to the success of public diplomacy, U.S. universities contribute $30 million a year in cost-sharing.

The problem with exchanges, however, is that they are expensive. To succeed in the future, public diplomacy will need to find ways to use technology to reach a wider audience with each individual exchange – through video, for example, or sophisticated use of social networking media – and to find ways to engage more private-sector partners.

As for English, the United States teaches it because the world wants to learn it – because governments and people in practically every country in the world see English as a way to move up economically. Everywhere, including difficult neighborhoods like Yemen, the West Bank and Gaza. In teaching English, we teach a language and tell America's story. Spending on English-teaching programs by the State Department has risen from $6.8 million in fiscal 2004 to $46.6 million this year.

Educational and cultural (including sports) exchanges, plus the outreach activities (such as sending speakers aboard and operating America.gov websites in seven different languages) of the Bureau of International Information Programs, comprise what I term "traditional public diplomacy." These programs are important. They work, as recent assessments and evaluations have shown. The challenge is to improve efficiency and flexibility.

TWO URGENT TASKS

But, to return to Strategic Public Diplomacy and the war of ideas: What are the urgent tasks today? Here are two....

A New Narrative: The most pernicious idea in Muslim societies is that the United States wants to destroy Islam and replace it with Christianity. Vast majorities in many countries believe this narrative, and it is the prism through which they view almost all U.S. activities.[23]

But to try to refute this narrative head-on is not easy. A better approach is to promote a different narrative – one that reflects the truth. The State Department's new strategic plan for public diplomacy lists "Shape the narrative" as one of five strategic objectives. That's encouraging, but the narrative that the plan has in mind appears, from the document, to be U.S.-centric and difficult to convey and sustain. The objective appears to be to explain American policies better and to "counter misinformation and disinformation."[24] Certainly, those activities must be part of any public diplomacy strategy, but the more valuable narrative to spread is not about the U.S. at all.

The indispensable narrative is the real story of what is happening in Muslim societies. It is a narrative of three conflicts that are within Muslim societies. Yes, the U.S. is deeply affected by them, but they are intra-Muslim conflicts and need to be understood that way. They are:

- Religion and terror. A small group of violent reactionaries -- led by Al Qaeda, the Taliban, and allied groups -- is trying, through horrifying brutality, to bring more than one billion Muslims into line with a sweeping totalitarian doctrine, inconsistent with the tenets of Islam.

Growing numbers of Muslims are waking up to threat and are opposing and ostracizing the violent extremists in their midst -- even in Pakistan, where a terrible threat had been widely ignored. Even as U.S. favorability has slipped, support for Al Qaeda and the Taliban has plummeted. In spring 2008, some 25 percent of Pakistanis had a favorable opinion of al Qaeda, with 34 percent unfavorable -- a disturbingly close split. Today, just 9 percent have a favorable opinion, with 61 percent unfavorable. So too with the Taliban: The ratings shifted from 27 percent favorable and 33 percent unfavorable in 2008 to 10 percent favorable and 70 percent unfavorable today.[25] Our job in public diplomacy should be to help spread information about these reactionary groups trying to destroy Islam.

- Iran and proxies. Along with its proxies Syria, Hezbollah, and Hamas, Iran is confronting the vast majority of Arab nations, including Saudi Arabia, Jordan, and Egypt. This Iran-vs.-Arab conflict is also part of the Sunni-Shia conflict that is playing out elsewhere, including Iraq, but Iran's threat transcends religion. Regardless of sectarian bent, Muslim communities are rising to oppose the attempts by Iran and its intelligence services – in particular the Qods Force - - to extend Shia extremism and influence throughout the world. Here, public diplomacy can support those who are struggling to change the policies of the Iranian regime.
- Democracy and human rights, especially the rights of women. Many Arab governments have denied their citizens what Egyptian activist Saad Eddin Ibrahim has called "the infrastructure of democracy": rule of law, independent judiciary, free media, gender equality, and autonomous civil society. These necessities of liberty are more important than ballots dropped in a box, as we have seen by the actions of the terrorist Hamas regime in Gaza.

A widespread criticism among Muslims is that the United States has not pressed authoritarian allies to democratize. For both moral and strategic reasons, we have a stake in supporting free societies with accountable governments. The reality of democracies thriving in Muslim societies -- like Turkey and Indonesia -- is a powerful counterweight to the canard that Islam and political freedom can't coexist. Here, public diplomacy can remind those advancing freedom and democracy that they aren't alone and that history, including our own, is replete with examples of brave advocates.

For the immediate future, our job in public diplomacy is to promote this accurate narrative in everything we do. We can do it while at the same time emphasizing America's values -- concepts of pluralism, freedom, and opportunity that run counter to the extremists' ideology. We should emphasize that the United States won't be a passive bystander in these struggles. We will advance our own ideals and interests - - which include promoting a comprehensive two-state solution between Israel and the Palestinians.

But it is challenging and empowering Muslim communities to take on the three great struggles themselves, with the United States as a constructive partner, that is an approach that will overturn the extremists' narrative and help shape a new, honest, and positive storyline --

in which Muslims see themselves not as victims but as central protagonists in global struggles for justice.[26]

Strategic Public Diplomacy in Iran: The second example is one I laid out in a recent article with Mike Doran, a former colleague who now teaches at NYU. It concerns Iran.

Here we are squandering a great opportunity. Our objective is an Iran free of nuclear weapons. Two routes to achieving the objective appear highly unlikely: armed conflict or successful official diplomacy. But public diplomacy can work – mainly because of the brave opposition movement that developed after the June elections. What are we doing to help? It's hard to see. Doran and I urge:

- Providing moral and educational support for the Green Movement in Iran by publicizing what worked in Ukraine or Georgia, dubbing into Farsi documentaries on the fall of Ceausescu, Milosevic and Pinochet; the transitions in South Africa and Poland; and the achievements of the U.S. civil-rights movement. The great fear of the Iranian regime is that a nonviolent civil resistance in the form of a color movement, like those in states of the former Soviet Union, will gain authority and legitimacy and, ultimately, power through democratic means. The regime is right to be afraid.

- Tightening sanctions on the Iranian economy and publicizing the connection between regime belligerence and economic malaise. The slogans of the protesters demonstrate that they are connecting the dots between the regime's foreign policy and economic privation.

- Doing all we can to increase communications within Iran, as well as between Iran and the outside world, including boosting broadcasting by Radio Farda and Voice of America satellite TV and spreading tools to facilitate mobile-phone messaging and social networking -- and helping Iranians get the technology to overcome regime attempts to block and censor. In testimony in February in the House, Mehdi Khalaji and J. Scott Carpenter urged this approach as well. They state that Ayatollah "Khamenei often expresses his belief that he is in a soft war with the West. For him, all new telecommunication, Internet and satellite technology are Western tools to defeat him in this war."[27] We should be furnishing that technology. We should also be vigorously opposing Iranian interference with satellite transmissions, in violation of international agreements.[28]

- Finally, aggressively refuting, in campaign style, the key propositions of Iranian propaganda, such as that the Green Movement is marginal and lacks support and that the West wants Iran to be a technological backwater. A serious strategic communications program for Iran could have dozens, even hundreds, of programs. They might range from a campaign, including posters and TV commercials featuring Gov. Arnold Schwarzenegger, to encourage Iranians to come to California to be trained as high-tech experts; to an aggressive effort to expose the Iranian agents who beat and seize demonstrators; to support for an interactive satellite TV station that appeals to young people and urges them to express free choice in cultural and social, as well as political matters; to financial aid to the families of victims of the crackdown on demonstrators.

RECOMMENDATIONS AND CONCLUSION

Here, then are seven recommendations for a more effective public diplomacy:

1. Make public diplomacy a top priority. The entire government should know that the President sees public diplomacy as a critical part of America"s overall national security strategy.
2. Make a distinction between what I call Strategic Public Diplomacy – that is, PD with clear objectives that can be achieved in a definable period, such as war-of-ideas goals – and long-term ongoing public diplomacy, which may be shaped strategically (with emphasis on exchanges with Muslim-majority nations, for example) but which is more general in its effects.
3. Institute a strong interagency structure and process led by an official with a close connection to the President. During the Bush Administration, that official was the Under Secretary of State for Public Diplomacy and Public Affairs, but other structures are possible.
4. Launch an inter-agency program quickly to show that public diplomacy can achieve national security goals. Iran should be the immediate focus.
5. Promote the successes and enhance the understanding of the function and purpose of the Broadcasting Board of Governors. Confirm the new slate of governors. The BBG is a precious asset that must not be ignored or denigrated.
6. Expand Public Diplomacy 2.0, using technology to facilitate and convene a broad and deep global conversation in which we can more effectively influence and inform. At the same time, put teeth into Secretary Clintons affirmation that the U.S. supports open global communications. One step would be to challenge Iranian jamming of satellite broadcasts.
7. Establish a culture of measurable results. All public diplomacy programs must be assessed and evaluated to see how well they "move the needle." Measuring can be difficult and expensive, but, without it, we can"t tell whether work is succeeding or failing.

Finally, remember that public diplomacy performs its mission of achieving the national interest in a particular way: by understanding, informing, engaging, and influencing foreign publics. While the "influencing" part may be the most important, the "understanding" part comes first. You can't persuade if you don't truly understand the people you are trying to persuade.

Senator J. William Fulbright, who created the Fulbright exchanges in 1946, put it well: The "essence of intercultural education," he said, referring to what would become one of our most effective public diplomacy programs, is "empathy, the ability to see the world as others see it, and to allow for the possibility that others may see something we have failed to see...."[29]

Another key word in public diplomacy is compassion. At the Bush Institute, we base our programs on four key principles of the former president: freedom, responsibility, opportunity, and compassion. Americans are compassionate people, and that trait needs to be reflected in all that we do in public diplomacy. It is the foundation of Public Diplomacy 2.0, and, in the goals we seek, it is the driving force behind Strategic Public Diplomacy.

I ended my testimony before this committee in January 2008 with the following sentence, which I believe bears repeating:

The task ahead is to tell the world the story of a good and compassionate nation and, at the same time, to engage in the most important ideological contest of our time – a contest that we will win.

Thank you.

End Notes

[1] "Changing Minds, Winning Peace," report of the Advisory Group on Public Diplomacy for the Arab and Muslim World, submitted to the Committee on Appropriations, U.S. House of Representatives, Oct. 1, 2003, p. 8.

[2] See many examples, including this speech last year by Yale Richmond, a retired foreign service officer: http://whirledview.typepad.com/whirledview/2009/12/cultural-exchange-andthe-cold-war

[3] "Changing Minds, Winning Peace," pp. 8 and 13. I served on this panel, created by Congress and chaired by Ambassador Edward Djerejian.

[4] http://www.defense

[5] http://www.nytimes.com/2008/10/19/world/asia/19iht-19afghan.17083733.html

[6] http://www.memri.org/report/en/0/0/0/0/0/0/2892.htm

[7] "Afghanistan and Pakistan Regional Stabilization Strategy," as updated Feb. 2010, Office of the Special Representative for Afghanistan and Pakistan, U.S. Department of State.

[8] http://www.icrd.org/

[9] http://www.layalina.tv/productions/lifeafterdeath.html

[10] http://georgewbush-whitehouse.archives.gov/nsc/nsct/2006/

[11] www.whitehouse.gov/blog

[12] For a more complete exposition of this subject, see my article, "It's Not About Us," on ForeignPolicy.com: http://www.foreignpolicy.com/articles/2009/09/01/its_not_about_us?page=0,0

[13] President Zardari of Pakistan has made this statement many times, for example: http://www.memri.org/report/en/0/0/0/0/0/0/2892.htm

[14] Secretary Clinton immediately supported the Alliance of Youth Movements and in January gave a speech on Internet freedom and met with high-tech executives on improving the use of social media in public diplomacy: http://voices.washingtonpost.com/posttech/2010/01/sec_clinton_dines_hightech_ti.html?wprss=posttech

[15] Joseph S. Nye, Jr., *Soft Power: The Means to Success in World Politics*, PublicAffairs, 2004, p. 7.

[16] http://connect.state.gov/

[17] http://connectcontest.state.gov/contests/change-your-climate-

[18] Oscar Morales in February became a Visiting Fellow of the George W. Bush Institute in Dallas.

[19] http://youthmovements.howcast.com/

[20] www.nytimes.com/2008/06/26/opinion/26kimmage.html

[21] The source of these data is the BBG itself, which contracts with a firm which independently engages such respected survey organizations. Most of the Middle East research was done by ACNielsen. The BBG uses the standard audience measurement for international broadcasters, asking whether the respondent watched or listened in the past week.

[22] www.fulbright.org/conference. Marianne Craven is Managing Director for Academic Programs at the Bureau of Educational and Cultural Affairs, U.S. Department of State.

[23] See sources that I cited in my confirmation testimony in January 2008: WorldPublicOpinion.org, Program on International Policy Attitudes, University of Maryland, "Muslim Opinion on US Policy, Attacks on Civilians and al Qaeda," April 24, 2007. A press release summarizing the study began, "An in-depth poll of four major Muslim countries has found that in all of them large majorities believe that undermining Islam is a key goal of US foreign policy." See http://worldpublicopinion.org/pipa/articles/brmiddleeastnafricara/346.php?lb=brme&pnt=346 &nid=&id=. Also, "America's Image in the World: Findings from the Pew Global Attitudes Project, Testimony of Andrew Kohut, Pew Research Center, before the Committee on Foreign Affairs, U.S. House of Representatives, March 14, 2007.

[24] "Public Diplomacy: Strengthening U.S. Engagement With the World," Office of the Under Secretary of State for Public Diplomacy and Public Affairs, 2010, pp. 8-11.

[25] http://pewresearch.org/pubs/1148/pakistan-little-support-for-terrorists-

[26] See "What Obama Should Tell Muslims," my op-ed from the Boston Globe, with Juan Zarate: http://www.boston.com/bostonglobe/editorial_opinion/oped/articles/2009/05/27/what_obama_s hould_tell_muslims/

[27] http://www.washingtoninstitute.org/templateC14.php?CID=512. Testimony before the House Committee on Foreign Affairs Subcommittee on the Middle East and South Asia. Both Khalaji, who was trained in the seminars of Qom before moving to the United States, and Carpenter, a former Deputy Assistant Secretary of State, are fellows of the Washington Institute for Near East Policy.

[28] http://www.bbg.gov/pressroom/printerfr.cfm?articleID=443. VOA and BBC transmissions were both jammed, leading a European satellite operator to take down Persian TV (PTV), the BBC Farsi network. VOA's Persian News Network is also sporadically removed. "Iranians keep asking me why the west is so powerless," Sadeq Saba, head of PTV, wrote on his blog. "They say: 'This is a rogue government jamming international signals. How will the west stop Iran getting nuclear weapons if they can't deal with this?'" (http://www.guardian 0/j an/14/bbc-joins-iran-tv-protest)

[29] www.fulbright.org/ifad/manual/quotes.pdf

In: U.S. Public Diplomacy: Background and Issues
Editor: Matthew B. Morrison

ISBN: 978-1-61728-888-3
© 2010 Nova Science Publishers, Inc.

Chapter 7

STATEMENT OF JUDITH MCHALE, UNDER SECRETARY FOR PUBLIC DIPLOMACY AND PUBLIC AFFAIRS, SENATE FOREIGN RELATIONS COMMITTEE, SUBCOMMITTEE ON INTERNATIONAL OPERATIONS AND ORGANIZATIONS, HUMAN RIGHTS, DEMOCRACY, AND GLOBAL WOMEN'S ISSUES

Judith Mchale

Chairman Kaufman, Members of the Subcommittee, thank you for your invitation to appear before you this morning.

I appreciate this opportunity to discuss with you the state of America's public diplomacy, the framework that we are developing to more closely align our activities with the nation's foreign policy objectives, and the challenges we continue to face.

Before I begin, I want to acknowledge the legacies of my predecessors, several of whom testified before you this morning. In a span of just a few years, they put our nation's public diplomacy on a trajectory that laid the foundation for a new approach to public diplomacy for the 21st Century.

Throughout the past year we have witnessed the strong, energetic, and consistent commitment of President Obama and Secretary Clinton to public diplomacy. From the President's speeches in Cairo and Accra, to the many events that the Secretary has held directly with international audiences around the world, they have made public diplomacy an integral part of their approach to foreign policy. Both understand that engagement with global publics must be an essential part of our foreign policy apparatus as we pursue our policy objectives, seek to advance our national interests, and strive to ensure our national security.

THE WORLD WE FACE

The communications revolution that has rocketed around the world has had an impact on the attitudes, behaviors, and aspirations of people everywhere. Public opinion is influencing foreign governments and shaping world affairs to an unprecedented degree. In the past 25 years 40 new electoral democracies have emerged. This is a great triumph for our belief in the democratic form of government. As citizens in these countries exercise their rights, their decisions affect not only the future of their own countries but also the future of the United States and that of the rest of the world. In this context, our efforts to engage foreign publics through public diplomacy are more important than ever before.

Today, 45 percent of the world's population is under the age of 25. These young people —many of whom face enormous social and economic challenges— have come of age during a period of limited direct engagement with the United States.

They communicate in new ways and with tools which are constantly evolving. As we reach out to this new generation we must develop strategies to engage and inspire them. Increasingly our opponents and adversaries are developing sophisticated media strategies to spread disinformation and rumors which ignite hatred and spur acts of terror and destruction. We must be ever vigilant and respond rapidly to their attacks against us.

Women account for over 50% of the world's population and yet in too many parts of the world they lack access to education and fundamental rights. Countless reports and studies demonstrate that increased participation by women in the social, economic, and political lives of their countries results in more stable productive societies. We must continue to develop and deploy new programs to support and empower women as they seek to improve their lives and communities.

The global challenges we face today require a complex, multi-dimensional approach to public diplomacy. Our Government must develop new ways to communicate and engage with foreign publics at all levels of society. In doing so, we must do a better job of listening; learn how people in other countries and cultures listen to us; understand their desires and aspirations; and provide them with information and services of value to them. In essence, we must develop ways to become woven into the fabric of the daily lives of people around the world as we seek to create strong and lasting relationships with them.

A STRATEGIC APPROACH FOR THE 21ST CENTURY

We must act boldly and decisively to develop a clear, consistent, and comprehensive approach to public diplomacy. Over the past eight months we have undertaken a focused and disciplined review of the current state of public diplomacy and public affairs at the Department of State. As part of that review, we have consulted with individuals involved in public diplomacy here on Capitol Hill, at the National Security Council and the Department of Defense, and at all levels within the Department of State. We have also met with representatives of academia, nongovernmental organizations and the private sector. I have traveled to embassies and consulates in Europe, the Middle East, South Asia, and East Asia. And in October we hosted a global conference attended by all our Public Affairs Officers to ensure that we understood the needs of our Posts around the world.

This process showed that in significant ways our public diplomacy was working well to advance America's interests. But it also revealed a great degree of consensus about what needs to be changed to align it to current priorities and guide our efforts going forward. Last month, we began rolling out the results of our review: a new global strategic framework for public diplomacy that I believe will give us the focus and capabilities we need in the complex environment of the 21st Century.

The new framework rests on the core mission of public diplomacy to support the achievement of U.S. foreign policy goals and objectives, advance national interests, and enhance national security by informing and influencing foreign publics and by expanding and strengthening the relationship between the people and government of the United States and citizens of the rest of the world.

As part of our review we identified five strategic imperatives: to pro-actively shape global narratives; expand and strengthen people-to-people relationships; counter violent extremism; better inform policy-making; and, redeploy resources in strategic alignment with shifting priorities. Moving forward, we are taking steps to ensure that all our activities support these requirements.

First, in this information saturated age we must do a better job of framing our national narrative. We must become more pro-active and less reactive. We are bolstering our communications outreach—locally, nationally, regionally, and globally—to inform, inspire, and persuade our target audiences and to counter misinformation. We are working with our posts around the world to develop and implement targeted media engagement plans to both push positive stories and to respond rapidly to negative attacks against us. We will expand the role of our regional Media Hubs, and enhance their capabilities as digital engagement centers to ensure that we are fully represented in dialogues in both traditional and new venues for information and debate.

In December , I sent a cable to our Public Affairs Officers worldwide directing them to be more aggressive and strategic in their communications efforts. As an example of our new forward-leaning stance across the range of issues, our Embassies successfully changed the global narrative about our rescue and relief efforts following the tragic earthquake in Haiti. In support of these efforts, we are creating the new position of Deputy Assistant Secretary of State for International Media Support within State's Bureau of Public Affairs to facilitate coordinated and high level attention to foreign media.

Second, we are expanding and strengthening people-to-people relationships— relationships based on mutual trust and respect—through our public diplomacy programs and platforms. In addition to growing our highly successful exchange programs, we are broadening the demographic base of those with whom we engage beyond traditional elites. We are using social networking and connective technologies such as Facebook, YouTube, and Twitter to expand our reach and ensure that we are represented in new media and conversation spaces. Last year, in connection with the President's speech in Ghana, we used a combination of traditional and new media to actively engage with millions of individuals across Africa. And in January, I participated in a Skype enabled video conference which allowed high school students in Boston to talk to their peers in Jalalabad.

We will continue to support programs that simultaneously advance U.S. national interests and offer desired skills to targeted audiences. These programs include expanded English language teaching and teacher training, collaboration and skill- building in science, technology, and entrepreneurship, programs designed to provide women with the skills they need to advance within their societies, and, educational advising that promotes the broad array of education opportunities offered by US academic institutions.

We are evaluating opportunities to revitalize and establish American Centers and Corners as spaces for public engagement. And we are working with organizations across the country to expand our cultural programs to showcase the breadth and depth of America's cultural heritage. Recognizing that participants in our programs are among our best ambassadors, we are investing new resources both to enable us to remain better connected to alumni of our exchange programs and to enable them to better connect with each other so that they can build upon their shared experiences.

Third, we are expanding our efforts to respond rapidly to terrorist and violent extremist messages and proactively counter the narrative that has allowed them to disseminate misinformation and recruit new followers. In Washington and at our Embassies and Consulates overseas, we will aggressively harness new and traditional media to communicate U.S. perspectives and counter misinformation and disinformation. We will redouble our efforts to empower credible voices within societies. To do so, we will continue to provide tools and platforms for independent voices to expand their reach, and leverage partnerships to train religious and secular leaders with local influence in issues of development, health, and education.

Fourth, we are taking steps to ensure that our policies and programs are informed upfront by a clear understanding of attitudes and opinions of foreign publics. We are establishing the position of Deputy Assistant Secretary of State for Public Diplomacy in each of the regional bureaus. These officers will be responsible for ensuring that a public diplomacy perspective is incorporated as part of senior policy deliberations and for coordinating all our public diplomacy initiatives throughout their respective regions. We are also strengthening our research and planning capacity. In doing so we will draw on the resources of the Bureau of Intelligence and Research at the State Department , the Broadcasting Board of Governors, media reporting from the Open Source Center, and others to provide us with the information and data we need for this critical task.

Finally, we are taking steps to ensure a strategic allocation of resources in support of today's foreign policy priorities. We are strengthening the Policy, Planning and Resource function within my office and we are reestablishing multi-year public diplomacy plans for all Posts. These plans will set forth our public diplomacy mission in the host country, analyze target audiences, inventory continuing and innovative tactics to achieve our goals, identify the resources necessary for success, and integrate realistic measurements of effectiveness. In Washington we will examine each plan to ensure congruence with our global objectives and allocation of public diplomacy resources in line with current priorities.

COORDINATION AT ALL LEVELS

As we implement the new global strategic framework for public diplomacy, we have placed renewed emphasis on coordination both in Washington and overseas to ensure that our efforts complement and, where possible, reinforce the activities of other departments and agencies.

We participate in the National Security Council (NSC) -led Interagency Policy Coordination (IPC) process. The NSC brings together senior working-level stakeholders from across the interagency for a Strategic Communications IPC meeting on a weekly basis. These meetings address a wide range of issues including global, regional, and country-specific matters. They are designed to coordinate, develop, and de-conflict communications programs and activities across U.S. government agencies. My staff also takes part in a variety of other staff-level coordination bodies, including the bi-weekly Small Table Group at the National Counterterrorism Center.

The Global Strategic Engagement Center (GSEC), which is part of my office, is specifically chartered to support the NSC's Global Engagement Directorate. We are expanding and upgrading GSEC to strengthen its ability to contribute across a broad range of U.S. government strategic communications and global engagement activities. To head the new GSEC, I have recruited Ambassador Richard LeBaron, formerly our Ambassador to Kuwait and one of our senior-most Foreign Service officers. He will arrive on the job this summer.

We also enjoy a close and productive working relationship with our partners at the Department of Defense. I talk and meet regularly with my counterparts there on both specific programs and on broader strategic issues, such as potential rebalancing of the respective roles, responsibilities, and resources of State and Defense in the public diplomacy and strategic communications arenas. I recently visited General Petraeus in Tampa to discuss challenges and opportunities in his region of responsibility and how we can work more effectively with CENTCOM. I have also met several times with Admiral Olson of the Special Operations Command (SOCOM) to put our heads together on ways to improve current cooperation between State and SOCOM.

THE NEW APPROACH: A CASE STUDY --- PAKISTAN

Last summer, my office worked closely with our Embassy in Islamabad, Special Representative for Afghanistan and Pakistan Richard Holbrooke, USAID, and DoD to draft the Pakistan Communications Plan, a copy of which has been provided to the Committee.

The Pakistan Plan has four broad goals: expand media outreach, counter extremist propaganda, build communications capacity, and strengthen people-to-people ties. Our plan links elements of traditional public diplomacy with innovative new tools.

For instance, recognizing that extremist voices dominate in some of Pakistan's media markets, we instituted a rapid response unit and a 24-hour multilingual hotline for the Embassy to respond to attacks, threats, and propaganda from the Taliban, al Qaeda, and their sympathizers. This approach reversed a previous approach of not actively countering such propaganda. It has been an uphill battle but, as our voice gets more frequent play, the impact on the discourse in Pakistan's media has been noticeable.

As we strengthen our people-to-people ties with Pakistanis, our aim has been to increase positive American presence on the ground in Pakistan. To do this we are focusing on more exchanges, more presence, more Lincoln Centers, more face-to- face meetings with engaged citizens in Pakistan, and more non-official contacts between Pakistanis and Americans in Pakistan.

Secretary Clinton's October 2009 visit to Pakistan was planned and executed in coordination with the themes of our strategic plan. Her focus on issues of education, jobs, and reliable electric power responded to what we had identified as central concerns of Pakistanis. Her extensive series of public engagement activities carried out the Plan's emphasis on rejuvenating our personal, face-to-face diplomacy. Her visits to historical and cultural venues underscored American respect for and desire for partnership with the people of Pakistan. Perhaps the most telling moment came during a press conference during which Pakistani Foreign Minister Qureshi stated that the Secretary's visit had been a success precisely because it had manifested a "policy shift" toward a focus on "people-centric" relations. This was and is precisely our message.

While very few countries will require plans on the order of Pakistan, henceforth we will ensure that our public diplomacy strategic plans for each Mission incorporate rigorous strategic analysis to drive focus and coordination at the post level.

Mr. Chairman, let me say in closing that I believe this is a moment of great opportunity to redefine our relationship with people around the world and to build bridges of knowledge and understanding with people everywhere. In doing so, I believe we will improve lives and support our national interests. I look forward to working with you as we seek to achieve these goals.

In: U.S. Public Diplomacy: Background and Issues
Editor: Matthew B. Morrison

ISBN: 978-1-61728-888-3
© 2010 Nova Science Publishers, Inc.

Chapter 8

NATIONAL FRAMEWORK FOR STRATEGIC COMMUNICATION

The White House

Dear Mr. President:
Pursuant to section 1055 of the Duncan Hunter National Defense Authorization Act for Fiscal Year 2009, I am providing a report on my Administration's comprehensive interagency strategy for public diplomacy and strategic communication of the Federal government.
Sincerely,

The Honorable Joseph R. Biden, Jr.
President of the Senate
Washington, D.C. 20510

Dear Madam Speaker:

Pursuant to section 1055 of the Duncan Hunter National Defense Authorization Act for Fiscal Year 2009, I am providing a report on my Administration's comprehensive interagency strategy for public diplomacy and strategic communication of the Federal government.

Sincerely,

The Honorable Nancy Pelosi
Speaker of the
House of Representatives
Washington, D.C. 20515-0508

PURPOSE OF REPORT

The Duncan Hunter National Defense Authorization Act for Fiscal Year 2009 requires the President to submit to the appropriate committees of Congress a report on a comprehensive interagency strategy for public diplomacy and strategic communication.

EXECUTIVE SUMMARY

Across all of our efforts, effective strategic communications are essential to sustaining global legitimacy and supporting our policy aims. Aligning our actions with our words is a shared responsibility that must be fostered by a culture of communication throughout the government. We must also be more effective in our deliberate communication and engagement, and do a better job understanding the attitudes, opinions, grievances, and concerns of peoples -- not just elites -- around the world. Doing so is critical to allow us to convey credible, consistent messages, develop effective plans and to better understand how our actions will be perceived.

Our study has revealed the need to clarify what strategic communication means and how we guide and coordinate our communications efforts. In this chapter, we describe "strategic communication" as the synchronization of our words and deeds as well as deliberate efforts to communicate and engage with intended audiences. We also explain the positions, processes, and interagency working groups we have created to improve our ability to better synchronize words and deeds, and better coordinate communications and engagement programs and activities. These changes are already producing visible results; however, we still have much ground to cover.

We recognize the need to ensure an appropriate balance between civilian and military efforts. As a result, a process has been initiated to review existing programs and resources to identify current military programs that might be better executed by other Departments and Agencies. This process includes an interagency working group tasked to develop short-, medium-, and long-term options for addressing issues pertaining to budgets, personnel, and future programs and activities.

DEFINING STRATEGIC COMMUNICATION

Over the last few years, the term "strategic communication" has become increasingly popular. However, different uses of the term "strategic communication" have led to significant confusion. As a result, we believe it is necessary to begin this chapter by clarifying what we mean by strategic communication. By "strategic communication(s)" we refer to: (a) the synchronization of words and deeds and how they will be perceived by selected audiences, as well as (b) programs and activities deliberately aimed at communicating and engaging with intended audiences, including those implemented by public affairs, public diplomacy, and information operations professionals.

- *Synchronization.* Coordinating words and deeds, including the active consideration of how our actions and policies will be interpreted by public audiences as an organic part of decision-making, is an important task. This understanding of strategic communication is driven by a recognition that what we do is often more important than what we say because actions have communicative value and send messages. Achieving strategic communication, in this sense, is a shared responsibility. It requires fostering a culture of communication that values this type of synchronization and encourages decision-makers to take the communicative value of actions into account during their decision-making. The most senior levels of government must advocate and implement a culture of communication that is reinforced through mechanisms and processes.
- *Deliberate Communication and Engagement.* The United States Government has a wide range of programs and activities deliberately focused on understanding, engaging, informing, influencing, and communicating with people through public affairs, public diplomacy, information operations and other efforts.

To be clear, we are not creating or advocating for the creation of new terms, concepts, organizations, or capabilities. We are, for the purposes of this chapter, clarifying different aspects of strategic communication. In short, we have taken steps to reinforce the importance of synchronizing words and deeds while simultaneously establishing coordination mechanisms and processes to improve the United States Government's ability to deliberately communicate and engage with intended audiences. The steps we have taken have already borne fruit, but both of these tasks are complex and we acknowledge that more remains to be done.

STRATEGY FOR SYNCHRONIZATION

Synchronizing deeds and words to advance United States Government interests, policies, and objectives is an important part of effective strategic communication and strategy more generally. In the past, the burden for synchronizing words and deeds has often been placed on the shoulders of the communications community, which only controls and executes a subset of the capabilities and activities that need to be synchronized. A key lesson we have learned is that actions well beyond those managed by the communications community have communicative value and impact.

Every action that the United States Government takes sends a message. Synchronization is therefore a shared responsibility that begins with senior leaders and specifically Department- level leadership. They must foster a "culture of communication" that recognizes and incentivizes the importance of identifying, evaluating, and coordinating the communicative value of actions as a proactive and organic part of planning and decision-making at all levels. The communications community supports senior leaders by leading the development of mechanisms and processes that enable and sustain synchronization. These mechanisms include processes designed to: ensure strategic goals and messages are well understood at all levels; raise awareness about the communicative impact of decisions and actions; emphasize the importance of considering such impacts proactively; and ensure that forums exist for deliberating these impacts on high-priority issues and coordinating actions with deliberate communication and engagement.

STRATEGY FOR DELIBERATE COMMUNICATION AND ENGAGEMENT

Deliberate communication and engagement with intended audiences is an important part of the United States Government's ability to meet its national security goals and objectives. Programs and activities focused on communicating and engaging with the public need to be strategic and long-term, not just reactive and tactical. They should also focus on articulating what the United. States is for, not just what we are against. For example, our efforts to communicate and engage with Muslim communities around the world must be defined primarily by a focus on mutual respect and mutual interest, even as we continue to counter violent extremism by focusing on discrediting and delegitimizing violent extremist networks and ideology.

Deliberate communication also helps establish the strategic messages against which our actions are often judged by the public, and deliberate engagement helps identify how our actions are being interpreted and perceived. It is vital that the United States is not focused solely on one-way communication, which is why we have consciously emphasized the importance of "engagement" -- connecting with, listening to, and building long-term relationships with key stakeholders.

The communications community is comprised of a wide variety of organizations and capabilities including, but not limited to: public affairs (PA), public diplomacy (PD), military information operations (I0), and defense support to public diplomacy (DSPD). Planning, development, and execution of engagement programs and activities need to be better coordinated, integrated, and driven by research, information, and intelligence. Steps are being taken to do this, including by specifying roles and responsibilities within departments and across the interagency, piloting an interagency planning process for key policy priorities, and strengthening the coordination of and improving access to relevant research, information, and intelligence.

Interagency Planning and Coordination

Strategic Planning

Across the United States Government, there are a variety of perspectives, models, and approaches used in strategic planning. Over the past year, the interagency communications community has been piloting an intuitive planning process for national-level priorities that attempts to bridge the individual processes of departments and agencies and allows both traditional and nontraditional partners to voluntarily bring their respective capabilities to affect common objectives. This process will be utilized for planning communication and engagement regarding strategic policy priorities. We will continue to monitor, evaluate, and adjust this planning process as necessary.

National-level Interagency Coordination

Interagency Policy Committees (IPCs) led by the NSS coordinate the development and implementation of national security policies by multiple agencies of the United States Government. The Strategic Communication IPC is the main forum for interagency deliberation and coordination of national security policy relating to strategic communications issues. The Strategic Communication IPC also provides policy analysis for consideration by more senior committees of the NSC/HSC system and ensures timely responses to decisions made by the President. The Strategic Communication IPC forms Sub-IPCs as required.

Operational-level Interagency Coordination

The Country Team and the Joint Interagency Coordination Group are the two standing interagency coordination bodies at the operational level. One holds operational responsibility, while the second serves to advise planning efforts.

- The Country Team, headed by the chief of the U.S. diplomatic mission, is the United States Government's senior coordinating and supervising body in-country. Achieving strategic communication, including through synchronization of words and deeds, as well as the effective execution of deliberate communication and engagement, is the responsibility of the Chief of Mission.
- Joint Interagency Coordination Groups (JIACG), established at each Geographic Combatant Command (GCC) headquarters, coordinate with United States Government civilian agencies to conduct operational planning. JIACGs support day-to-day planning at the GCC headquarters, and advise planners regarding civilian agency operations, capabilities, and limitations. While the JIACG has no operational authority, it does provide perspective in the coordinated use of national power and can serve as a referral resource for military planners seeking information and input from communication practitioners in theater or at the national-level.

Information, 'Intelligence, Research and Analysis Support Deliberate Communication and Engagement

Information, intelligence, research, and analysis are key enablers for policy development and strategic planning. Various agencies and offices across the United States Government support efforts to communicate and engage with publics by conducting research and analysis on foreign public opinion, key audiences, the most effective mechanisms for communicating with and engaging them, and violent extremist communications and messages when 'appropriate. However, these efforts should be better coordinated and easier to access, especially in the field. The United States Government's efforts to communicate and engage with foreign publics should be shaped by information, research, and analysis about key audiences.

PRIORITIES FOR STRATEGIC COMMUNICATION

Although the United States Government carries out deliberate communication and engagement worldwide, the priorities for our communication and engagement efforts are the same as overall national security priorities. Communication and engagement, like all other elements of national power, should be designed to support policy goals as well as to achieve specific effects to include:

- Foreign audiences recognize areas of mutual interest with the United States;
- Foreign audiences believe the United States plays a constructive role in global affairs; and
- Foreign audiences see the United States as a respectful partner in efforts to meet complex global challenges.

Our communication and engagement with foreign audiences should emphasize mutual respect and mutual interest. The United States should articulate a positive vision, identifying what we are for, whenever possible, and engage foreign audiences on positive terms. At the same time, our countering violent extremism (CVE) efforts should focus more directly on discrediting, denigrating, and delegitimizing al-Qa'ida and violent extremist ideology.

RESOURCES

It is essential that we balance and optimize investment across the communications community. Resource decisions and applications must be shaped by national priorities and be consistent with existing roles and missions and the capacity of each stakeholder to effectively execute validated tasks and programs. Accountability, assessment, and reporting are critical aspects of our newly established planning process to ensure all major deliberate communication and enaagement efforts are coordinated and effective.

We are aware of concerns that the resources for our efforts need to be "re-balanced" according to established roles and responsibilities. An interagency working group has been formed to evaluate military communication and engagement programs, activities, and investments to identify those that .may be more appropriately funded or implemented by civilian departments and agencies, especially outside theaters of conflict. This review will be framed by four inter-related elements key to the success of "re-balancing" our programs: (a) how best to allocate financial resources; (b) how quickly to streamline or eliminate programs to reduce unnecessary duplication; (c) how to ensure we preserve important military communication and engagement capacities; and (d) how best to expedite revitalizing and strengthening civilian department and agency capabilities, both qualitatively and quantitatively, to enable them to effectively execute these programs and activities.

ROLES AND RESPONSIBILITIES

National Security Staff

The Deputy National Security Advisor for Strategic Communications (DNSA/SC) serves as the National Security Advisor's principal advisor for strategic communications. The Senior Director for Global Engagement (SDGE) is the principal deputy to the DNSA/SC. Together, they are responsible for ensuring that (a) the message-value and communicative impact of actions are considered during decision-making by the National Security Council and Homeland Security Council, (b) the mechanisms to promote strategic communication are in place within the National Security Staff (NSS), and (c) similar mechanisms are developed across the interagency. The DNSA/SC and SDGE are also responsible for guiding and coordinating interagency deliberate communication and engagement efforts, and execute this responsibility through the NSS Directorate for Global Engagement (NSS/GE) and through the Interagency Policy Committee (IPCs) on Strategic Communication, which they chair.

Department of State

The Department of State carries out Public Diplomacy as an essential part of foreign policy. Public Diplomacy (PD) within the State Department is led by the Under Secretary of State for Public Diplomacy and Public Affairs (R). The Department of State distinguishes between Public Affairs, which includes Outreach to domestic publics, and Public Diplomacy (PD), which seeks to promote the national interest of the United States through understanding, engaging, informing, and influencing foreign publics, and by promoting mutual understanding between the people of the United States and people from other nations around the world.

- The Office of the Under Secretary of State for Public Diplomacy and Public Affairs engages functional and regional bureaus within the Department of State to ensure coordination and integration between policy, communication, and engagement objectives.
- The Under Secretary's Office of Policy, Planning, and Resources for Public Diplomacy and Public Affairs (R/PPR) provides long-term strategic planning and performance measurement capability for public diplomacy and public affairs programs. The Under Secretary's Policy Planning Staff oversees implementation of the Department's global strategic plan for public diplomacy and devises plans for discrete events such as Presidential speeches and initiatives and longterm engagement on such areas as climate change, nonproliferation, and global health issues. To achieve these objectives, R/PPR ensures coordination among global PD resources, including the Bureaus of International Information Programs (IIP), Educational and Cultural Affairs (ECA), and Public Affairs (PA), and Public Affairs Officers at overseas missions.
  - The Global Strategic Engagement Center (GSEC) supports interagency efforts on global engagement and strategic communication. GSEC represents the State

Department in the coordination of communications and engagement planning and activities by contributing to the discussions in, disseminating the decisions of, and executing projects as requested by the IPCs for Global Engagement and Strategic Communication. GSEC promulgates interagency decisions and objectives to relevant bureaus and offices in the Department of State and connects decision-makers with government-wide expertise on strategic communication.

- The Public Diplomacy Office Director (PDOD) is the senior U.S.-based PD official in each geographic regional bureau and the International Organizations bureau of the Department of State. PDODs are responsible for integrating communication into decision-making and helping to ensure policies and plans developed at the bureau-level are coordinated with deliberate messaging and engagement programs and activities. PDODs manage and supervise the operations of their respective bureau's PD office. They work closely with Public Affairs Officers overseas, the regional bureau leadership, other bureaus, and the Office of the Under Secretary for Public Diplomacy and Public Affairs to develop PD strategies for their regions and formulate and implement PD initiatives. In conjunction with their bureau Front Office and Executive Office, PDODs propose and manage regional PD budgets and the assignments process for staffing PD positions in the bureaus and the field. The PDOD reports to the bureau Deputy Assistant Secretary designated to oversee PD and PA.

Department of Defense

The Department of Defense (DOD) is a key contributor to our communication and engagement efforts. The key elements of DOD involved include, but are not limited to: information operations (IQ), defense support to public diplomacy (DSPD), public affairs (PA), and civil affairs (CA) -- all working together to accomplish military objectives that support national objectives.

- The Under Secretary of Defense for Policy (USD(P)) is the principal staff assistant and advisor to the Secretary of Defense for all matters on the formulation of national security and defense policy, and the integration and oversight of DoD policy and plans to achieve national security objectives.
  - The Senior Advisor to the USD(P) advises the USD(P) on strategic communication and heads the OUSD(P) Global Strategic Engagement Team (GSET). This team is tasked with facilitating the strategic communication process within OUSD(P) and liaising with other DOD components as appropriate.
  - Primary responsibility for Defense Support for Public Diplomacy is placed with the appropriate regional and functional offices within OUSD(P).
  - OUSD(P) DASD for Plans has the primary responsibility, in close coordination with CUSD(P) GSET and OASD(PA) for ensuring that guidance for strategic communication is included in strategic planning guidance documents, such as

the GEF and Global Force Posture, and for reviewing Combatant Command plans directed by the GEF to ensure strategic communication considerations have been integrated in the plans.

- Within OUSD(P), the Assistant. Secretary of Defense for Special Operations/Low Intensity Conflict and Interdependent Capabilities (ASD (SO/LIC&IC)) serves as the principal staff assistant and advisor to the Secretary of Defense on Special Operations and Low Intensity Conflict matters. The ASD (SO/LIC&IC) exercises policy oversight for Psychological Operations (PSYOP) activities within the DoD, including Military Information Support Teams, ASD (SO/LIC&IC) is responsible for development, coordination, and oversight of the implementation of policy and plans for DoD participation in all United States Government combating terrorism activities, including programs designed to counter violent extremism. The ASD (SO/LIC&IC) coordinates closely with the OUSD(P) GSET.

- The USD(I) is the principal staff assistant and advisor to the Secretary of Defense for Information Operations (IC)). DOD Directive 3600.01 defines Information Operations as "the integrated employment of the core capabilities of Electronic Warfare (EW), Computer Network Operations (CNO), Psychological Operations (PSYOP), Military Deception (MILDEC), and Operations Security (OPSEC), in concert with specified supporting and related capabilities, to influence, disrupt, corrupt, or usurp adversarial human and automated decision making while protecting our own." The USD(I) exercises authority for oversight of IO in coordination with the USD(P) and other OSD offices. OUSD(I) also works with the Military Departments to develop an Information Operations Career Force. Information operations personnel are key participants in the strategic communication process at Combatant Commands and across the Department.

- The ASD(PA) is the principal staff assistant and advisor to the Secretary of Defense for communications activities including, but not exclusively, DOD news media relations, public liaison, and public affairs. ASD(PA) conducts short-, mid-, and long-term communication planning in support of policy objectives. These plans are coordinated extensively across the Department, and with interagency partners as applicable. ASD(PA) also coordinates media engagement and prepares speeches and talking points for the Secretary, Deputy Secretary, and OSD principals, provides media and audience analysis for use by DOD components, and approves public affairs guidance for the Combatant Commands and other DOD components.

- The Joint Staff contributes to the communications enterprise at many levels. The Current Operations Directorate (J-3) provides Information Operations (I0)/Psychological Operations (PSYOP) expertise and advice to leadership to achieve national, strategic, and theater military objectives. The Plans and Policy Directorate (J-5), in conjunction with the Combatant Commands and Services, develops policy guidance, strategic plans, and enduring communications themes and narratives for senior leadership, based upon policy guidance and directives from OSD. The J-5 also serves as the Joint Staff representative in the interagency process.

- The Chairman of the Joint Chiefs of Staff Public Affairs Office (CJCS PAO) is the principal staff assistant and advisor to the CJCS for news media relations, public liaison, and public affairs.
- DOD's Global Engagement Strategy Coordination Committee (GESCC), created in June 2009, is evolving into the central body for facilitating the strategic communication integrating process within the Department. The GESCC meets on a biweekly basis to identify emerging issues, exchanges information on key actions being worked across the staffs (including strategic communication studies, reports and long-term planning documents), and facilitates the proper integration and deconfliction of DOD activities. The GESCC is co-chaired by OUSD(P) and OASD(PA), and brings together all of the key Don offices mentioned above (OUSD(P), OASD(PA), OUSD(I), Joint Staff). Other regular GESCC attendees include representatives from the Office of the Assistant Secretary of Defense for Legislative Affairs and the Office of the Under Secretary of Defense for Acquisition, Technology & Logistics. Other DOD offices, including Combatant Command representatives, are invited to participate in GESCC meetings and GESCC representatives and also work closely with the Department of State's Global Strategic Engagement Center.

Broadcasting Board of Governors

The Broadcasting Board of Governors (BBG) is responsible for non-military, international broadcasting sponsored by the United States Government, including the Voice of America (VOA), Radio Free Europe/Radio Liberty (RFE/RL), Radio Free Asia (RFA), Radio and TV Marti, and the Middle East Broadcasting Networks (MBN)—Radio Sawa and Alhurra Television. BBG broadcasters distribute programming in 60 languages to an estimated weekly audience of 175 million people via radio, TV, the Internet and other new media. The BBG works to serve as an example of a free and professional press, reaching a worldwide audience with news, information, and relevant discussions. An independent federal agency, the BBG is headed by a nine-person bipartisan board that serves as a firewall against political interference in the journalistic product. The Secretary of State delegates her ex officio seat to the Under Secretary of State for Public Diplomacy and Public Affairs.

United States Agency for International Development

The United States Agency for International Development (USAID) works to inform recipients and partners of U.S. humanitarian and development aid initiatives. USAID directly engages with local stakeholders as part of development and foreign assistance activities. USAID also designs and implements communications capacity building programs including infrastructure development and media training.

Intelligence Community

In its role as the head of the Intelligence Community (IC), the Office of the Director for National Intelligence (ODNI) is responsible for coordinating the efforts of intelligence agencies to conduct research and analysis on foreign public opinion, communication modes and mechanisms, and violent extremist communication as appropriate.

National Counterterrorism Center

The Global Engagement Group in the Directorate of Strategic Operational Planning at the National Counterterrorism Center coordinates, integrates, and synchronizes United States Government efforts to counter violent extremism and deny terrorists the next generation of recruits. The Global Engagement Group operates in accordance with Section 1021 of the Intelligence Reform and Terrorism Prevention Act and the direction provided by the National Implementation Plan. Utilizing these unique authorities, NCTC often serves as the interagency coordinator for counterterrorism-related deliberate communications and engagement planning efforts at the request of the SC IPC, NSS, and individual departments and agencies.

Other Departments and Agencies

Other departments and agencies with specific subject matter expertise and related communication and engagement capabilities may be asked to participate in communication and engagement strategy development and implementation as needed.

MEASURING SUCCESS

It is important to the effectiveness of our programs that we develop the capacity to measure success and emphasize accountability. Measuring the results of a plan or activity requires the identification of indicators for the plan or activity's investment, products, and outcomes. These indicators are evidence of the activity's achievements and can be used to build assessments of costs and benefits over time. There are two types of indicators. Measures of Performance (MOP) show the amount of investment compared to the quantity of product produced by an activity. Meanwhile, Measures of Effectiveness (MOE) give some insight into whether a plan, program, or activity is achieving the desired impact.

In measuring success, the greater emphasis should always be on obtaining valid, accurate measures of effectiveness, since they help determine which efforts deserve continued funding; which efforts should be used as templates for future efforts; and which efforts should be adjusted or even abandoned. Programs that are meeting performance metrics but are not having the desired effect should be re-evaluated. In choosing the most appropriate indicators, departments and agencies should consider all relevant subject-matter expertise and should involve all relevant stakeholders. Program development should also include specific budgeting and resourcing for measurement activities that are needed to evaluate success.

There are difficult challenges to measuring the success of communication and engagement efforts. First, these efforts often target audiences' perceptions, which are not easily observed and, therefore, not easily measured. While there are some methods of measuring success, such as opinion polling, these methods are subject to many different types of uncertainty and margins of error and, therefore, cannot accurately predict behavior. Second, it is difficult to isolate the effect of communication and engagement from other influences including other policy decisions. Lastly, communication and engagement effects are long-term and require persistent measurement. Because of these challenges, it is best to develop phased, layered plans for measuring success that are specific to a given plan or program.

ASSESSMENT OF THE NEED FOR AN INDEPENDENT, NOT-FOR-PROFIT ORGANIZATION

The National Security Staff currently sees no need to establish a new, independent, not-for--profit organization responsible for providing independent assessment and strategic guidance on strategic communication and public diplomacy, as recommended by the Task Force on Strategic Communication of the Defense Science Board. At this time, the existing enterprise either already meets or is working to meet the recommended purposes of the organization prescribed by the Task Force as follows:

- There are a variety of offices across the United States Government that provide an abundance of information and analysis on a regular basis to civilian and military decision- makers on global public opinion; the role of culture, values, and religion in shaping human behavior; media trends and influences on audiences; and information technologies. However, this information and analysis could be better coordinated and shared across the community. An additional entity would only produce more information and analysis to be coordinated and made accessible. The Strategic Communication IPC has formed a Sub-IPC on Information, Research, and Analysis to better coordinate and aggregate relevant information and analysis, and develop mechanisms for improving access across departments and agencies.
- As stated previously, an interagency process for communication and engagement planning was formalized and approved by the Strategic Communication IPC in November 2009. This process allows the interagency to develop strategies to address current and emergent areas of national security concern.

The ability to establish public-private partnerships is a critical issue. However, at this time, there are a number of key pending reviews, including the Presidential Study Directive on Development and the Department of State's Quadrennial Diplomacy and Development Review, that are examining the issue of public-private partnerships. As a result, we do not believe this chapter is the correct mechanism for addressing the United States Government's abilities   to   form   public-private   partnership.

INDEX

D

H

I

J

K